MICROECONOMICS
STUDY GUIDE

Boyes/Melvin

MICROECONOMICS
STUDY GUIDE

James E. Clark
Wichita State University

Janet L. Wolcutt
Wichita State University

Houghton Mifflin Company   **Boston**

Dallas   Geneva, Illinois   Palo Alto   Princeton, New Jersey

Cover photograph by Ralph Mercer, Boston, MA.

Fundamental Questions, Key Terms, and Idea Maps from William Boyes and Michael Melvin, *Economics*.
Copyright © 1991 by Houghton Mifflin Company. Used with permission.

Printed in the U.S.A.

Library of Congress Catalog Card Number: 90–83023

ISBN: 0–395–58067–6

ABCDEFGHIJ-CS-99876543210

CONTENTS

Using the Study Guide   vii

Idea Map   ix

Chapter 1   Economics: The World Around You   1

Chapter 2   Choice, Opportunity Costs, and Specialization   17

Chapter 3   Markets, Demand and Supply, and the Price System   29

Chapter 4   The Price System, Market Failures, and Alternatives   57

Chapter 5   Households, Businesses, Government, and the International Sector   67

Chapter 6   Consumer Choice   77

Chapter 7   Elasticities of Demand and Supply   107

Chapter 8   The Costs of Doing Business   129

Chapter 9   An Overview of Product Markets   151

Chapter 10   Perfect Competition   165

Chapter 11   Monopoly   181

Chapter 12   Monopolistic Competition, Oligopoly, and the Economics of Information   193

Chapter 13   Antitrust Policy and the Regulation of Monopoly   209

Chapter 14   An Overview of Resource Markets   221

Chapter 15   The Labor Market   239

Chapter 16   Unions   255

Chapter 17   Land, Capital, and the Entrepreneurial Ability   267

Chapter 18   The Economics of Aging and Health Care   281

Chapter 19   Income Distribution, Poverty, and Government Policy   293

Chapter 20   The Environment   303

Chapter 21   The Government and Public Choice   313

Chapter 22   World Trade Equilibrium   319

Chapter 23   Commercial Policy   337

Chapter 24   Exchange-Rate Systems and Practices   349

Chapter 25   Foreign-Exchange Risk and International Lending   359

USING THE STUDY GUIDE

WHAT'S IN THE STUDY GUIDE

All Study Guide chapters are organized the same way; each includes the following:

- *Fundamental Questions* are repeated from the text chapter and are briefly answered. The questions and their answers give you an overview of the chapter's main points.
- *Key Terms* from the chapter are listed to remind you of new vocabulary presented in the chapter.
- A *Quick Check Quiz* focuses on vocabulary and key concepts from the chapter. These multiple-choice questions allow you to see whether you understand the material and are ready to move on or whether you need to review some of the text before continuing.
- *Practice Questions and Problems* provide in-depth coverage of important ideas from the chapter and give you the opportunity to apply concepts and work out problems.
- The *Thinking About and Applying* section covers one or more topics in greater depth and will help you learn to apply economics to real-world situations. This section will also show you how various economic concepts are related to one another and, as a result, will help you to think economically.
- The *Answers* section may be the most important part of the Study Guide. Answers to all questions and problems are provided with explanations of how to arrive at the correct answer. In many cases, explanations are given for what you did wrong if you arrived at certain wrong answers.

HOW TO STUDY ECONOMICS

No one ever said that economics is an easy subject, and many students tell us it is the most challenging subject they have studied. Despite the challenge, most students manage to learn a great deal of economics, and we're sure you can too. But doing well in economics requires a commitment from you to *keep up* your studying and to *study properly.*

Keeping up: Although there may be subjects that can be learned reasonably well by cramming the night before an exam, economics is *not* one of them. Learning economics is like building a house: first you need to lay a solid foundation and then you must carefully build the walls. To master economics you must first learn the early concepts, vocabulary, and ideas; if you do not, the later ones will not make any sense.

Studying properly: Listening in class, reading the text, and going through the Study Guide are not enough to really learn economics—you must also organize your studying. The textbook and the Study Guide have been designed to help you organize your thinking and your studying. Used together, they will help you learn.

We recommend following these steps for each chapter:

1. Skim the text chapter before your instructor discusses it in class to get a general idea of what the chapter covers.
   a. Look at the idea map first to see how the chapter fits in with what you've learned already. The idea map is printed in full color in your textbook and is reproduced in black and white in the Study Guide.
   b. Read through the Fundamental Questions and the Preview to get a sense of what is to come.
   c. Skim through the chapter, looking only at the section headings and the section Recaps.
   d. Read the chapter Summary. By this point, you should have a good idea of what topics the chapter covers.

2. Read the text chapter and Study Guide one section at a time. Both the text and the Study Guide break down each chapter into several sections so that you will not need to juggle too many new ideas at once.

   a. Read through one section of the text chapter. Pay attention to the marginal notes containing definitions of Key Terms, highlights of important concepts, and Fundamental Questions.

   b. Study the section Recap. If parts of the Recap are not clear to you, review those parts of the section.

   c. In the Study Guide, read the answers to the Fundamental Questions covered in the section you are studying.

   d. Take the Quick Check Quiz for the section. Write your answers on a separate sheet of paper so that you can use the quiz again later. If you missed any questions, review the applicable section in the text.

   e. Work through the Practice Questions and Problems for the section, writing your answers in the spaces provided. Check your answers; then review what you missed. Read through the explanations in the Answers section, even if you answered the question or problem correctly.

   f. If there are ideas that are not clear or problems you do not understand, talk to your instructor. Economics instructors are interested in helping their students.

3. Review the chapter as a whole. Although each section should initially be studied alone, you will need to put the pieces together.

   a. Read through the chapter again, paying special attention to the idea map, the Fundamental Questions, the section Recaps, the Economic Insight boxes, and the chapter Summary. If you like to outline chapters on paper, now is the time to do so. The section headings and subheadings provide an ideal framework for outlining the text.

   b. In the Study Guide, read through the Fundamental Questions and their answers.

   c. Review the list of Key Terms. Write down the definition of each one at this point, and check your definitions against the marginal notes or the glossary. Study any terms you missed.

   d. Work through the Exercises at the end of the text chapter.

   e. Read through the Economically Speaking section in the text to see how the real world contains examples of economic thinking.

   f. Work through the Thinking About and Applying section of the Study Guide.

4. Ideally, studying for exams should be a repetition of steps 1, 2, and 3 above. However, economists recognize the existence of opportunity costs, and you have many other things to do with your time in addition to studying economics. If you cannot study for an exam as thoroughly as you should, you can use some techniques to help refresh your memory. These techniques assume that you *did* study the materials at least once (there is no magic way to learn economics without doing some serious studying).

   a. Review the Fundamental Questions, the idea maps, the section Recaps, the Key Term lists, and the chapter Summaries in the text.

   b. Read again the Fundamental Questions and their answers in the Study Guide.

   c. Take the Quick Check Quiz again, writing your answers in the Study Guide this time. Questions that you miss will direct you to the areas you need to study most.

If you follow these suggestions, you are sure to meet with success in your study of economics.

T his text presents all the key concepts of economics. In addition it explains how people use these concepts—in business, in government, and in ordinary households. In both the world of theory and the real world of application, knowing the relationships of ideas is crucial. No one can move about in either world without knowing the pathways that relationships form. When studying, it helps a great deal to have some picture of these pathways. That is why a map to show you the important conceptual and real-world pathways of microeconomics is presented on the following pages. Using this map will help you

- pull together and manage a large subject
- learn the process of economic thinking
- improve your own critical thinking.

TAKE MORE THAN ONE VIEW

As you work through the chapters of this book, you will examine in close-up each particular concept. Yet to understand the material, and to get a feel for how economists think, you need to have a second point of view too—an overview. Keeping yourself "up above it" at the same time you are "down in it" will help you remember what you are reading much better and also help you understand and use the concepts you learn more easily. Taking more than one view of your subject has another benefit; it is an ingredient of good critical thinking.

MAKE YOUR OWN CONNECTIONS

To understand economics you need to keep track of how one thing changes in response to another, to see relationships more than fixed ideas. And this requires another ingredient of critical thinking, a sense of independence. With the idea map you can get around on your own (just as different classes may follow different sequences of chapters). Use it to get a feel for how ideas connect and then make your own connections as you read, actively asking yourself questions that cause you to evaluate, structure, and personalize the ideas. Work toward finding your own pathways, from idea to idea and from idea to reality.

USE THIS TEXT AS A SYSTEM

The other features of the text also show pathways, but they do it in a verbal way instead of the visual way the map does. The *Fundamental Questions* point to main issues and help you categorize details, examples, and theories accordingly. Colors in the *graphs* help you classify curves and see relationships to data in the *tables*. The *Recaps* reinforce overarching ideas; they orient you before you go on to the next big section. (Using them, in fact, is a lot like pausing to look at a map.) The *system of referencing* sections and headings by number will help you group concepts and also keep track of what level of ideas you are working with. If you use the idea map and the other features of the text, this text can be more than an authoritative source of information—it can be a system for comprehension. ▶

Making Sense of Microeconomics

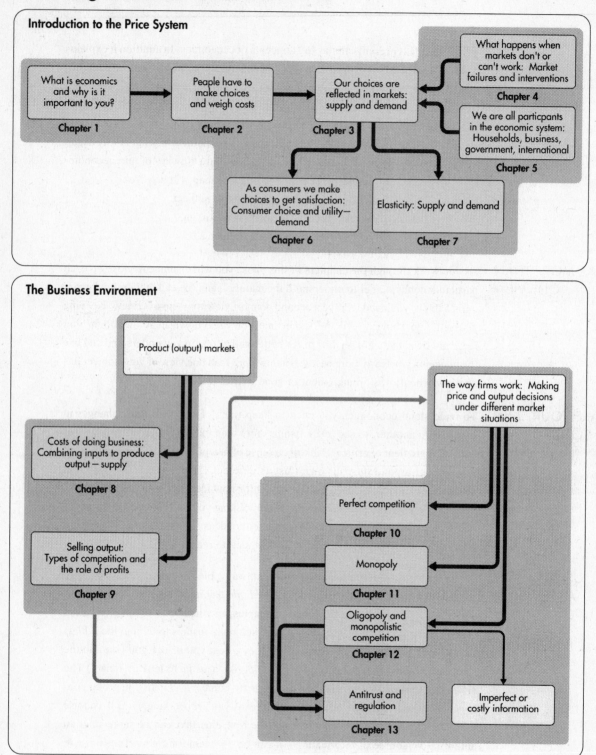

Introduction to the Price System

What is economics and why is it important to you?
Chapter 1

People have to make choices and weigh costs
Chapter 2

Our choices are reflected in markets: supply and demand
Chapter 3

What happens when markets don't or can't work: Market failures and interventions
Chapter 4

We are all particpants in the economic system: Households, business, government, international
Chapter 5

As consumers we make choices to get satisfaction: Consumer choice and utility—demand
Chapter 6

Elasticity: Supply and demand
Chapter 7

The Business Environment

Product (output) markets

Costs of doing business: Combining inputs to produce output — supply
Chapter 8

Selling output: Types of competition and the role of profits
Chapter 9

The way firms work: Making price and output decisions under different market situations

Perfect competition
Chapter 10

Monopoly
Chapter 11

Oligopoly and monopolistic competition
Chapter 12

Antitrust and regulation
Chapter 13

Imperfect or costly information

The Business Environment (continued)

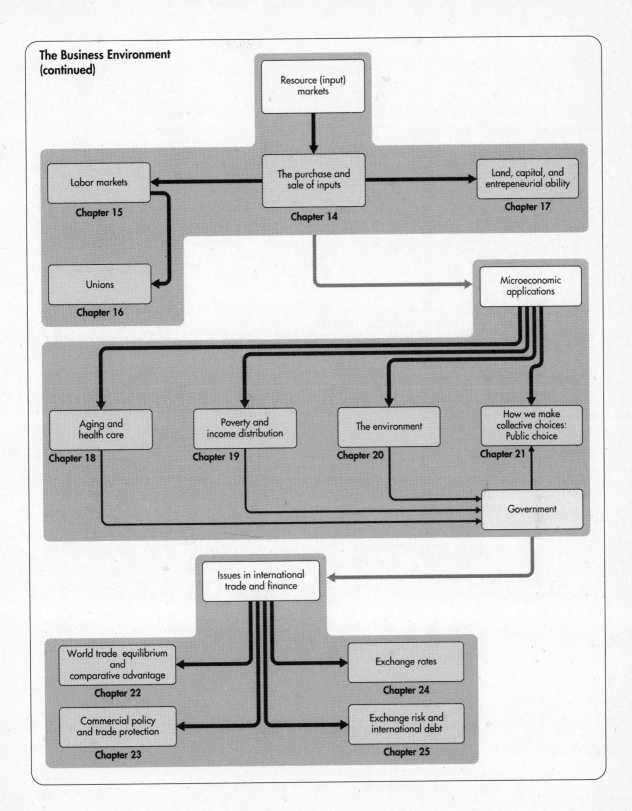

MICROECONOMICS
STUDY GUIDE

CHAPTER 1
Economics: The World Around You

1. What is economics?

   Economics is the study of how people choose to allocate scarce resources to satisfy their unlimited wants. There are several words in this definition that should be emphasized. First, people allocate **scarce** resources. If there were enough of a resource to go around so that everyone could have as much as he or she wanted, there would be no need to allocate.

   The definition states that people have **unlimited wants.** Note that it says "wants," not "needs." People *act* on the basis of their wants, not necessarily on the basis of their needs. (Otherwise they would not buy strawberry sundaes.) If each of us made a list right now of the top ten things we would like to have and our fairy godmother popped out of the air and gave us what we wanted, most of us would immediately find that there are ten *more* things we'd like to have. Since resources are scarce and wants are unlimited, economics studies the best way to allocate these resources so that none of them are wasted.

2. What is scarcity?

   To an economist, a good is scarce if people want more of it than is available when its price is zero. So any item that is not available for free is scarce.

3. What is rational self-interest?

   People acting on the basis of **rational self-interest** will make the choices that, at the time and with the information they have at their disposal, will give them the greatest amount of satisfaction. Economists say "rational" to imply that the self-interest of each individual makes sense or is logical. People do not purposely make themselves less happy. It is important to note that these decisions are made under uncertainty. If you buy a new stereo system and then the same system goes on sale next week, of course you will wish that you had waited. But you didn't know it would go on sale next week—if you had known, you would have waited. People act on the information that they have on hand, which may not be complete or accurate.

4. What is the difference between positive and normative analysis?

   Positive analysis makes no value judgments; it is the study of things the way they are. **Normative analysis** brings value judgments into play; it is the study of what ought to be. Economists usually agree on aspects of positive economics but disagree on issues of normative economics. For example, economists will agree that an increase in the sales tax on cigarettes will reduce the consumption of cigarettes, but they will disagree about whether such a tax ought to be imposed.

KEY TERMS

scarcity
economic good
free good
bad
unlimited wants
rational self-interest
land
labor
capital

entrepreneurial ability
entrepreneur
durables
nondurables
services
microeconomics
macroeconomics
positive analysis
normative analysis

theory
model
test
scientific method
assumptions
ceteris paribus
hypothesis
fallacy of composition
association as causation

QUICK CHECK QUIZ

Section 1: What Is Economics?

1. Which of the following is NOT an economic good?
   a. steaks
   b. houses
   c. cars
   d. garbage
   e. t-shirts

2. Which of the following is NOT one of the four categories of resources?
   a. land
   b. automobiles
   c. capital
   d. entrepreneurial ability
   e. labor

3. The payment for capital is called
   a. rent.
   b. wages.
   c. salaries.
   d. interest.
   e. profit.

4. Which of the following is a durable good?
   a. grapes
   b. wine
   c. refrigerators
   d. disposable razors
   e. bathroom tissue

5. Microeconomics includes the study of
   a. how an individual firm decides the price of its product.
   b. inflation in the United States.
   c. how much output will be produced in the U.S. economy.
   d. how many workers will be unemployed in the U.S. economy.
   e. how the U.S. banking system works.

6. The payment for entrepreneurial ability is called
   a. wages and salaries.
   b. rent.
   c. interest.
   d. profit.
   e. financial capital.

Section 2: The Economic Approach

1. Analysis that does not impose the value judgments of one individual on the decisions of others is called _____ analysis.
   a. positive
   b. normative
   c. economic
   d. noneconomic
   e. the scientific method of

2. Which of the following is NOT one of the five steps in the scientific method?
   a. Recognize the problem.
   b. Make assumptions in order to cut away unnecessary detail.
   c. Develop a model of the problem.
   d. Test the hypothesis.
   e. Make a value judgment based on the results of the hypothesis test.

3. If an individual decides to save more, he or she can save more. Therefore, if the society as a whole decides to save more, it will be able to save more. This reasoning is mistaken and as such is an example of
   a. ceteris paribus.
   b. the fallacy of composition.
   c. the interpretation of association as causation.
   d. the scientific method.
   e. none of the above—this reasoning is not mistaken.

4. Tim has noticed that every time he washes his car in the morning, it rains that afternoon. He has therefore decided to sell his services to farmers in drought-stricken areas, since he believes he can cause it to rain by washing his car. Tim's error is called
   a. ceteris paribus.
   b. the fallacy of composition.
   c. the mistaken interpretation of association as causation.
   d. the scientific method.
   e. none of the above—this reasoning is not mistaken.

5. Which of the following is a normative statement?
   a. Lower interest rates encourage people to borrow.
   b. Higher prices for cigarettes discourage people from buying cigarettes.
   c. If the price of eggs fell, people would probably buy more eggs.
   d. There should be a higher tax on cigarettes, alcohol, and other "sin" items to discourage people from buying these products.
   e. A higher interest rate encourages people to save more.

PRACTICE QUESTIONS AND PROBLEMS

Section 1: What Is Economics?

1. _____ exists when people want more of an item than is available when the price of the item is zero.

2. Any good that is scarce is an _____ good.

3. If there is enough of a good available at a zero price to satisfy wants, the good is called a _____ good.

4. A good that people will pay to have less of is called a _____ .

5. People use scarce resources to satisfy their _____ wants.

6. _____ means that people will make the choices that will give them the greatest amount of satisfaction.

7. List the four categories of resources and the payments associated with each.

   _____

   _____

   _____

   _____

8. _____ includes all natural resources, such as minerals, timber, and water, as well as the land itself.

9. _____ refers to the physical and intellectual services of people.

10. _____ is a manufactured or created product used solely to produce goods and services.

11. _____ capital refers to the money value of capital as represented by stocks and bonds.

12. _____ is the ability to recognize a profitable opportunity and the willingness and ability to organize land, labor, and capital and to assume the risk associated with the opportunity.

13. Goods that are used over a period of one or more years are called _____.

14. _____ are work that is done for others that does not involve the production of goods.

15. _____ is the study of economics at the level of the individual economic entity.

16. The study of the economy at the aggregate level is called _____.

17. What is economics?

_____

_____

_____

_____

Section 2: The Economic Approach

1. Analysis that does not impose the value judgments of one individual on the decisions of others is called _____ analysis.

2. _____ analysis involves imposing value judgments on the decisions of others.

3. Economists generally agree on the _____ aspects of economics.

4. List the five steps in the scientific method.

_____

_____

_____

_____

_____

5. The role of _____ is to reduce the complexity of a problem.

6. _____ means "other things being equal."

7. A theory, or _____, is a simple, logical story based on positive analysis that is used to explain an event.

8. A _____ is an explanation that accounts for a set of facts and allows us to make predictions in similar situations.

9. The _____ is the error of attributing what applies to one to the case of many.

10. The mistaken interpretation of _____ occurs when unrelated or coincidental events that occur at about the same time are believed to have a cause-and-effect relationship.

THINKING ABOUT AND APPLYING ECONOMICS: THE WORLD AROUND YOU

I. The Relationship Between Speed Limits and Highway Deaths

1. The "Economically Speaking" article in the text states that in twenty-two of the thirty-eight states that chose to raise the speed limit on rural highways, highway deaths jumped 46 percent between May and July over the same three months in 1986. Transportation Committee Chairman James Howard attributes the increase in deaths to the higher speed limit. Can you think of any other reasons that highway deaths might have increased? If states that did not increase rural speed limits experienced a similar increase in highway deaths, what common mistake might Chairman Howard be making?

_____

_____

_____

_____

ANSWERS

Quick Check Quiz

Section 1: What Is Economics?

1. d; 2. b; 3. d; 4. c; 5. a; 6. d
   If you missed any of these questions, you should go back and review pages 4–7 in Chapter 1.

Section 2: The Economic Approach

1. a; 2. e; 3. b; 4. c; 5. d
   If you missed any of these questions, you should go back and review pages 7–12 in Chapter 1.

Practice Questions and Problems

Section 1: What Is Economics?

1. Scarcity
2. economic
3. free
4. bad
5. unlimited
6. Rational self-interest
7. land; rent
   labor; wages and salaries
   capital; interest
   entrepreneurial ability; profit

8. Land
9. Labor
10. Capital
11. Financial
12. Entrepreneurial ability
13. durables
14. Services
15. Microeconomics
16. macroeconomics
17. Economics is the study of how people choose to use their scarce resources to satisfy their unlimited wants.

Section 2: The Economic Approach

1. positive
2. Normative
3. positive
4. Recognize the problem.
   Make assumptions in order to cut away unnecessary detail.
   Develop a model of the problem.
   Present a hypothesis.
   Test the hypothesis.
5. assumptions
6. Ceteris paribus
7. model
8. hypothesis
9. fallacy of composition
10. association as causation

Thinking About and Applying Economics: The World Around You

I. The Relationship Between Speed Limits and Highway Deaths

1. Other factors that might increase highway deaths include the following:

   a. Has there been an increase in population? It seems reasonable to expect more accidents as congestion increases.
   b. Are Americans buying more smaller cars? If so, auto deaths would be expected to increase because smaller cars provide less protection in the event of a crash.
   c. Has there been an increase in the number of people drinking (or being otherwise impaired) and driving? If so, we would expect an increase in the number of traffic fatalities no matter what the speed limit was.

   Perhaps you can think of other factors that might account for the increase in traffic fatalities that Howard attributes to the higher speed limit. If Howard has wrongly attributed the higher death toll to the higher speed limit, he has mistaken association for causation.

APPENDIX TO CHAPTER 1
Working with Graphs

SUMMARY

Most people are visually oriented: they are better able to understand things that they can "picture." The pictures that economists use to explain concepts are called graphs.

There are three commonly used types of graphs: the line graph, the bar graph, and the pie chart. The pie chart is used to show the relative magnitude of the parts that make up a whole. Line graphs and bar graphs are used to show the relationship between two variables. One of the variables, the **independent variable,** has values that do not depend on the values of other variables. The values of **dependent variables** do depend on the values of other variables.

If two variables move in the same direction together, the relationship is called a **direct,** or **positive relationship,** and the **slope** of the line or curve relating the two variables will be positive. If two variables move together but in opposite directions, the relationship is an **inverse,** or **negative relationship,** and the slope of the line or curve relating the two variables will be negative. A curve **shifts** when, for each combination of variables measured on the horizontal and vertical axes, one of the variables changes by a certain amount while the other variable remains the same. Shifts occur when variables other than those on the axes are allowed to change.

The slope of a line or curve is the rise over the run. The **45-degree line** is a special line that bisects the origin and has a slope equal to 1. At every point on the 45-degree line, the variable on the horizontal axis has the same value as the variable on the vertical axis.

We can find the maximum or minimum point on a curve by finding where the slope of the curve is equal to zero. If the slope goes from positive to zero to negative, a maximum occurs. If the slope goes from negative to zero to positive, a minimum occurs.

KEY TERMS

independent variable	positive relationship	shift
dependent variable	inverse relationship	slope
direct relationship	negative relationship	45-degree line

PRACTICE QUESTIONS AND PROBLEMS

1. The owner of a business that sells home heating oil has noticed that the amount of heating oil sold increases as the temperature outside decreases. Heating oil is the _____ (dependent, independent) variable. The relationship between the two variables is _____ (direct, inverse), and the slope of the line will be _____ (positive, negative.) Use the graph

below to show the nature of the relationship between home heating oil sales and outside temperature. Be sure to label your axes.

2. What might make the curve you drew in question 1 shift?

_____

_____

_____

_____

3. The table below shows the relationship between the quantity of milk that dairy farmers are willing to offer for sale and the price of milk. This relationship is _____ (direct, inverse). The slope of the line will be _____ (positive, negative). Plot the curves on the graph on the following page.

Price of Milk	Quantity of Milk Offered for Sale
$ .50	0
.75	2
1.00	4
1.25	6
1.50	8

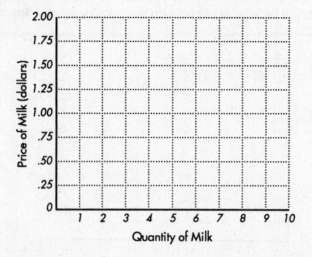

4. Consider the relationship between household spending (called "Consumption") and National Income on the graph below, and answer the following questions.

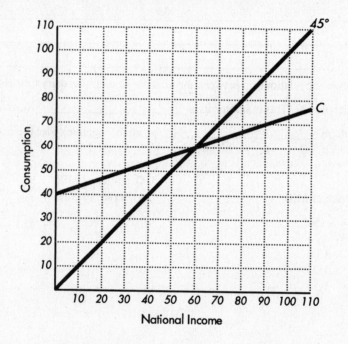

a. The relationship between consumption and income is _____ (direct, inverse).

b. What is the slope of the line? _____

The intercept? _____

c. What is the equation for this line? _____

d. At what point does consumption equal income? _____

5. The maximum point of the total revenue curve below occurs at the quantity _____ . The slope of the curve is _____ at quantities less than this amount and is _____ at quantities greater than this amount.

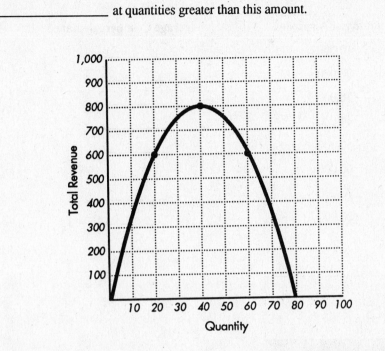

6. The graph below shows the percentages of income that the King family spends, pays in taxes, and saves. What kind of graph is this? _____

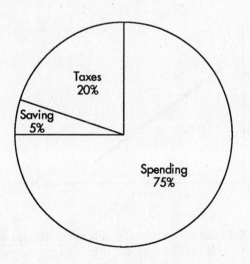

7. The table below shows the relationship between the quantity of airplanes built at a production plant in Wichita and the average cost (cost per airplane). Make up a set of figures that will show that a minimum average cost occurs at 40,000 airplanes.

Quantity of Airplanes	Average Cost per Airplane
10,000	_____
20,000	_____
30,000	_____
40,000	_____
50,000	_____
60,000	_____
70,000	_____
80,000	_____

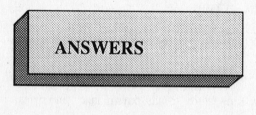

ANSWERS

1. dependent; inverse; negative

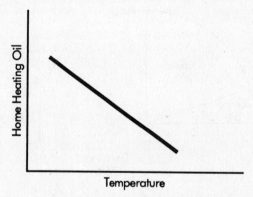

2. Anything other than temperature that affects the sales of home heating oil will cause this curve to shift. One such variable might be the cost of electricity. If it decreases significantly, people may turn to electric space heaters to heat parts of their homes and buy less home heating oil at every price.
3. direct; positive

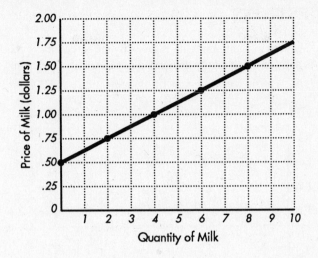

4. a. direct
   b. 1/3; 40
   c. $C = 40 + 1/3Y$
   d. 60
5. 40; positive; negative
6. pie chart
7. There are many possible solutions. The numbers need to decrease until you reach the quantity 40,000, and increase thereafter. Here is one possible solution.

Quantity of Airplanes	Average Cost per Airplane
10,000	40
20,000	30
30,000	20
40,000	10
50,000	20
60,000	30
70,000	40
80,000	50

ADDITIONAL QUESTIONS

1. The demand for Mardi's Tacos in Hammondville is given by the equation $P = \$2.00 - .02Q$, where P is the price of tacos in dollars and Q is the quantity demanded of tacos. Plot the demand for Mardi's Tacos on the graph below.

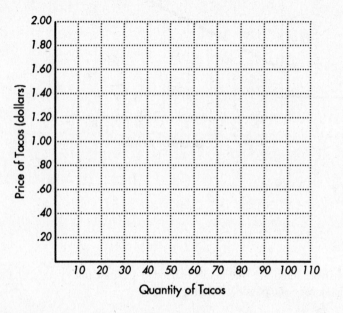

The relationship between price and quantity demanded is _____ (direct, inverse).

2. The supply for tacos in Hammondville is given by the equation $P = \$.40 + .005Q$, where P is the price of tacos in dollars and Q is the quantity supplied of tacos. Plot the supply of tacos on the graph below.

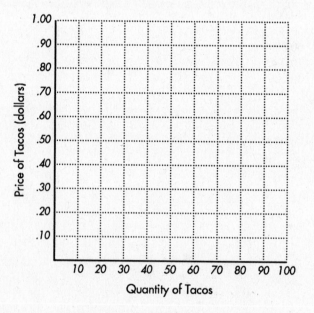

The relationship between price and quantity supplied is _____ (direct, inverse).

3. Plot the total revenue function $TR = -10Q^2 + 600Q$ on the graph below. The maximum total revenue is obtained by selling _____ units.

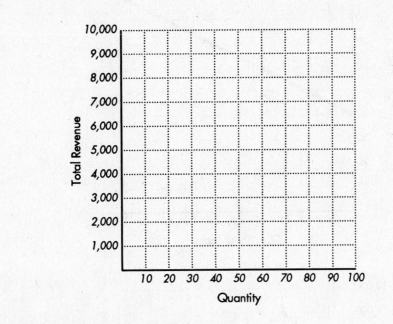

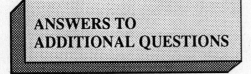

1. inverse

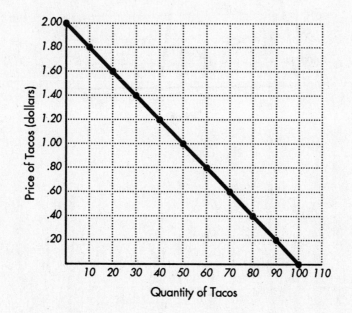

2. direct

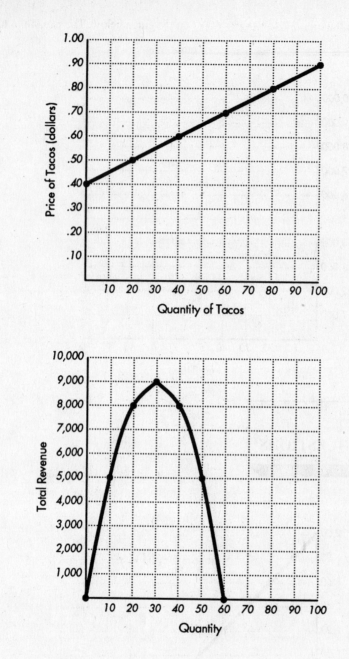

3. 30

CHAPTER 2
Choice, Opportunity Costs, and Specialization

FUNDAMENTAL
QUESTIONS

1. What are opportunity costs?

    The **opportunity cost** of something is what you need to give up in order to get it. For example, if you would prefer to be sleeping now instead of studying economics, the opportunity cost of studying is the sleep you could be enjoying.

2. What is the full cost of any purchase?

    The full cost of any purchase is whatever you have to forgo to make the purchase. Part of the cost is the price of the good or service, but it may also include the value of the time you had to give up to stand in line to make the purchase or the time you spent comparing prices and products.

3. What is the production possibilities curve?

    A **production possibilities curve** shows all the combinations of output that could be produced with a given set of resources, assuming that the resources are fully and efficiently used.

4. What accounts for increasing marginal opportunity costs?

    Resources tend to be specialized—that is, better at producing one kind of good or service than another. For example, suppose that Vickeryland can produce either guns or butter. If Vickeryland throws all its resources into producing guns, some resources will not be good at producing guns. If some cows are switched over from making guns to making butter, they will probably be much better at making butter than at making guns. Vickeryland will gain a lot of butter and lose very few guns. But as more and more butter is produced, eventually some resources that were very good at making guns will have to be switched into making butter. If these resources are very good at making guns and not so good at making butter, Vickeryland will give up lots of guns and gain very little butter. If you must give up an increasing number of guns to get each additional unit of butter, then the opportunity cost of each additional unit of butter is increasing. If resources were equally adaptable among uses, the opportunity cost of each additional unit of butter would remain constant. The **marginal opportunity cost** would be constant.

5. What accounts for specialization?

    It pays to specialize whenever opportunity costs are *different*. Two parties can specialize and then trade, which makes both parties better off. Even if one person or nation has an **absolute advantage** over another (does something more efficiently than the other) in the production of a good or service, it does not mean that that person or nation will produce that good or service. Specialization occurs as a result of **comparative**, not absolute, **advantage**. Specialization according to comparative advantage minimizes opportunity cost.

6. What is comparative advantage?

   A has a comparative advantage over *B* in the production of a good or service if *A*'s opportunity cost for producing the good or service is lower than *B*'s.

KEY TERMS

opportunity costs	constant marginal opportunity cost
trade off	increasing marginal opportunity cost
specialist	decreasing marginal opportunity cost
production possibilities curve (PPC)	sunk costs
marginal opportunity cost	comparative advantage
marginal	absolute advantage

QUICK CHECK QUIZ

Section 1: Opportunity Costs

1. Janine is an accountant who makes $30,000 a year. Robert is a college student who makes $8,000 a year. All other things being equal, who is more likely to stand in a long line to get a concert ticket?
   a. Janine, because her opportunity cost is lower
   b. Janine, because her opportunity cost is higher
   c. Robert, because his opportunity cost is lower
   d. Robert, because his opportunity cost is higher
   e. Janine, because she is better able to afford the cost of the ticket

2. Which of the following statements is false?
   a. Points inside the production possibilities curve represent combinations where resources are not being fully or efficiently used.
   b. Points outside the production possibilities curve represent combinations that are not attainable with the current level of resources.
   c. If an individual is producing a combination on his or her production possibilities curve, in order to get more of one good, he or she must give up some of the other.
   d. If a nation obtains more resources, the production possibilities curve will shift outward.
   e. Marginal opportunity costs are always constant.

3. At point *A* on a production possibilities curve, there are 50 tons of corn and 60 tons of wheat. At point *B* on the same curve, there are 40 tons of corn and 80 tons of wheat. If the farmer is currently at point *A*, the opportunity cost of moving to point *B* is
   a. 10 tons of corn.
   b. 20 tons of wheat.
   c. 1 ton of corn.
   d. 2 tons of wheat.
   e. 40 tons of corn.

4. President Johnson thought it was possible to spend more resources in Vietnam without having to give up consumer goods at home. President Johnson must have believed that
   a. the American economy was operating at top efficiency.
   b. the American economy was operating at a point inside its production possibilities curve.
   c. the American economy was operating at a point on its production possibilities curve.
   d. the American economy was operating at a point outside its production possibilities curve.
   e. marginal opportunity costs were constant.

Use the table below to answer questions 5 through 8.

Combination	Clothing	Food
A	0	110
B	10	105
C	20	95
D	30	80
E	40	60
F	50	35
G	60	0

5. If the economy is currently producing at point *F*, the opportunity cost of 10 additional units of clothing is approximately
   a. 25 units of food.
   b. 5 units of food.
   c. 10 units of food.
   d. 35 units of food.
   e. 3.5 units of food.

6. A combination of 20 units of clothing and 80 units of food is
   a. unattainable.
   b. inefficient.
   c. possible by giving up 15 units of food.
   d. possible if the economy obtains more resources.
   e. possible if an improvement in technology makes the production possibilities curve shift in.

7. The marginal opportunity cost of 10 units of clothing is
   a. constant.
   b. decreasing.
   c. increasing.
   d. the same for each 10 units of food.
   e. decreasing for clothing but increasing for food.

8. A combination of 50 units of clothing and 70 units of food is
   a. inefficient.
   b. obtainable by giving up 35 units of food.
   c. a combination where resources are not fully utilized.
   d. unattainable.
   e. possible if an improvement in technology shifts the production possibilities curve in.

Section 2: Specialization

Use the table below to answer questions 1 through 4.

Combination	Alpha		Beta	
	Beef	Microchips	Beef	Microchips
A	0	200	0	300
B	25	150	25	225
C	50	100	50	150
D	75	50	75	75
E	100	0	100	0

1. The opportunity cost of a microchip in Alpha is _____ units of beef, and the opportunity cost of a microchip in Beta is _____ units of beef. The opportunity cost of a unit of beef is _____ units of microchips in Alpha and _____ units of microchips in Beta.
   a. 1/3; 1/2; 3; 2
   b. 2; 3; 1/2; 1/3
   c. 1/2; 1/3; 2; 3
   d. 3; 2; 1/3; 1/2
   e. 1/2; 3; 1/3; 2

2. Marginal opportunity costs are
   a. constant for Alpha but increasing for Beta.
   b. constant for Alpha but decreasing for Beta.
   c. constant for Alpha and for Beta.
   d. increasing for Alpha but decreasing for Beta.
   e. decreasing for Alpha but increasing for Beta.

3. Alpha has a comparative advantage in _____ , and Beta has a comparative advantage in _____ . Alpha should produce _____ , and Beta should produce _____ .
   a. beef; microchips; beef; microchips
   b. beef; microchips; microchips; beef
   c. microchips; beef; microchips; beef
   d. microchips; beef; beef; microchips
   e. There is no basis for specialization and trade between these two countries, since Beta can produce just as much beef and more microchips than Alpha.

4. Which of the following statements is true?
   a. Alpha has an absolute advantage in the production of beef.
   b. Alpha has an absolute advantage in the production of microchips.
   c. Beta has an absolute advantage in the production of beef.
   d. Beta has an absolute advantage in the production of microchips.
   e. Alpha has no absolute advantage over Beta, and Beta has no absolute advantage over Alpha.

5. Which of the following statements is true?
   a. Individuals, firms, and nations will specialize in the production of the good or service that has the highest opportunity cost.
   b. An individual, firm, or nation must first have an absolute advantage in the production of a good or service before it can have a comparative advantage in the production of that good or service.
   c. Comparative advantage exists whenever one person, firm, or nation engaging in an activity incurs lower absolute costs than does some other individual, firm, or nation.
   d. An individual, firm, or nation specializes according to absolute advantage.
   e. An individual, firm, or nation need not have an absolute advantage to have a comparative advantage.

PRACTICE QUESTIONS AND PROBLEMS

Section 1: Opportunity Costs

1. _____ are forgone opportunities or forgone benefits.

2. People purchase items and participate in activities that _____ (maximize, minimize) opportunity costs.

3. A _____ is someone whose opportunity cost of switching to an activity other than the one he or she specializes in is very high relative to the opportunity cost of the activity in which he or she specializes.

4. A _____ is a graph that illustrates the trade-offs facing a society.

5. A point that lies _____ the production possibilities curve indicates that resources are not being fully or efficiently used.

6. Points outside the production possibilities curve represent combinations of goods and services that are

   _____ .

7. The _____ is the amount of one good or service that must be given up to obtain one additional unit of another good or service.

8. A straight-line production possibilities curve illustrates _____ (increasing, constant, decreasing) marginal opportunity costs.

9. A bowed-out production possibilities curve illustrates _____ (increasing, constant, decreasing) marginal opportunity costs.

10. A bowed-in production possibilities curve illustrates _____ (increasing, constant, decreasing) marginal opportunity costs.

11. Because resources tend to be specialized, the production possibilities curve is likely to be

    _____ (bowed in, bowed out, straight line), indicating that marginal opportunity

    costs are _____ (increasing, decreasing, constant).

12. People trade off one activity for another until the marginal opportunity cost of an additional amount of the first activity _____ (is greater than, equals, is less than) the marginal benefits of that additional amount.

13. People make decisions based on the _____ (marginal, total) opportunity cost.

14. Costs borne in the past are known as _____ costs.

15. Opportunity cost is a(n) _____ (objective, subjective) concept.

16. Use the graph below to answer the following questions.

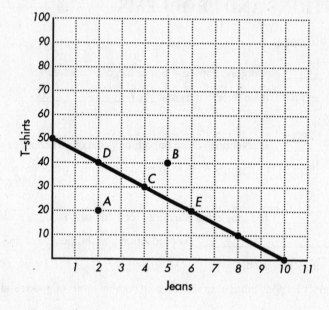

a. The marginal opportunity cost is _____ (increasing, constant, decreasing).

b. Point A represents a combination of t-shirts and jeans that is _____ .

c. Point B represents a combination of t-shirts and jeans that is _____ .

d. If an individual is currently producing the combination of t-shirts and jeans at point C, the marginal opportunity cost of an additional t-shirt is _____ jean(s).

e. If an individual is currently producing the combination of t-shirts and jeans at point D, the marginal opportunity cost of 1 pair of jeans is _____ t-shirt(s).

17. Use the graph below to answer the following questions.

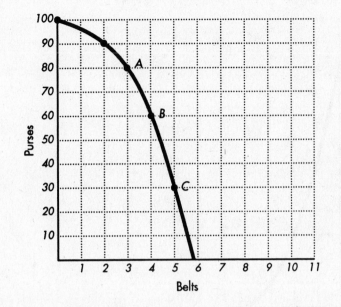

a. The marginal opportunity cost is _____ (increasing, constant, decreasing).

b. If an individual is currently producing the combination of purses and belts at point B, the marginal opportunity cost of an additional purse is approximately _____ belt(s).

c. If an individual is currently producing the combination of purses and belts at point A, the marginal opportunity cost of an additional purse is approximately _____ belt(s).

d. If an individual is currently producing the combination of purses and belts at Point B, the marginal opportunity cost of an additional belt is _____ purse(s).

18. Use the graph below to answer the following questions.

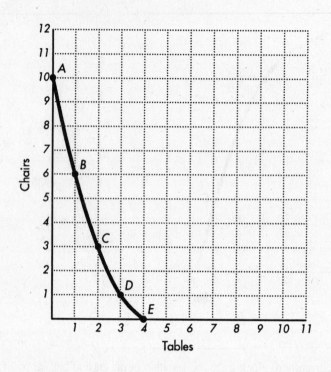

a. The marginal opportunity cost is _____ (increasing, constant, decreasing).

b. If an individual is currently producing the combination of chairs and tables at point C, the marginal opportunity cost of an additional chair is approximately _____ table(s).

c. If an individual is currently producing the combination of chairs and tables at point B, the marginal opportunity cost of an additional chair is approximately _____ table(s).

d. If an individual is currently producing the combination of chairs and tables at point B, the marginal opportunity cost of an additional table is _____ chair(s).

19. Roger Southby was almost finished with his accounting degree when he discovered the wonderful world of marketing. Roger would like to switch majors but does not want to waste the years of schooling he already has. What can you tell Roger to help him make his decision?

_____

_____

_____

_____

20. Mardi and Martin paid $20 each to see a new foreign film. Halfway through the film, Mardi got disgusted and wanted to leave. Martin insisted that they stay, because they paid $40 altogether to see the film, and he wanted to get his money's worth out of it. Can you offer them some economic insight to help them resolve this argument?

_____

_____

_____

_____

Section 2: Specialization

1. It is in your best interest to specialize where your opportunity costs are _____ (highest, constant, lowest).

2. When one person, firm, or nation is more skillful than another person, firm, or nation, that person, firm, or nation has an _____ advantage in producing that good.

3. A nation has a comparative advantage in those activities in which it has _____ (the highest, constant, the lowest) opportunity costs.

4. People specialize according to their _____ (absolute, comparative) advantage.

5. If a country specializes in the production of goods and services in which it has a comparative advantage, it can trade with other countries and enjoy a combination of goods and services that lies _____ its production possibilities curve.

6. Use the table below to answer the following questions.

	Robinson Crusoe		Man Friday	
Combination	Coconuts	Fish	Coconuts	Fish
A	5	0	10	0
B	4	1	8	1
C	3	2	6	2
D	2	3	4	3
E	1	4	2	4
F	0	5	0	5

a. The marginal opportunity costs for Robinson Crusoe and his Man Friday are _____ (increasing, constant, decreasing).

b. The marginal opportunity cost of a coconut is _____ fish for Robinson Crusoe and _____ fish for his Man Friday.

c. The marginal opportunity cost of a fish is _____ coconut(s) for Robinson Crusoe and _____ coconut(s) for his Man Friday.

    d. His Man Friday has an absolute advantage in the production of _____ .

        Robinson Crusoe has an absolute advantage in _____ .

    e. Robinson Crusoe has a comparative advantage in _____ , and Friday has a

        comparative advantage in _____ .

    f. Robinson Crusoe should specialize in producing _____ , and Friday should

        specialize in producing _____ .

THINKING ABOUT AND APPLYING CHOICE, OPPORTUNITY COSTS, AND SPECIALIZATION

I. More on Opportunity Costs

Marc and Shelly Colby are a couple in their thirties with two children. Marc owns his own company and makes $70,000 a year, and Shelly has been responsible for raising their children. Now that the children are in school all day, Shelly is considering going back to school to finish her degree. She estimates that tuition will cost about $3,000. Marc likes carpentry and is thinking about going to a special school for a year to learn more about it. He estimates that the school will cost about $1,500. After they discuss it, they decide that Shelly should go back to school but that it costs too much for Marc to go to carpentry school. Explain.

_____

_____

_____

_____

II. Still More on Opportunity Costs

The "Economically Speaking" article in your text suggests that some entrepreneurs may actually increase their incomes by selling their firms. The text presents an example of an entrepreneur who could earn $330,310 per year by selling his company as opposed to $125,000 per year by continuing to run it. If money were the only consideration, the entrepreneur would clearly be better off to sell.

    What if the situation were reversed, and the entrepreneur would make $125,000 by selling the company and $330,310 per year by continuing to run the company? Why might the entrepreneur sell the company?

_____

_____

_____

_____

ANSWERS

Quick Check Quiz

Section 1: Opportunity Costs

1. c; 2. e; 3. a; 4. b; 5. d; 6. b; 7. c; 8. d
   If you missed any of these questions, you should go back and review pages 34–44 in Chapter 2.

Section 2: Specialization

1. c; 2. c; 3. a; 4. d; 5. e
   If you missed any of these questions, you should go back and review pages 44–48 in Chapter 2.

Practice Questions and Problems

Section 1: Opportunity Costs

1. Opportunity costs
2. minimize
3. specialist
4. production possibilities curve (PPC)
5. inside
6. unattainable
7. marginal opportunity cost
8. constant
9. increasing
10. decreasing
11. bowed out; increasing
12. equals
13. marginal
14. sunk
15. subjective
16. a. constant
    b. inefficient (or does not fully utilize all resources)
    c. unattainable
    d. .2 (We must move to point D to get additional t-shirts. Moving from C to D, we get 10 t-shirts by giving up 2 pairs of jeans. To get 1 t-shirt, we must give up 2/10 jean, or .2 jean.)
    e. 5 (We must move toward point C to get additional jeans. Moving from D to C, we get 2 pairs of jeans by giving up 10 t-shirts. For 1 pair of jeans, we must give up 10/2 t-shirts, or 5 t-shirts.)
17. a. increasing
    b. .05 (We must move toward point A to get additional purses. Moving from B to A, we give up 1 belt for 20 purses. For 1 purse, we give up approximately 1/20 or .05 belt.)
    c. .1 (We must move up the curve to get additional purses. At point A we have 80 purses and 3 belts. Moving up the curve, we have 90 purses and 2 belts. We gave up 1 belt for 10 purses. For 1 purse, we give up approximately 1/10 or .1 belts.) Note that as we make more purses, the opportunity cost in terms of belts increases.
    d. 30 (To get an additional belt, we must move from B to C. At B, we had 60 purses and 4 belts. At C, we have 30 purses and 5 belts. We gave up 30 purses for 1 belt.)

18. a. decreasing
    b. 1/3 (To get more chairs, we must move toward point B. At point C we had 2 tables and 3 chairs. At point B we have 1 table and 6 chairs. We gave up 1 table for 3 chairs. To get 1 chair, we give up approximately 1/3 table.)
    c. 1/4 (To get more chairs, we must move toward point A. At point B we had 1 table and 6 chairs. At point A we have no tables and 10 chairs. We gave up 1 table for 4 chairs. To get 1 chair, we give up approximately 1/4 table.)
    d. 3 (To get more tables, we must move from B to C. At B, we had 6 chairs and 1 table. At C, we have 3 chairs and 2 tables. we gave up 3 chairs for 1 table.)

19. The years of schooling Roger already has are a *sunk* cost—he cannot get them back whether he continues as an accounting major or switches to marketing. These costs should have no effect on his decision to change majors, since he cannot change what has already happened. The relevant costs are the opportunity costs of continuing his accounting major versus the opportunity costs of switching to marketing.

20. Whether they stay or leave, they cannot get their $40 back. It is a sunk cost and should not enter the decision-making process. The relevant costs are the opportunity costs of staying versus the opportunity costs of leaving.

Section 2: Specialization

1. lowest
2. absolute
3. the lowest
4. comparative
5. outside
6. a. constant
   b. 1; 1/2
   c. 1; 2
   d. coconuts; neither fish nor coconuts
   e. fish; coconuts
   f. fish; coconuts

Thinking About and Applying Choice, Opportunity Costs, and Specialization

I. More on Opportunity Costs

Tuition isn't the only cost. If Marc has to give up $70,000 a year to go to carpentry school for a year, he and Shelly may feel that the benefits from carpentry school are not worth $70,000. Carpentry school costs too much. Since Shelly is not working outside the home, her major cost is the leisure time she will have now that their children are in school. She may feel that the benefits of having her degree are worth giving up her leisure time.

II. Still More Opportunity Costs

There are nonmonetary costs to running your own business: the hours you put in, the strain and worry of being in charge of the business, and so forth. An entrepreneur may feel that it is worth giving up some income to get more leisure time and peace of mind.

CHAPTER 3
Markets, Demand and Supply, and the Price System

1. What is a market?

    A **market** is a place or service that allows buyers and sellers to exchange goods and services. A market may refer to a specific place or may be the exchange of a particular good or service at many different locations. Market transactions may involve the use of money or **barter.** Markets dealing with illegal goods and services are called **black markets.** Markets whose transactions are not recorded are known as **underground markets.** In all markets, goods and services are exchanged and prices are determined.

2. What is demand?

    Demand is a schedule showing the quantities of a good or service that consumers are willing and able to buy at each possible price during a specific period of time, all other things being equal. People often confuse *demand* with *quantity demanded. Demand* refers to a list of prices and corresponding quantities. It is similar to a bus schedule in that it gives many price and quantity options, just as a bus schedule gives many time and location options. *Quantity demanded* indicates how much of a good or service will be bought at *one* particular price. It is correct to say "If the price of a hair dryer is $15, the *quantity demanded* is 20." It is not correct to say "If the price of a hair dryer is $15, the *demand* is 20." Quantity demanded would be analogous to one particular time on the bus schedule: "At 1:10 the bus will be at Lion's Head."

    The **law of demand** states that as the price of a good decreases, people will buy more. That's why stores have sales to get rid of merchandise they can't sell: they know that if they lower the price, people will buy more.

    When economists construct a **demand schedule,** they hold everything except the price of the good constant and determine what quantity consumers will buy at all the possible prices. However, things other than price affect how much of a good or service people are willing to buy. These other **determinants of demand** are income, tastes, prices of related goods or services, expectations, and number of buyers. When one of these determinants of demand changes, the whole demand schedule changes.

    Economists take seriously the adage "A picture is worth a thousand words," so they draw pictures of demand schedules. Such pictures are called **demand curves.** Price is put on the vertical axis and quantity on the horizontal axis. Demand curves slope down from left to right because of the **substitution and income effects.** When one of the five determinants of demand (income, tastes, etc.) changes, the demand curve shifts to the left or the right. Increases in demand shift the curve to the right, and decreases in demand shift the curve to the left. A change in the price of a good or service does not shift the demand curve but instead is represented by a movement from one point to another along the same curve.

3. What is supply?

    Supply is a schedule showing the quantities of a good or service that producers are willing and able to offer at each possible price during a specific period of time, all other things being equal. People often confuse *supply* with *quantity supplied. Supply* refers to a list of prices and corresponding quantities. *Quantity supplied* indicates how much of a good or service will be offered for sale at *one* particular price. It is correct to say "If the price of a hair dryer is $15, the *quantity supplied* will be 10." It is not correct to say "If the price of a hair dryer is $15, the *supply* is 10."

    The **law of supply** states that as the price of a good increases, producers will offer more for sale. That's why people offer a seller a higher price for the product when there is a shortage: they know the higher price will entice the producer to produce more.

    When economists construct a **supply schedule,** they hold everything except the price of the good constant, and determine what quantity producers will offer for sale at all the possible prices. However, things other than price affect how much of a good or service producers are willing to supply. These other **determinants of supply** are prices of resources, technology and **productivity,** expectations of producers, number of producers, and prices of related goods or services. When one of these determinants of supply changes, the whole supply schedule changes.

    A picture of a supply schedule is called a **supply curve.** As before, price goes on the vertical axis and quantity on the horizontal axis. Supply curves slope up from left to right. When one of the five determinants of supply (prices of resources, etc.) changes, the supply curve shifts to the left or the right. Increases in supply shift the curve to the right and decreases in supply shift the curve to the left. A change in the price of a good or service does not shift the supply curve but instead is represented by a movement from one point to another along the same curve.

4. How is price determined by demand and supply?

    The price of a good or service will change until the equilibrium price is reached. **Equilibrium** occurs when the quantity demanded is equal to the quantity supplied at a particular price. At prices above the equilibrium price, quantity supplied is greater than quantity demanded, so a **surplus** develops. Sellers must lower their prices to get rid of the goods and services that accumulate. At prices below the equilibrium price, quantity demanded is greater than quantity supplied, and a **shortage** develops. Sellers see the goods and services quickly disappear and realize they could have asked a higher price. The price goes up until the shortage disappears. The price continues to adjust until quantity demanded and quantity supplied are equal.

5. What causes price to change?

    The price may change when demand, supply, or both change. A change in demand causes price to change in the same direction: an increase in demand causes price to increase. A change in supply causes price to change in the opposite direction: an increase in supply causes price to decrease. If supply and demand both change, the direction of the change in price depends on the relative sizes of the changes in demand and supply. For example, if demand and supply both increase but the demand change is larger, price will increase: it will act as if the only change had been a change in demand. If demand and supply both increase but the supply change is larger, price will decrease: it will act as if the only change had been a change in supply.

KEY TERMS

market
black market
underground market
barter
double coincidence of wants
transaction costs
relative price
nominal price
purchasing power
demand

law of demand
determinants of demand
substitution effect
income effect
demand schedule
demand curve
substitute goods
complementary goods
supply

law of supply
supply schedule
supply curve
determinants of supply
productivity
equilibrium
surplus
shortage
disequilibrium

QUICK CHECK QUIZ

Section 1: Markets

1. Which of the following is an example of an underground market activity?
   a. A trader buys IBM stock on the New York Stock Exchange.
   b. The United Mine Workers negotiate a wage contract with a mine owner.
   c. A hair stylist cuts a manicurist's hair in exchange for a manicure.
   d. The Mertzes have lunch at the Dew Drop Inn.
   e. The Federal Reserve buys bonds from the public.

2. Which of the following is NOT a black market activity?
   a. A street addict buys cocaine from a drug dealer.
   b. A yuppie stockbroker buys marijuana from a neighbor.
   c. A fifteen-year-old girl does not report her paper route earnings to the IRS.
   d. A liquor store sells whiskey to a minor.
   e. A prostitute performs her services in a major hotel.

3. In Mongoverna this year, apples cost fifty cents each and oranges cost thirty-five cents each. Suppose that next year, inflation runs rampant in Mongoverna. The price of apples increases to one dollar each, and the price of oranges increases to seventy cents each. Which of the following statements is true?
   a. The relative price of an apple has not changed.
   b. The relative price of an orange has changed.
   c. The absolute price of an apple has not changed.
   d. The absolute price of an orange has not changed.
   e. Both c and d are correct.

4. Which of the following statements is true?
   a. The transaction costs of finding a double coincidence of wants in order to barter are usually quite low.
   b. Money reduces transaction costs.
   c. People base economic decisions on nominal prices.
   d. If all money prices doubled, nominal prices would not change.
   e. A double coincidence of wants is necessary to conduct money transactions.

5. If the price of a t-shirt is $12 and the price of a pair of designer jeans is $66, the relative price of a pair of designer jeans is
   a. 5 1/2 t-shirts.
   b. 2/11 t-shirts.
   c. 5 1/2 jeans.
   d. 2/11 jeans.
   e. $66.

Section 2: Demand

1. Which of the following will NOT cause a decrease in the demand for bananas?
   a. Reports surface that imported bananas are infected with a deadly virus.
   b. Consumers' incomes drop.
   c. The price of bananas rises.
   d. A deadly virus kills monkeys in zoos across the United States.
   e. Consumers expect the price of bananas to decrease in the future.

2. An increase in demand
   a. shifts the demand curve to the left.
   b. causes an increase in equilibrium price.
   c. causes a decrease in equilibrium price.
   d. causes a decrease in equilibrium quantity.
   e. does not affect equilibrium quantity.

3. Which of the following is NOT a determinant of demand?
   a. incomes
   b. tastes
   c. prices of resources
   d. prices of complements
   e. consumers' expectations about future prices

4. If demand decreases,
   a. price and quantity increase.
   b. price and quantity decrease.
   c. price increases and quantity decreases.
   d. price decreases and quantity increases.
   e. the supply will decrease.

5. A decrease in quantity demanded could be caused by
   a. a decrease in consumers' incomes.
   b. a decrease in the price of a substitute good.
   c. an increase in the price of a complementary good.
   d. a decrease in the price of the good.
   e. an increase in the price of the good.

6. A consumer buys more of a good or service when its price falls because it becomes cheaper relative to other goods. This is called
   a. the income effect.
   b. the substitution effect.
   c. a decrease in quantity demanded.
   d. a decrease in quantity supplied.
   e. a change in tastes.

7. The law of demand states that
   a. as the price of a good rises, the quantity demanded will fall, ceteris paribus.
   b. as the price of a good rises, the quantity supplied will fall, ceteris paribus.
   c. as the price of a good rises, the quantity demanded will rise, ceteris paribus.
   d. as the price of a good rises, the quantity supplied will rise, ceteris paribus.
   e. as the price of a good falls, the quantity demanded will fall, ceteris paribus.

8. Which of the following will cause an increase in the demand for eggs?
   a. The price of eggs drops.
   b. The price of bacon rises.
   c. A government report indicates that eating eggs three times a week increases the chances of having a heart attack.
   d. A decrease in the cost of chicken feed makes eggs less costly to produce.
   e. None of the above will increase the demand for eggs.

9. When the price of a good that a consumer typically buys goes up, the purchasing power of that consumer's income goes down. The consumer will buy less of that good and all other goods. This is called
   a. the substitution effect.
   b. the income effect.
   c. a decrease in quantity demanded.
   d. a decrease in quantity supplied.
   e. a change in tastes.

10. A freeze in Peru causes the price of coffee to skyrocket. Which of the following will happen?
    a. The demand for coffee will increase, and the demand for tea will increase.
    b. The demand for coffee will increase, and the quantity demanded of tea will increase.
    c. The quantity demanded of coffee will increase, and the demand for tea will increase.
    d. The quantity demanded of coffee will increase, and the quantity demanded of tea will increase.
    e. The quantity demanded of coffee will decrease, and the demand for tea will increase.

Section 3: Supply

1. According to the law of supply,
   a. as the price of a good or service rises, the quantity supplied will decrease, ceteris paribus.
   b. as the price of a good or service rises, the quantity supplied will increase, ceteris paribus.
   c. as the price of a good or service rises, the quantity demanded will increase, ceteris paribus.
   d. as the price of a good or service rises, the quantity demanded will decrease, ceteris paribus.
   e. as the price of a good or service falls, the quantity supplied of the good or service will increase.

2. Which of the following is NOT a determinant of supply?
   a. prices of resources
   b. technology and productivity
   c. prices of complements
   d. expectations of producers
   e. the number of producers

3. Japanese producers of a type of microchip offered such low prices that U.S. producers of the chip were driven out of business. As the number of producers decreased,
   a. the market supply of microchips increased; that is, the supply curve shifted to the right.
   b. the market supply of microchips increased; that is, the supply curve shifted to the left.
   c. the market supply of microchips decreased; that is, the supply curve shifted to the right.
   d. the market supply of microchips decreased; that is, the supply curve shifted to the left.
   e. there was no change in the supply of microchips; this event is represented by a movement from one point to another on the same supply curve.

4. Electronics firms can produce more than one type of good. Suppose that electronics firms are producing both military radios and microchips. A war breaks out, and the price of military radios skyrockets. The electronics firms throw more resources into making military radios and fewer resources into making microchips. Which of the statements below is true?
   a. The supply of microchips has decreased, and the quantity supplied of military radios has increased.
   b. The supply of microchips has decreased, and the supply of military radios has increased.
   c. The quantity supplied of microchips has decreased, and the supply of military radios has decreased.
   d. The quantity supplied of microchips has decreased, and the quantity supplied of military radios has decreased.
   e. There has been no change in the supply of microchips or in the supply of military radios.

5. Suppose that a change in technology makes car phones cheaper to produce. Which of the following will happen?
   a. The supply curve will shift to the left.
   b. The supply curve will shift to the right.
   c. The supply of car phones will increase.
   d. The supply of car phones will decrease.
   e. Both b and c are correct.

6. If supply decreases,
   a. the supply curve shifts to the right.
   b. equilibrium price increases.
   c. equilibrium price decreases.
   d. equilibrium price decreases and equilibrium quantity increases.
   e. equilibrium price increases and equilibrium quantity decreases.

7. Suppose that automakers expect car prices to be lower in the future. What will happen now?
   a. Supply will increase.
   b. Supply will decrease.
   c. Supply will not change.
   d. Demand will increase.
   e. Demand will decrease.

8. Which of the following will NOT cause an increase in the supply of milk?
   a. an increase in the number of dairy farmers
   b. a change in technology that reduces the cost of milking cows
   c. a decrease in the price of cheese
   d. a decrease in the price of milk
   e. a decrease in the price of cow feed

9. Which of the following will NOT change the supply of beef?
    a. The U.S. government decides to give a subsidy to beef producers.
    b. An epidemic of cow flu renders many cattle unfit for slaughter.
    c. The price of fish increases.
    d. A new hormone makes cows fatter and requires less feed.
    e. Beef producers expect lower beef prices next year.

Section 4: Equilibrium: Putting Demand and Supply Together

1. If demand increases and supply does not change,
    a. equilibrium price and quantity increase.
    b. equilibrium price and quantity decrease.
    c. equilibrium price increases and equilibrium quantity decreases.
    d. equilibrium price decreases and equilibrium quantity increases.
    e. the demand curve shifts to the left.

2. If supply decreases and demand does not change,
    a. equilibrium price and quantity increase.
    b. equilibrium price and quantity decrease.
    c. equilibrium price increases and equilibrium quantity decreases.
    d. equilibrium price decreases and equilibrium quantity increases.
    e. the supply curve shifts to the right.

3. Prices above the equilibrium price
    a. cause a shortage to develop and drive prices up.
    b. cause a shortage to develop and drive prices down.
    c. cause a surplus to develop and drive prices up.
    d. cause a surplus to develop and drive prices down.
    e. cause an increase in supply.

4. Prices below the equilibrium price
    a. cause a shortage to develop and drive prices up.
    b. cause a shortage to develop and drive prices down.
    c. cause a surplus to develop and drive prices up.
    d. cause a surplus to develop and drive prices down.
    e. cause an increase in demand.

5. Utility regulators in some states are considering forcing operators of coal-fired generators to be responsible for cleaning up air and water pollution resulting from the generators. Utilities in these states do not currently pay the costs of the cleanup. If this law goes into effect,
    a. demand for electricity will increase, and price and quantity will increase.
    b. demand for electricity will decrease, and price and quantity will decrease.
    c. the supply of electricity will decrease, and price and quantity will decrease.
    d. the supply of electricity will increase, the price will decrease, and the quantity will decrease.
    e. the supply of electricity will decrease, the price of electricity will increase, and the quantity will decrease.

6. Medical research from South Africa indicates that vitamin A may be useful in treating measles. If the research can be substantiated,
   a. the supply of vitamin A will increase, causing equilibrium price and quantity to increase.
   b. the supply of vitamin A will increase, causing equilibrium price to fall and quantity to increase.
   c. the demand for vitamin A will increase, causing equilibrium price and quantity to increase.
   d. the demand for vitamin A will increase, causing equilibrium price to rise and quantity to fall.
   e. the supply of vitamin A will increase, causing equilibrium price to rise and quantity to fall.

7. Since 1900, changes in technology have greatly reduced the costs of growing wheat. The population has also increased since then. If you know that the changes in technology had a greater effect than the increase in population, then since 1900
   a. the price of wheat has increased and the quantity of wheat has decreased.
   b. the price and quantity of wheat have increased.
   c. the price and quantity of wheat have decreased.
   d. the price of wheat has decreased and the quantity of wheat has increased.
   e. the quantity of wheat has increased, and you haven't got the faintest idea what happened to the price.

8. Which of the following statements is false?
   a. Disequilibrium may persist in some markets because it is too costly to change prices rapidly.
   b. Most concert promoters believe it is better to have low ticket prices and long lines rather than high ticket prices and empty seats.
   c. Money prices set by governments are typically lower than equilibrium prices.
   d. Part of the cost of a restaurant meal is the opportunity cost of the time spent waiting for a table.
   e. All of the above are true.

Use the table below to answer questions 9 through 12.

Price	Quantity Demanded	Quantity Supplied
$0	24	0
1	20	2
2	16	4
3	12	6
4	8	8
5	4	10
6	0	12

9. The equilibrium price is
   a. $1.
   b. $2.
   c. $3.
   d. $4.
   e. $5.

10. The equilibrium quantity is
    a. 2.
    b. 4.
    c. 6.
    d. 8.
    e. 10.

11. If the price is $2, a ____ of ____ units will develop, causing the price to ____ .
    a. shortage; 12; increase
    b. shortage; 12; decrease
    c. surplus; 12; increase
    d. surplus; 12; decrease
    e. surplus; 19; decrease

12. If the price is $5, a ____ of ____ units will develop, causing the price to ____ .
    a. shortage; 6; increase
    b. shortage; 6; decrease
    c. surplus; 6; increase
    d. surplus; 6; decrease
    e. shortage; 12; increase

Use the graph below to answer questions 13 through 16.

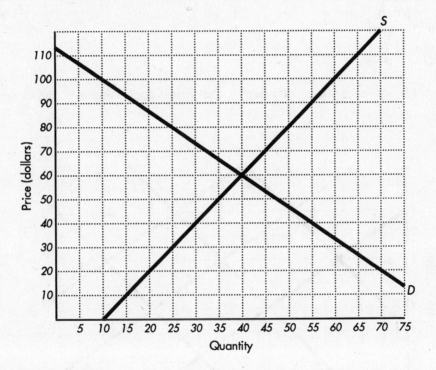

13. The equilibrium price is
    a. $20.
    b. $40.
    c. $60.
    d. $80.
    e. $100.

14. The equilibrium quantity is
    a. 25.
    b. 30.
    c. 35.
    d. 40.
    e. 45.

15. A price of $80 would cause a _____ of _____ units to develop, driving the price _____ .
    a. shortage; 6; up
    b. shortage; 25; up
    c. surplus; 6; down
    d. surplus; 25; down
    e. surplus; 25; up

16. A price of $20 would result in a _____ of _____ units, driving the price _____ .
    a. shortage; 10; up
    b. shortage; 50; up
    c. surplus; 10; down
    d. surplus; 50; down
    e. shortage; 50; down

Use the graph below to answer questions 17 through 20. The original supply curve is S_1, and the original demand curve is D_1.

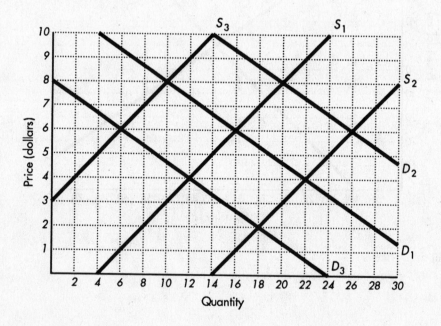

17. The original equilibrium price is _____ , and the original equilibrium quantity is _____ units.
    a. $6; 6
    b. $4; 12
    c. $8; 20
    d. $6; 16
    e. $8; 20

18. An increase in the price of a resource causes _____ to shift to _____ . The new equilibrium price is _____ , and the new equilibrium quantity is _____ units.
    a. demand; D_2; $8; 20
    b. demand; D_3; $4; 12
    c. supply; S_2; $4; 22
    d. supply; S_3; $8; 10
    e. supply; S_3; $10; 14

19. Begin at the original equilibrium position at the intersection of D_1 and S_1. Now a decrease in the price of a complementary good causes the _____ to shift to _____ . The new equilibrium price is _____ , and the equilibrium quantity is _____ units.
    a. demand; D_2; $8; 20
    b. demand; D_3; $4; 12
    c. supply; S_2; $4; 22
    d. supply; S_3; $8; 10
    e. supply; S_3; $10; 14

20. Begin at the original equilibrium position at the intersection of D_1 and S_1. An increase in income occurs at the same time as a change in technology decreases the costs of production. The new equilibrium price will be _____ , and the new equilibrium quantity will be _____ units.
    a. $6; 26
    b. $$4; 22
    c. $8; 20
    d. $10; 14
    e. $6; 8

PRACTICE QUESTIONS AND PROBLEMS

Section 1: Markets

1. A _____ is a place or service that enables buyers and sellers to exchange goods and services.

2. Another name for exchanges that violate the law is the _____ market.

3. The name given to unrecorded transactions, whether legal or illegal, is the _____ market.

4. The exchange of goods and services directly, without money, is called _____ .

5. In a barter economy, trade cannot occur unless there is a _____ of wants.

6. Another name for the money price of a good or service is the _____ price.

7. _____ prices, as opposed to money prices, affect economic behavior.

8. A person who chooses not to report his or her earnings to the IRS in order to avoid paying taxes would be part of the _____ market.

9. _____ occurs when an auto mechanic tunes up an accountant's car in exchange for the accountant doing the mechanic's income taxes.

10. The costs involved in making a barter exchange are called _____ costs.

11. The price established when an exchange occurs is called the _____ price.

12. If all nominal prices double, relative prices _____ (do, do not) change.

Section 2: Demand

1. _____ refers to the quantities of a well-defined commodity that consumers are willing and able to buy at each possible price during a given time period, ceteris paribus.

2. According to the law of demand, if you _____ your price, people will buy more, ceteris paribus.

3. _____ is Latin for "other things being equal."

4. List the five determinants of demand.

_____

_____

_____

_____

_____

5. Demand curves slope down because of the _____ and _____ effects.

6. Suppose that an increase in the price of Nohr Cola causes you to switch to Sooby Cola. You therefore buy less Nohr Cola. This is an example of the _____ effect.

7. Suppose that the price of steak decreases and your income does not change. You therefore can buy more steak than you did before. This is an example of the _____ effect.

8. A _____ is a graph of a demand schedule.

9. _____ goods can be used in place of each other; such goods would not be consumed at the same time.

10. Goods that are used together are called _____ goods.

11. Mardi, Dot, and Diane are college students who share an apartment. Dot loves strawberries and will buy them whenever they are available. Diane is a fair-weather strawberry eater: she only buys them if she thinks she is getting a good price. Mardi will eat strawberries for their vitamin C content but isn't crazy about them. The table on the following page shows the individual demand schedules for Mardi, Dot, and Diane. Suppose that these three are the only consumers in the local market for strawberries. Sum their individual demands to get the market demand schedule.

Price per Quart	Quantity for Dot	Quantity for Diane	Quantity for Mardi	Market
$0	6.00	4.00	2.00	_____
1	5.00	3.50	1.50	_____
2	4.00	3.00	1.00	_____
3	3.25	2.00	0.75	_____
4	2.00	1.50	0.50	_____
5	1.25	0.50	0.25	_____
6	0	0	0	_____

Plot the market demand for strawberries on the graph below.

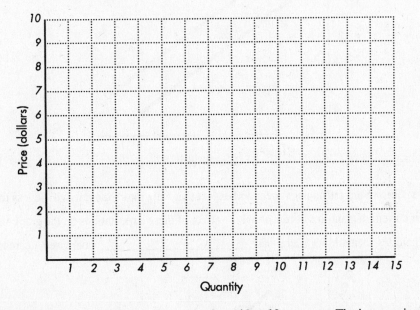

12. Suppose that the price of strawberries increases from $2 to $3 per quart. The increase in price would cause a decrease in the _____ (demand, quantity demanded) of strawberries. Show the effect of a change in the price of strawberries on the graph above.

13. Suppose that Dot reads in the paper that eating strawberries increases the sexual attractiveness of females. As a group, Dot and her friends decide to buy twice as many strawberries as they did before at every price. Plot the new market demand curve in the graph above, and label it D_2. This change in tastes has caused a/an _____ (increase, decrease) in _____ (demand, quantity demanded).

14. An increase in income _____ (increases, decreases) the _____ (demand, quantity demanded) for haircuts.

15. Many Americans have decreased their consumption of beef and switched to chicken in the belief that eating chicken instead of beef will lower their cholesterol. This change in tastes has

_____ (increased, decreased) the _____ (demand, quantity demanded) for beef and _____ (increased, decreased) the _____ (demand, quantity demanded) for chicken.

16. In the graph below, the price of good X increased, causing the demand for good Y to change from D_1 to D_2. The demand for good Y _____ (increased, decreased). X and Y are _____ (substitutes, complements).

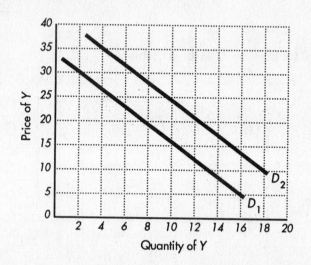

17. Mr. and Mrs. Gertsen are retiring next year and expect that their future income will be less than it is now. If D_1 is their current demand for bacon, show the effect of these expectations on the graph below. Label your new curve D_2. Demand for bacon has _____ (increased, decreased).

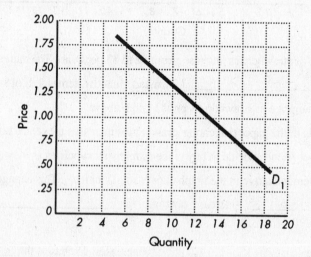

18. In the year 2000, one out of every five Americans will be over 65 years old. The demand for healthcare facilities for the elderly will _____ (increase, not change, decrease).

19. A crisis in the Middle East causes people to expect the price of gasoline to increase in the future. The demand for gasoline today will _____ (increase, not change, decrease).

20. If the price of Pepsi increases, the demand for Coke and other substitutes will

_____ .

Section 3: Supply

1. _____ is the amount of a good or service that producers are willing and able to offer for sale at each possible price during a period of time, ceteris paribus.

2. According to the law of supply, as the price _____, the quantity supplied decreases.

3. A table or list of the prices and corresponding quantity supplied of a well-defined good or service is called a _____ .

4. A _____ is a graph of a supply schedule.

5. Market supply curves have _____ slopes.

6. There are only two strawberry producers in the little town where Dot, Diane, and Mardi live. Their individual supply schedules are shown below. Sum the individual supplies to get market supply, and plot market supply on the graph on the following page.

Price per Quart	Quantity Supplied by Farmer Dave	Quantity Supplied by Farmer Ruth	Market
$0	2	2	_____
1	3	3	_____
2	4	4	_____
3	5	5	_____
4	6	6	_____
5	7	7	_____
6	8	8	_____

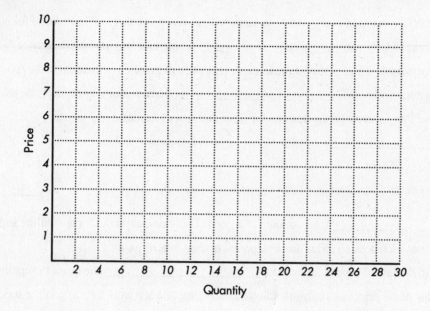

7. List the five determinants of supply.

_____

_____

_____

_____

_____

8. Suppose that a crisis in the Middle East cuts off the supply of oil from Saudi Arabia. If S_1 is the original market supply of oil, draw another supply curve, S_2, on the graph below to show the effect of Saudi Arabia's departure from the market. The _____ (quantity supplied, supply) has _____ (increased, decreased).

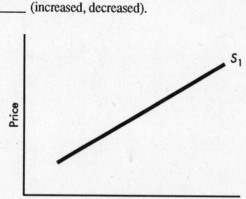

9. If the price of tomato sauce increases, the _____ (supply, quantity supplied) of pizza will _____ (increase, decrease).

10. _____ is the quantity of output produced per unit of resource.

11. A new process for producing microchips is discovered that will decrease the cost of production by 10 percent. The supply of microchips will _____ (increase, decrease, not change), causing the supply curve to _____ (shift to the right, shift to the left, not change).

12. A paper manufacturer can produce notebook paper or wedding invitations. If the price of wedding invitations skyrockets, we can expect the supply of _____ (notebook paper, wedding invitations) to _____ (increase, decrease).

13. A real estate developer who specializes in two-bedroom homes believes that the incomes of young couples will decline in the future. We can expect the supply of this realtor's two-bedroom homes to _____ (increase, decrease).

14. Changes in quantity supplied are caused by changes in the _____ of the good.

Section 4: Equilibrium: Putting Demand and Supply Together

1. The point at which the quantity demanded equals the quantity supplied at a particular price is known as the point of _____.

2. Whenever the price is greater than the equilibrium price, a _____ arises.

3. A _____ arises when the quantity demanded is greater than the quantity supplied at a particular price.

4. Shortages lead to _____ in price and quantity supplied and _____ in quantity demanded.

5. Surpluses lead to _____ in price and quantity supplied and _____ in quantity demanded.

6. The only goods that are not scarce are _____ goods.

7. The change in equilibrium price and quantity is in the _____ (same, opposite) direction as the change in demand.

8. Balloon manufacturers are nervous about a children's movement that may affect their product. The children are lobbying state legislatures to ban launchings of more than ten balloons at a time, citing the danger that balloons can do to wildlife. If the children are successful, we can expect the _____ (demand for, supply of) balloons to _____ (increase, decrease), causing the equilibrium price to _____ and the equilibrium quantity to _____.

9. If design changes in the construction of milk cartons cause the cost of production to decrease, we can expect the _____ (demand for, supply of) such cartons to _____ (increase, decrease), and the equilibrium price to _____ and the equilibrium quantity to _____.

10. A decrease in supply leads to a(n) _____ in price and a(n) _____ in quantity.

11. Remember Dot, Diane, and Mardi and the strawberry farmers Dave and Ruth? The local market for straw-berries (before Dot read about the effects of strawberries on sexual attractiveness) is reproduced on the graph below. The original demand is D_1, and the original supply is S. The equilibrium price is _____, and the equilibrium quantity is _____.

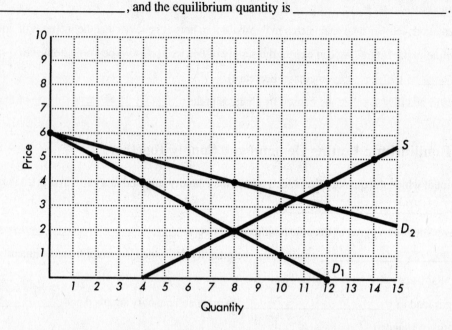

After Dot read the article on strawberries and sexual attractiveness, the market demand curve shifted to D_2. The new equilibrium price is _____, and the equilibrium quantity is _____. There was also a change in _____ (supply, quantity supplied).

12. _____ occurs when the quantity demanded and the quantity supplied are not equal.

13. The graph on the following page shows the market for corn. The equilibrium price is _____, and the equilibrium quantity is _____.

If the price of corn is $14, the quantity demanded will be _____, and the quanti-ty supplied will be _____. A _____ of _____ units will develop, causing the price and quantity supplied to _____ and the quantity demanded to _____.

If the price is $4, the quantity demanded will be _____, and the quantity supplied will be _____. A _____ of _____ units will develop, causing the price and quantity supplied to _____ and the quantity demanded to _____.

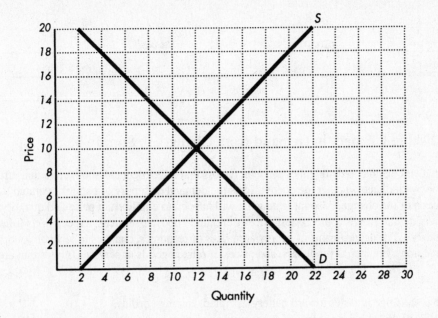

14. List three reasons why markets do not clear all the time.

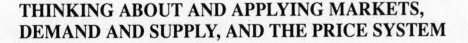

_____

_____

_____

THINKING ABOUT AND APPLYING MARKETS, DEMAND AND SUPPLY, AND THE PRICE SYSTEM

I. Wooden Bats Versus Metal Bats

1. The "Economically Speaking" section in Chapter 3 suggests an exercise for you to do. The supply of wooden bats is shown as S_w on the graph below. It has a steeper slope than the supply of metal bats, S_m, reflecting the fact that it is easier to produce additional metal bats than additional wooden bats. Suppose that D_m is the demand for metal bats. If baseball purists are willing to pay more for a "sweet crack" sound than for a dull metallic "ping" when they connect with a fastball, draw a demand curve for wooden bats and label it D_w. What are the consequences for the relative prices of wooden and metal bats?

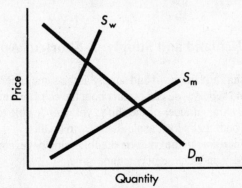

_____

_____

_____

_____

II. Distinguishing Changes in Demand from Changes in Supply

It is important that you be able to distinguish between factors that affect demand and factors that affect supply. For each event below, indicate whether the event affects the demand or supply of battery-operated dancing flowers and the direction of the change. Also indicate what will happen to equilibrium price and quantity. Remember, the determinants of demand are income, tastes, prices of related goods or services, expectations (of consumers), and number of buyers. The determinants of supply are prices of resources, changes in technology or productivity, producers' expectations, number of producers, and prices of related goods or services (goods that are substitutes in production).

1. There is a change in tastes toward battery-operated dancing gorillas.
2. The price of plastic rises.
3. A technological breakthrough makes it cheaper to produce plastic flowers.
4. Consumers' incomes rise.
5. The price of battery-operated dancing gorillas rises.
6. The price of batteries skyrockets.
7. A fire destroys a major production facility for dancing flowers.
8. Consumers expect lower prices for dancing flowers in the future.

	Demand	Supply	Price	Quantity
1.	_____	_____	_____	_____
2.	_____	_____	_____	_____
3.	_____	_____	_____	_____
4.	_____	_____	_____	_____
5.	_____	_____	_____	_____
6.	_____	_____	_____	_____
7.	_____	_____	_____	_____
8.	_____	_____	_____	_____

III. Simultaneous Shifts in Demand and Supply: A Shortcut Approach

What do you do if events occur that shift both demand and supply at the same time? If you know the relative magnitudes of the shifts in demand and supply, you can predict both the equilibrium price and the equilibrium quantity. If you do not know the relative magnitudes of the shifts, you will be able to predict either equilibrium price or equilibrium quantity, but not both. Let's look at a quick way to do this.

Suppose demand and supply both increase. In the chart on the following page, consider what will happen to price and quantity if you consider ONLY an increase in demand.

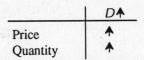

Now consider what will happen to price and quantity if you consider ONLY an increase in supply.

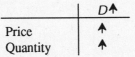

It's easy to see now that the quantity will increase but that the effect on price will be uncertain. If the demand change is larger than the supply change, price will increase. If the supply change is larger than the demand change, price will decrease.

Let's try it again. Suppose demand increases and supply decreases. First, consider what will happen to price and quantity if you consider ONLY an increase in demand.

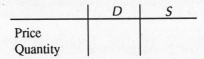

Now consider what will happen to price and quantity if you consider ONLY a decrease in supply.

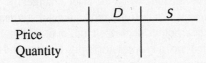

Can you see that the price will increase but that the effect on quantity will be uncertain? If the demand change is larger than the supply change, quantity will increase. If the supply change is larger than the demand change, quantity will decrease.

1. In the chart below, indicate a decrease in demand coupled with an increase in supply.

	D	S
Price		
Quantity		

2. Now try a decrease in demand coupled with a decrease in supply.

	D	S
Price		
Quantity		

3. Now let's try a more concrete example. We are analyzing the market for home computers. We foresee three main events coming up that will affect this market:
   a. Consumers' incomes are likely to increase.
   b. There will be an increase in the number of buyers as more schoolchildren become familiar with home computers in the classroom.
   c. We expect improvements in technology that will decrease the costs of production.

   Use the chart to determine what will happen to the equilibrium price and equilibrium quantity of home computers.

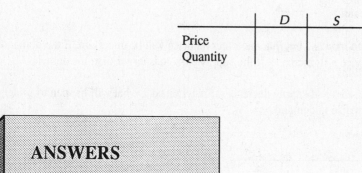

	D	S
Price		
Quantity		

ANSWERS

Quick Check Quiz

Section 1: Markets

1. c; 2. c (This is an underground market activity and not necessarily illegal.); 3. a; 4. b; 5. a
   If you missed any of these questions, you should go back and review pages 56–60 in Chapter 3.

Section 2: Demand

1. c (A change in the price of a good causes a movement along the curve—a change in quantity demanded—not a change in demand.); 2. b; 3. c; 4. b; 5. e (Items a, b, and c are determinants of demand and cause the demand curve to shift. Item d causes an *increase* in quantity demanded.); 6. b; 7. a; 8. e (Item a causes an increase in quantity demanded. Items b and c cause decreases in demand. Item d affects the *supply* of bacon.); 9. b; 10. e (The demand for coffee is designed to tell us the quantity demanded when the price changes, so it does not shift when price changes: you move from one price to another on the same curve. Coffee and tea are substitutes in consumption. When the price of coffee rises, people buy less coffee and substitute tea. They buy more tea at every price, so the demand for tea increases.)
   If you missed any of these questions, you should go back and review pages 60–68 in Chapter 3.

Section 3: Supply

1. b; 2. c; 3. d; 4. a (The supply of military radios exists to tell us the quantity supplied of military radios when the price of radios changes. Supply doesn't change when the price changes: you simply move from one price to another on the same curve. Since microchips and military radios are substitutes in production, when the price of military radios increases, the supply of microchips decreases.); 5. e; 6. e; 7. a; 8. d (A change in the price of a good causes a change in quantity supplied, not a change in supply. Cheese and milk are substitutes in production, so if the price of cheese decreases, the supply of milk increases.); 9. c
   If you missed any of these questions, you should go back and review pages 68–74 in Chapter 3.

Section 4: Equilibrium: Putting Demand and Supply Together

1. a; 2. c; 3. d; 4. a; 5. e; 6. c; 7. d (Item e would be correct if you did not know that the supply change was greater than the demand change.), 8. b; 9. d; 10. d; 11. a; 12. d; 13. c; 14. d; 15. d; 16. b; 17. d; 18. d; 19. a; 20. a

If you missed any of these questions, you should go back and review pages 74–80 in Chapter 3.

Practice Questions and Problems

Section 1: Markets

1. market
2. black
3. underground
4. barter
5. double coincidence
6. nominal
7. Relative
8. underground
9. Barter
10. transaction
11. relative
12. do not

Section 2: Demand

1. Demand
2. lower
3. Ceteris paribus
4. income
   tastes
   prices of related goods or services
   expectations (of consumers)
   number of buyers
5. income; substitution
6. substitution
7. income
8. demand curve
9. Substitute
10. complementary
11.

Price per Quart	Market
$0	12
1	10
2	8
3	6
4	4
5	2
6	0

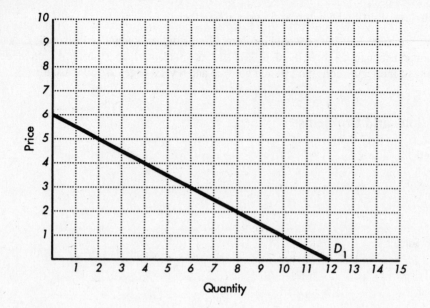

12. quantity demanded

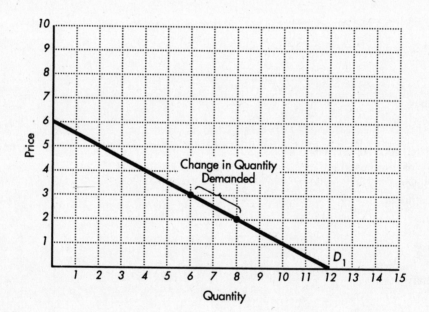

13. increase; demand

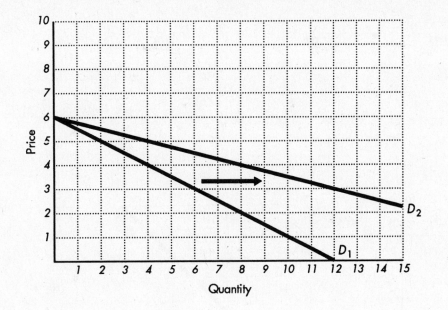

14. increases; demand
15. decreased; demand; increased; demand
16. increased; substitutes
17. decreased

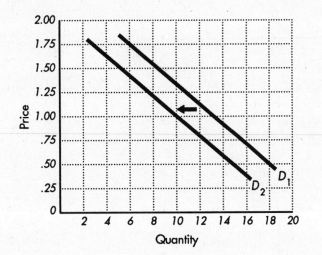

18. increase
19. increase
20. increase

Section 3: Supply

1. Supply
2. decreases
3. supply schedule
4. supply curve
5. positive

6.

Price per Quart	Market
$0	4
1	6
2	8
3	10
4	12
5	14
6	16

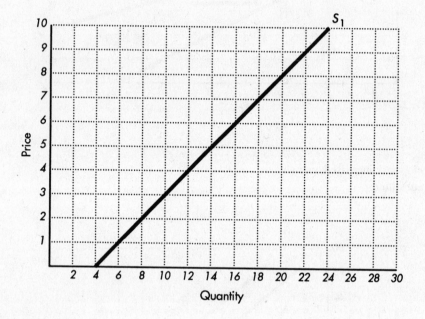

7. prices of resources
   technology and productivity
   expectations of producers
   number of producers
   prices of related goods or services
8. supply; decreased

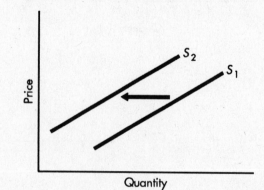

9. supply; decrease
10. Productivity
11. increase; shift to the right
12. notebook paper; decrease
13. increase (The real estate developer will try to offer as many homes for sale *now*, before incomes drop and the prices of houses drop.)
14. price

Section 4: Equilibrium: Putting Demand and Supply Together

1. equilibrium
2. surplus
3. shortage
4. increases; decreases
5. decreases; increases
6. free
7. same
8. demand for; decrease; decrease; decrease
9. supply of; increase; decrease; increase
10. increase; decrease
11. $2; 8; $3 1/3; 10 2/3 (These two values are eyeballed from the graph.); quantity supplied
12. Disequilibrium
13. $10; 12; 8; 16; surplus; 8; decrease; increase; 18; 6; shortage; 12; increase; decrease
14. Price changes can be costly.
    Buyers and sellers may not want price changes.
    Government intervention affects prices.

Thinking About and Applying Markets, Demand and Supply, and the Price System

I. Wooden Bats Versus Metal Bats

1.

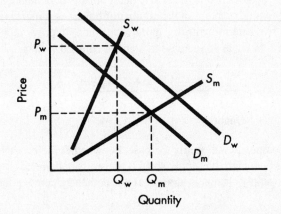

If baseball purists prefer wooden bats to metal bats, the demand for wooden bats will be to the right of the demand for metal bats. The price of wooden bats will be higher than the price of metal bats.

II. Distinguishing Changes in Demand from Changes in Supply

	Demand	Supply	Price	Quantity
1.	decrease	no change	decrease	decrease
2.	no change	decrease	increase	decrease
3.	no change	increase	decrease	increase
4.	increase	no change	increase	increase
5.	increase	no change	increase	increase
6.	no change	decrease	increase	decrease
7.	no change	decrease	increase	decrease
8.	decrease	no change	decrease	decrease

III. Simultaneous Shifts in Demand and Supply: A Shortcut Approach

1.

	$D\downarrow$	$S\uparrow$
Price	$\downarrow$	$\downarrow$
Quantity	$\downarrow$	$\uparrow$

Price will surely decrease, but the effect on quantity is uncertain. If the demand change is larger than the supply change, quantity will decrease. If the supply change is larger than the demand change, quantity will increase.

2.

	$D\downarrow$	$S\downarrow$
Price	$\downarrow$	$\uparrow$
Quantity	$\downarrow$	$\downarrow$

Quantity will surely decrease, but the effect on price is uncertain. If the demand change is larger than the supply change, price will decrease. If the supply change is larger than the demand change, price will increase.

3. An increase in consumers' incomes is one of the five determinants of demand, so this factor will cause demand to increase. Likewise, an increase in the number of buyers will increase demand. Improvements in technology are one of the five determinants of supply. Since these improvements lower costs, supply will increase. We are therefore looking at an increase in demand coupled with an increase in supply. Our chart looks like this:

	$D\uparrow$	$S\uparrow$
Price	$\uparrow$	$\downarrow$
Quantity	$\uparrow$	$\uparrow$

The quantity of home computers will surely increase, but whether the price rises or falls depends on whether the demand shifts outweigh the supply shift. If the shifts in demand overwhelm the shift in supply, prices will increase. If the supply change is larger than the demand change, prices will decrease.

CHAPTER 4
The Price System, Market Failures, and Alternatives

1. In a market system, who decides what goods and services are produced?

   In a **market system,** consumers decide what goods and services are produced by means of their purchases. If consumers want more of a good or service and are able to pay for it, demand increases and the price of the good or service increases. Higher profits then attract new producers to this industry. If consumers want less of an item, demand decreases and the price of the item decreases. Resources are attracted away from this industry.

   Under **socialism** and **communism,** central planners decide what goods and services are to be produced. In **traditional economies,** the same goods and services are produced now and in the same way as they were produced in the past.

2. How are goods and services produced?

   In a market system, the search for profit leads firms to use the least-cost combinations of resources to produce goods and services.

3. Who obtains the goods and services that are produced?

   In a market system, income and prices determine who gets what. Income is determined by the ownership of resources: those who own highly valued resources get more income. Output is then allocated to whoever is willing to pay the price.

4. What is a market failure?

   A **market failure** occurs when the price of a good or service does not fully reflect all the costs or benefits associated with the production or consumption of that good or service. It may result from imperfect information, **externalities,** the existence of **public goods,** or the existence of common ownership.

5. How do different economic systems answer the *what, how,* and *for whom* questions?

   Capitalist economies rely on prices to allocate resources and output. Socialist and communist economies rely on central planning boards. **Mixed economies** rely on a mixture of prices and government planning. Traditional societies produce the goods they have always produced and allocate output in the way it has always been allocated.

KEY TERMS

market system	market price	capitalism
price system	market imperfection	laissez faire
centrally planned system	long run	socialism
consumer sovereignty	externalities	communism
technical efficiency	public goods	mixed economies
economic efficiency	private property right	traditional economies
market failure	free ride	

QUICK CHECK QUIZ

Section 1: What Is Produced

1. In a market system, _____ decide what will be produced.
   a. producers
   b. consumers
   c. politicians
   d. government authorities
   e. central planning boards

2. Many fitness educators are advocating step exercise as a way to improve cardiovascular fitness. Special boxes are used by participants, who step up and down, from side to side, and so on. If these boxes catch on, the (demand for, supply of) these boxes will (increase, decrease), their price will (increase, decrease), and (more, fewer) boxes will be produced.
   a. demand for; increase; increase; more
   b. supply of; increase; increase; more
   c. supply of; increase; decrease; more
   d. demand for; increase; decrease; more
   e. supply of; increase; decrease; fewer

Section 2: How Goods and Services Are Produced

1. Assume that labor costs $3/unit, capital costs $2/unit, land costs $1/unit, and entrepreneurial ability costs $4/unit. All of the following combinations of resources will produce 35 units of good X. Which is the technically efficient way to produce good X?
   a. 3 units of land, 4 units of labor, 2 units of capital, and 1 unit of entrepreneurial ability
   b. 2 units of land, 1 unit of labor, 2 units of capital, and 1 unit of entrepreneurial ability
   c. 4 units of land, 1 unit of labor, 1 unit of capital, and 1 unit of entrepreneurial ability
   d. 1 unit of land, 2 units of labor, 3 units of capital, and 2 units of entrepreneurial ability
   e. 2 units of land, 2 units of labor, 3 units of capital, and 1 unit of entrepreneurial ability

2. Economic efficiency refers to
   a. the combination of inputs that result in the lowest costs.
   b. the allocation of resources in their most highly valued uses.
   c. the role of central planning boards in determining what goods and services are to be produced.
   d. the role of government in providing public goods.
   e. the role of government in imposing taxes on those goods and services that produce negative externalities.

Section 3: The Distribution of Goods and Services: For Whom

1. About 60 percent of national income comes from
   a. rent.
   b. wages and salaries.
   c. interest.
   d. profit.
   e. dividends.

2. Which of the following statements is true?
   a. In a communist system, income and prices allocate goods and services.
   b. Incomes are more equally distributed in less developed countries than in developed countries.
   c. About 26 percent of national income in the United States comes from profit, the return for entrepreneurial ability.
   d. In a market system, incomes are evenly distributed.
   e. Government-directed answers to the questions of what to produce, how to produce, and for whom to produce lead to a more equal distribution of income.

Section 4: Evaluating the Price System

1. Which of the following does NOT involve negative externalities?
   a. cigarette smoke in a crowded restaurant
   b. acid rain
   c. Amazon rain forests, which help to neutralize the effects of air pollution
   d. a blaring stereo
   e. the use of a highway by an additional vehicle

2. A lighthouse is an example of
   a. a negative externality.
   b. a positive externality.
   c. a public good.
   d. a commonly owned good.
   e. a private property right.

3. If negative externalities are involved in the production or consumption of a good, (too little, too much) of the good is produced or consumed. The government should (impose taxes, grant subsidies) to encourage producers to produce (more, less) of the good.
   a. too little; grant subsidies; more
   b. too little; impose taxes; less
   c. too much; impose taxes; more
   d. too much; impose taxes; less
   e. too much; grant subsidies; less

4. Which of the following statements is false?
   a. It is not possible to exclude people from the benefits of public goods.
   b. Education is an example of a good with positive externalities.
   c. People have an incentive to try for a free ride when goods are public goods.
   d. If a good has positive externalities, too little of the good is produced.
   e. The price system ensures that the appropriate amount of public goods will be produced.

5. Which of the following is an example of market failure?
   a. Lana hates her new haircut.
   b. Stan's new car turns out to be a clunker.
   c. Jan's neighbor blasts her out of bed with his new stereo at 4 A.M.
   d. Dan's new sweater falls apart the first time he washes it.
   e. Tim buys expensive basketball shoes that hurt his feet.

Section 5: Alternative Economic Systems

1. Which country(ies) come(s) closest to a purely socialist form of economic system?
   a. Cuba
   b. Italy
   c. Canada
   d. Vietnam
   e. Cuba and Vietnam

2. Laissez faire is associated with
   a. capitalist economies.
   b. socialist economies.
   c. communist economies.
   d. mixed economies.
   e. traditional economies.

3. Central planners answer the questions of *what, how,* and *for whom* to produce in
   a. capitalist economies.
   b. socialist economies.
   c. communist economies.
   d. traditional economies.
   e. socialist and communist economies.

4. _____ economies exist because people lack the opportunities or incentives to learn new ways.
   a. Capitalist
   b. Socialist
   c. Communist
   d. Traditional
   e. Mixed

PRACTICE QUESTIONS AND PROBLEMS

Section 1: What Is Produced

1. The _____, or price, system is an economic system in which supply and demand determine what goods and services are produced and the prices at which they are sold.

2. An economic system in which the government determines what goods and services are produced and the prices at which they are sold is called a _____ system.

3. _____ is the supreme authority of consumers to determine, by means of their purchases, what is produced.

4. Resources tend to flow from _____ -valued uses to _____ - valued uses as firms seek to make a profit.

5. If consumers' tastes change in favor of a good, _____ (demand, supply) will _____ (increase, decrease). A _____ (higher, lower) price will attract new firms to the production of that good.

6. If consumers' tastes change away from a good, _____ (demand, supply) will _____ (increase, decrease). A _____ (higher, lower) price will cause firms to leave the industry.

7. In a market system, _____ dictate what is to be produced by means of their purchases of goods and services.

Section 2: How Goods and Services Are Produced

1. _____ efficiency is the combination of inputs that results in the lowest cost.

2. _____ efficiency is the employment of resources in their most highly valued use in order to maximize the value of the output.

3. The search for _____ induces firms to use resources in their most efficient manner.

4. A small company continues to use an old mimeograph machine even though a new personal copier would cut the company's copying costs by 50 percent. This is an example of _____ inefficiency.

5. A black man is repeatedly passed over for promotion because of his race. This is an example of _____ inefficiency.

Section 3: The Distribution of Goods and Services: For Whom

1. Most income comes from _____ .

2. The most unequal distribution of income occurs in _____ (developed, less developed) countries.

3. _____ and _____ determine for whom to produce.

4. The price system _____ (does, does not) guarantee an equal distribution of income.

Section 4: Evaluating the Price System

1. _____ is the failure of the market system to achieve economic and technical efficiency.

2. The _____ price is the equilibrium price.

3. Situations in which the least-cost combination of resources is not used or in which a resource is not used where it has its highest value are called _____.

4. The _____ is a period of time in which something once believed to be fixed becomes variable.

5. _____ are the costs or benefits of a market activity borne by someone who is not a party to the market transaction.

6. When negative externalities exist, the market price _____ (overstates, understates) the full cost of the activity.

7. _____ are goods whose consumption benefits more than the person who purchased the good.

8. The limitation of ownership to an individual is called a _____.

9. A producer or consumer who enjoys the benefits of a good without having to pay for it is getting a _____.

10. Common ownership results in _____ (overutilization, underutilization).

11. Market imperfections may result from _____ or inaccurate information.

12. Once streetlights exist, people who have not paid for them cannot be excluded from their benefits. Streetlights are _____ goods.

Section 5: Alternative Economic Systems

1. _____ is an economic system characterized by private ownership of most resources, goods, and services.

2. _____ is a French phrase meaning "leave alone."

3. _____ is an economic system characterized by government ownership of resources other than labor and centralized economic decision making.

4. In socialist systems, incomes tend to be _____ (more, less) evenly distributed than in capitalist countries.

5. _____ is an economic system in which all resources are commonly owned and economic decision making is centrally planned.

6. _____ economies have the characteristics of more than one economic system.

7. In _____ economies, long-established customs provide answers to the *what, how,* and *for whom* questions.

THINKING ABOUT AND APPLYING THE PRICE SYSTEM, MARKET FAILURES, AND ALTERNATIVES

I. The Demand for Services in the Travel Industry

The "Economically Speaking" selection in the text looks at the economic incentives for travel firms to add services. These services add costs to the expenses of the firm but may also increase demand. If the demand shift is greater than the supply shift, it pays the firm to add the service. If the supply shift is greater than the demand shift, it does not pay the firm to add the service.

The graph below represents the demand for hotel rooms without daily delivery of newspapers. Plot new demand and supply curves that show the effects of providing daily newspapers, and construct your curves to make it profitable for hotels to provide the newspapers.

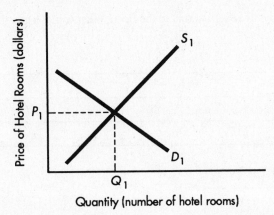

What happened to the price of hotel rooms?

_____

_____

_____

_____

II. Government Response to Externalities

The graph on the following page shows the demand and supply of an industry's product. This industry currently spews pollution into the air but bears no costs for its actions. If the industry is made responsible for the cleanup, show the effect on the market for this firm's product.

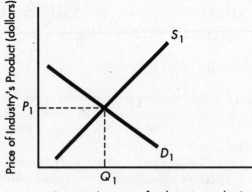

Quantity (amount of industry's product)

How could the government make this cost internal to the firm? What would happen to the price of the firm's output?

_____

_____

_____

_____

ANSWERS

Quick Check Quiz

Section 1: What Is Produced

1. b; 2. a

  If you missed any of these questions, you should go back and review pages 86–90 in Chapter 4.

Section 2: How Goods and Services Are Produced

1. b; 2. b

  If you missed any of these questions, you should go back and review page 91 in Chapter 4.

Section 3: The Distribution of Goods and Services: For Whom

1. b; 2. c

  If you missed any of these questions, you should go back and review pages 92–94 in Chapter 4.

Section 4: Evaluating the Price System

1. c; 2. c; 3. d; 4. e; 5. c

  If you missed any of these questions, you should go back and review pages 94–99 in Chapter 4.

Section 5: Alternative Economic Systems

1. e; 2. a; 3. e; 4. d
   If you missed any of these questions, you should go back and review pages 99–104 in Chapter 4.

Practice Questions and Problems

Section 1: What Is Produced

1. market
2. centrally planned
3. Consumer sovereignty
4. low; higher
5. demand; increase; higher
6. demand; decrease; lower
7. consumers

Section 2: How Goods and Services Are Produced

1. Technical
2. Economic
3. profit
4. technical
5. economic

Section 3: The Distribution of Goods and Services: For Whom

1. wages and salaries
2. less developed
3. Income; price
4. does not

Section 4: Evaluating the Price System

1. Market failure
2. market
3. market imperfections
4. long run
5. Externalities
6. understates
7. Public goods
8. private property right
9. free ride
10. overutilization
11. incomplete
12. public

Section 5: Alternative Economic Systems

1. Capitalism
2. *Laissez faire*
3. Socialism
4. more
5. Communism
6. Mixed
7. traditional

Thinking About and Applying the Price System, Market Failures, and Alternatives

I. The Demand for Services in the Travel Industry

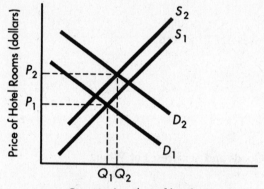

Quantity (number of hotel rooms)

If your graph is correct, the demand shift will be greater than the supply shift. If the new equilibrium price and quantity are greater than the original price and quantity, you have done it correctly.

The price of hotel rooms increased.

II. Government Response to Externalities

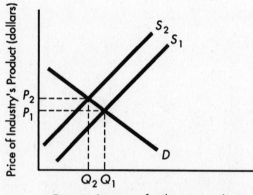

Quantity (amount of industry's product)

If the industry is forced to pay for the cleanup, costs will rise, shifting the supply curve to the left. The government could achieve this effect by imposing a tax on the industry or by setting quotas on its output.

CHAPTER 5
Households, Businesses, Government, and the International Sector

1. What is a household, and what is household income and spending?

   A **household** consists of one or more persons who occupy a unit of housing. Householders derive their incomes from ownership of the factors of production: land, labor, capital, and entrepreneurial ability. Household spending is called **consumption** and is the largest component of total spending in the economy.

2. What is a firm, and what is business spending?

   A firm is a business organization controlled by a single management. **Business firms** may be organized as **sole proprietorships, partnerships,** or **corporations.** Business spending by firms is called **investment** and consists of expenditures on capital goods to be used in producing goods and services.

3. What is the economic role of government?

   The economic role of government may be divided into two categories: microeconomic policy and macroeconomic policy. Microeconomic policy deals with providing public goods, correcting externalities, promoting competition, and redistributing income. Macroeconomic policy is divided into two categories, **fiscal policy** and **monetary policy**. Monetary policy is directed toward control of the money supply and credit. Fiscal policy deals with government spending and taxation.

4. How does the international sector affect the economy?

   The economies of industrialized nations are highly interdependent. As business conditions change in one country, business firms shift resources between countries so that economic conditions in one country spread to other countries.

   The international trade of the United States occurs primarily with the industrial countries, especially Canada and Japan. **Exports** are products the United States sells to foreign countries. **Imports** are products it buys from other countries. The United States had **trade surpluses** after World War II up until the 1980s.

5. How do the four sectors interact in the economy?

   Households own the **factors of production** and sell them to firms, the government, and the international sector in return for income. Business firms combine the factors of production into goods and services and sell them to households, the international sector, and the government in exchange for total revenue. The government receives income from households and firms in the form of taxes and uses these taxes to provide certain goods and services. The international sector buys and sells goods and services to business firms. The **circular flow diagram** is used to illustrate these relationships.

KEY TERMS

household
consumption
business firm
sole proprietorship
partnership
corporation
multinational business

venture capital
investment
monetary policy
Federal Reserve
fiscal policy
budget surplus (deficit)

imports
exports
trade surplus (deficit)
net exports
factors of production
circular flow diagram

QUICK CHECK QUIZ

Section 1: Households

1. Householders _____ years old make up the largest number of households.
   a. 15–24
   b. 25–34
   c. 35–44
   d. 45–54
   e. 55–64

2. Householders _____ years old have the largest median income.
   a. 15–24
   b. 25–34
   c. 35–44
   d. 45–54
   e. 55–64

3. The largest percentage of households consists of _____ person(s).
   a. one
   b. two
   c. three
   d. four
   e. five

4. Household spending, or consumption, is the _____ component of total spending in the economy.
   a. largest
   b. second largest
   c. third largest
   d. fourth largest
   e. smallest

Section 2: Business Firms

1. In _____ , the owners of the business are responsible for all the debts incurred by the business and may have to pay these debts from their personal wealth.
   a. sole proprietorships
   b. partnerships
   c. corporations
   d. sole proprietorships and partnerships
   e. sole proprietorships, partnerships, and corporations

2. _____ are the most numerous form of business organization, and _____ account for the largest share of total revenues.
   a. Sole proprietorships; partnerships
   b. Sole proprietorships; corporations
   c. Partnerships; corporations
   d. Corporations; sole proprietorships
   e. Partnerships; sole proprietorships

3. Investment, as used in the text, is NOT
   a. a financial transaction such as buying bonds or stock.
   b. business spending on capital goods.
   c. equal to about one-fourth of household spending.
   d. extremely volatile.
   e. All of the above describe investment.

4. The largest percentage of the cash needed to start new businesses comes from
   a. bank loans.
   b. relatives.
   c. friends.
   d. SBA loans.
   e. personal assets.

Section 3: Government

1. Which of the following is NOT a microeconomic function of government?
   a. provision of public goods
   b. control of money and credit
   c. correction of externalities
   d. promotion of competition
   e. redistribution of income

2. Which of the following is a macroeconomic function of government?
   a. redistribution of income
   b. promotion of competition
   c. determining the level of government spending and taxation
   d. provision of public goods
   e. correction of externalities

3. The _____ is/are responsible for fiscal policy, and the _____ is/are responsible for monetary policy.
   a. Federal Reserve; Congress
   b. Federal Reserve; Congress and the president
   c. Congress; Federal Reserve
   d. Congress and the president; Federal Reserve
   e. Congress; Federal Reserve and the president

Section 4: The International Sector

1. The United States tends to import primary products such as agricultural products or minerals from
   a. low-income countries.
   b. medium-income countries.
   c. high-income countries.
   d. industrialized countries.
   e. developing countries.

2. The United States does most of its trading with
   a. the United Kingdom and Germany.
   b. Eastern Europe.
   c. Canada and Japan.
   d. oil exporters.
   e. Western Europe.

Section 5: Linking the Sectors

1. Which of the following statements is false?
   a. Households own the factors of production.
   b. Firms buy the factors of production from households.
   c. The value of output must equal the value of income.
   d. The value of private production must equal the value of household income.
   e. Households receive income from the government in exchange for providing the factors of production for the government.

PRACTICE QUESTIONS AND PROBLEMS

Section 1: Households

1. A _____ consists of one or more persons who occupy a unit of housing.

2. Household spending is called _____.

3. Householders between _____ and _____ years old have the largest median incomes.

4. A household is most likely to consist of _____ persons.

Section 2: Business Firms

1. A _____ is a business organization controlled by a single management.

2. A _____ is a business owned by one person.

3. A _____ is a business owned by two or more individuals who share both the profits of the business and the responsibility for the firm's losses.

4. A _____ is a legal entity owned by shareholders whose liability for the firm's losses is limited to the value of the stock they own.

5. A _____ business is a firm that owns and operates producing units in foreign countries.

6. In the United States, the most common form of business organization is the _____.

7. _____ refers to a loan provided by an individual or firm that specializes in lending to new, unproven businesses.

8. The _____ is a government agency that assists small firms.

9. _____ is the expenditure by business firms for capital goods.

10. _____ account for the largest fraction of business revenue.

Section 3: Government

1. a. List the four microeconomic functions of government.

    _____

    _____

    _____

    _____

    b. Who is responsible for microeconomic policies? _____

2. The macroeconomic functions of government are _____ and _____ policy.

3. The _____ is the central bank of the United States.

4. Monetary policy is directed toward control of the _____.

5. Fiscal policy is directed toward _____ and _____.

6. Who is responsible for monetary policy? _____

7. Who is responsible for fiscal policy? _____

8. The _____ usually initiates major policy changes.

9. If federal government spending is less than tax revenue, a budget _____ exists.

10. If federal government spending is greater than tax revenue, a budget _____ exists.

Section 4: The International Sector

1. The _____ is an international organization that makes loans to developing countries.

2. Low-income economies are heavily concentrated in _____ and _____.

3. Products that a country buys from another country are called _____.

4. Products that a country sells to another country are called _____.

5. The United States trades mainly with two countries, _____ and _____.

6. A trade _____ exists when exports exceed imports.

7. A trade _____ exists when imports exceed exports.

8. _____ equal exports minus imports.

9. _____ net exports signal a trade surplus; _____ net exports signal a trade deficit.

Section 5: Linking the Sectors

1. List the four factors of production.

   _____

   _____

   _____   _____

   _____

2. _____ own the factors of production.

3. The _____ is a model showing the flow of output and income from one sector of the economy to another.

THINKING ABOUT AND APPLYING HOUSEHOLDS, BUSINESSES, GOVERNMENT, AND THE INTERNATIONAL SECTOR

I. The Circular Flow Diagram

Use the diagram below to see if you understand how the four sectors of the economy are linked together. Fill in the appropriate labels. Money flows are represented by broken lines. Flows of physical goods and services are represented by solid lines.

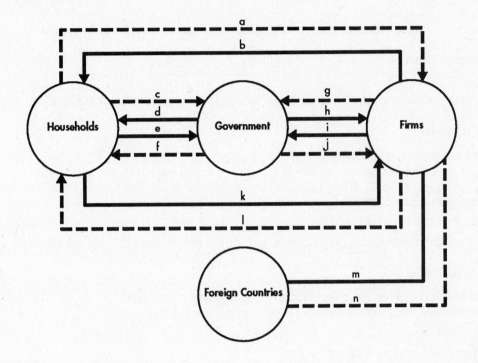

II. Student Entrepreneurs

The "Economically Speaking" article in your text describes some successful and not so successful ventures by student entrepreneurs. Consider student entrepreneurs as a group and compare them with entrepreneurs in general. What advantages might student entrepreneurs have because they are students? What disadvantages are they likely to have?

_____

_____

_____

_____

Quick Check Quiz

Section 1: Households

1. b; 2. d; 3. b; 4. a
   If you missed any of these questions, you should go back and review pages 110–112 in Chapter 5.

Section 2: Business Firms

1. d; 2. b; 3. a; 4. e
   If you missed any of these questions, you should go back and review pages 112–117 in Chapter 5.

Section 3: Government

1. b (It's a macroeconomic function.); 2. c; 3. d
   If you missed any of these questions, you should go back and review pages 117–123 in Chapter 5.

Section 4: The International Sector

1. e; 2. c
   If you missed either of these questions, you should go back and review pages 123–127 in Chapter 5.

Section 5: Linking the Sectors

1. d (This must be true only when the government and foreign sectors are excluded.)
   If you missed this question, you should go back and review pages 128–132 in Chapter 5.

Practice Questions and Problems

Section 1: Households

1. household
2. consumption
3. 45; 54
4. two

Section 2: Business Firms

1. business firm
2. sole proprietorship
3. partnership
4. corporation
5. multinational
6. sole proprietorship
7. Venture capital
8. Small Business Administration (SBA)
9. Investment
10. Corporations

Section 3: Government

1. a. provision of public goods
       correction of externalities
       promotion of competition
       redistribution of income
    b. Congress and the president
2. fiscal; monetary
3. Federal Reserve
4. money supply
5. government spending; taxation
6. Federal Reserve
7. Congress and the president
8. president
9. surplus
10. deficit

Section 4: The International Sector

1. World Bank
2. Africa; Asia
3. imports
4. exports
5. Canada; Japan
6. surplus
7. deficit
8. Net exports
9. Positive; negative

Section 5: Linking the Sectors

1. land
   labor
   capital
   entrepreneurial ability
2. Households
3. circular flow diagram

Thinking About and Applying Households, Businesses, Government, and the International Sector

I. The Circular Flow Diagram

line a—payments for goods and services
line b—goods and services
line c—taxes
line d—government services
line e—factors of production
line f—payments for factors of production
line g—taxes
line h—government services
line i—factors of production
line j—payments for factors of production

line k—factors of production
line l—payments for factors of production ($)
line m—net exports
line n—payments for net exports ($)

II. Student Entrepreneurs

Student entrepreneurs may be more in touch with the campus market than entrepreneurs as a group. It may be less expensive for students to get information about the student market (demographics, tastes, and so forth) and what products or services might appeal to that market. It may also be easier for them to disseminate information about their product or service and to find reliable, cheap employees. Finally, most students have not yet taken on family responsibilities, so they are at a point in their life cycle where they are the only ones who are hurt if the risk of opening their own business does not pay off.

Probably the biggest disadvantage in being a student entrepreneur is financing the firm. Students generally do not have many personal assets, and they may find that youth and inexperience hamper them in getting loans.

CHAPTER 6*
Consumer Choice

FUNDAMENTAL
QUESTIONS

1. Does one more dollar mean less to a millionaire than to a pauper?

    Just like paupers, millionaires (and all the rest of us, too) are subject to the laws of economics. Suppose you found a dollar bill on the sidewalk. Would you be happier about that if you had a million dollars already in the bank, or if you were broke and didn't know where your next meal was coming from? Consumer choice theory helps us understand why we care more about finding a dollar when we are poor than when we are rich.

    Using dollars to buy goods and services gives us satisfaction, or **utility.** As we consume more of anything during some period of time, the principle of **diminishing marginal utility** tells us that we will get less **marginal utility** (added satisfaction) from each unit. If you had no money at all, you would get a lot of utility from finding just one dollar bill but if you had a million dollars in the bank, you wouldn't care as much about finding another one.

    Since we can't measure utility, we can't really say whether one person gets more utility from something than another person does. If Joe and Jane are both paupers, we can't say which one would get more utility from one more dollar, and if Jane and Joe are both millionaires, we can't say either. Nor can we say which would get more utility if one were a millionaire and the other a pauper. We can be confident, though, that both Jane and Joe would rather be millionaires—and that each would get less satisfaction from a dollar if they were millionaires than if they were paupers.

2. How can a firm make a profit offering "all you can eat" specials?

    You probably know people who like to put sugar in their coffee. Have you ever seen them put five pounds of sugar in a single cup of coffee, even in places where sugar is free? They stop putting sugar into their coffee when they've had enough for their tastes: that is, when the marginal utility of sugar has become zero.

    People behave the same way about food—they stop eating when they are full. In economic language, they stop eating when their marginal utility for eating more at this meal declines to zero. At this point, eating more would give them **disutility.** To make a profit on "all you can eat" specials, the restaurant just has to set its price high enough to make a profit on the average consumer.

3. How do consumers allocate their limited incomes among the billions of goods and services that exist?

    When you walk into the mall, you don't just go into the first store and spend all your money on the first thing you see; you shop around and buy the things that give you the most value for your money. You probably don't think about it in these terms, but what you're doing is maximizing your utility by following the **equimarginal principle:** allocating your limited dollars among goods and services in such

Economics Chapter 20.

a way that the marginal utilities per dollar of expenditure on the last unit of each good purchased will be as nearly equal as possible.

This really is just common sense. If 7UP® has a marginal utility of 20 per dollar and Pepsi® has a marginal utility of 10 per dollar, 7UP is a better buy. If you were buying Pepsi now, you'd get more utility by switching to 7UP. The only time you can't get more utility by switching products is when the marginal utilities per dollar are the same.

4. Why do Disneyland, Sea World, and other businesses charge an admission fee and then provide the use of the facilities for no extra charge?

If the people managing Disneyland and Sea World know what they're doing, the answer must be that this method gives them more profit. The reason that it is more profitable goes back to the ideas of downward-sloping demand curves and **consumer surplus.** Suppose Jonathan will go to 1 movie next Saturday if the price is $6; he will buy tickets to 2 movies only if the price per movie drops to $4. If the movie theater charges $4 per ticket, they will take in $8 from Jonathan, even though those 2 movies were worth $10 to him ($6 for the first movie, plus $4 for the second); Jonathan has a consumer surplus of $2. But what if the theater runs a double feature: 2 movies for one $10 price? Jonathan will spend the $10, since the 2 movies are worth that much to him. By selling the 2 movies for a single price, the theater can collect Jonathan's consumer surplus.

KEY TERMS

utility	equimarginal principle	total utility
marginal utility	disutility	consumer surplus
diminishing marginal utility	consumer equilibrium	

QUICK CHECK QUIZ

Section 1: Utility

1. When economists use the term *utility*, they are talking about
   a. the usefulness of a good in everyday life: shovels have utility, but diamond rings don't have utility.
   b. a measure of the satisfaction received from possessing or consuming goods and services.
   c. businesses that sell electricity and natural gas.
   d. the satisfaction received from a good minus the price of the good.
   e. the satisfaction received from a good plus the price of the good.

2. Total utility measures the
   a. total satisfaction derived from consuming a good or service divided by the price of the good or service.
   b. extra utility derived from consuming one more unit of a good or service.
   c. total satisfaction derived from consuming a quantity of a good or service.
   d. extra utility derived from consuming one more unit of a good or service divided by the price of the good or service.
   e. total satisfaction derived from consuming a good or service divided by the price of the good or service.

3. Marginal utility measures the
   a. total satisfaction derived from consuming a good or service divided by the price of the good or service.
   b. extra utility derived from consuming one more unit of a good or service.
   c. total satisfaction derived from consuming a quantity of a good or service.
   d. extra utility derived from consuming one more unit of a good or service divided by the price of the good or service.
   e. total satisfaction derived from consuming a good or service multiplied by the price of the good or service.

4. As a consumer eats additional pieces of pie today, total utility will
   a. always keep increasing.
   b. always keep decreasing.
   c. keep increasing until dissatisfaction sets in.
   d. keep decreasing until dissatisfaction sets in.
   e. decrease until just before dissatisfaction sets in, then increase.

5. When marginal utility is zero, total utility is
   a. increasing.
   b. decreasing.
   c. at its maximum.
   d. at its minimun.
   e. zero.

6. According to the principle of diminishing marginal utility,
   a. total utility declines with each additional unit of a good or service that the consumer obtains.
   b. marginal utility declines with each additional unit of a good or service that the consumer obtains.
   c. total utility always grows with each additional unit of a good or service that the consumer obtains.
   d. marginal utility always grows with each additional unit of a good or service that the consumer obtains.
   e. marginal utility always remains constant.

Section 2: Utility and Choice

1. To decide which of two goods is the better buy, a consumer should compare the products'
   a. marginal utilities.
   b. total utilities.
   c. marginal utilities per dollar.
   d. total utilities per dollar.
   e. disutility.

2. Jennifer is trying to decide whether to buy a croissant or a bran muffin for tomorrow's breakfast. The croissant costs $2 and has a marginal utility of 30. The muffin costs $1 and has a marginal utility of 20. Which should she buy?
   a. the croissant, because it has a higher marginal utility
   b. the croissant, because it has a lower marginal utility per dollar
   c. the muffin, because it costs less
   d. the muffin, because it has a higher marginal utility per dollar
   e. It doesn't matter, because the croissant and the muffin have the same value to her.

3. Consumer equilibrium occurs when
   a. consumers have lots of money to spend.
   b. the marginal utilities per dollar obtained from the last unit of all products consumed are the same.
   c. consumers buy all goods that have a positive marginal utility.
   d. consumers buy all goods that have a positive total utility.
   e. consumers buy all goods that do not give disutility.

4. If a consumer is in equilibrium, then
   a. the consumer will not reallocate income.
   b. the consumer should buy more of all products.
   c. the consumer should buy more of some products and less of other products.
   d. the total utility obtained from all products consumed is the same.
   e. the consumer should buy less of all products.

Section 3: The Demand Curve Again

1. The relation between the price of a product and the quantity demanded is
   a. inverse.
   b. direct.
   c. reverse.
   d. complex.
   e. positive.

2. If the price of strawberries increases, then
   a. the marginal utility of strawberries will decrease.
   b. the marginal utility of strawberries will increase.
   c. the marginal utility per dollar of strawberries will decrease.
   d. the marginal utility per dollar of strawberries will increase.
   e. the total utility of strawberries will increase.

3. When a good becomes less expensive, it yields more satisfaction per dollar, so consumers buy more of it and less of other goods. This is called the
   a. substitution effect.
   b. income effect.
   c. replacement effect.
   d. augmentation effect.
   e. disbursement effect.

4. When a good becomes less expensive, consumers' real incomes increase and consumers purchase more of all goods. This is called the
   a. substitution effect.
   b. income effect.
   c. replacement effect.
   d. augmentation effect.
   e. disbursement effect.

5. Consumer surplus is the
   a. marginal utility divided by the price of a good.
   b. difference between what a consumer is willing to pay and the market price of a good.
   c. consumer's unspent income.
   d. consumer's total spending on a good.
   e. difference between the total utility and the marginal utility of a good.

Section 4: Market Demand

1. The market demand curve is obtained by
   a. summing individual demand curves.
   b. multiplying individual demand curves.
   c. dividing individual demand curves.
   d. subtracting individual demand curves.
   e. finding the ratios of the individual demand curves.

2. Which of the following is NOT held constant in determining the market demand for a good?
   a. individual consumers' incomes
   b. the number of consumers
   c. the prices of other goods
   d. the time period under consideration
   e. All of the above are held constant in determining the market demand for a good.

PRACTICE QUESTIONS AND PROBLEMS

Section 1: Utility

1. _____Total_____ (Total, Marginal) utility is the total satisfaction that a consumer obtains from consuming a quantity of some good or service, whereas _marginal_ (total, marginal) utility is the extra utility derived from consuming one more unit of a good or service.

2. According to the principle of _decreasing marginal utility_, marginal utility declines with each additional unit of a good or service.

3. Total utility increases until _disutility_ sets in.

4. The total utility of a good is at its maximum when marginal utility is _zero_.

5. Josephine gets 30 utils of satisfaction from eating 3 slices of cake in a day, and she gets 35 utils of satisfaction from eating 4 slices. What is her marginal utility for the fourth slice of cake?

   _____5_____ utils

6. Napolean gets 20 utils of satisfaction from eating 3 slices of bread in a day, and he gets 4 additional utils of satisfaction from eating a fourth slice. What is his total utility for 4 slices of bread?

   _____24_____ utils

The table below shows Napolean's total utility from eating slices of bread. Use the table to answer questions 7 through 9.

Slices of Bread per Day	Total Utility	Marginal Utility
1	4	4
2	14	10
3	20	6
4	24	4
5	24	0
6	21	–3

7. Fill in the blanks in the table with Napolean's marginal utility from eating slices of bread.

8. Using the same bar graph formats as Figures 1(a) and 1(b) in your text, plot Napolean's total and marginal utility from slices of bread on the graphs below.

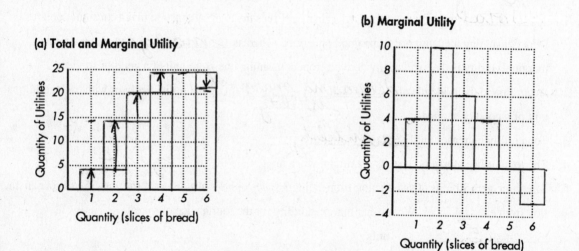

9. Explain how the principle of diminishing marginal utility applies to Napolean's consumption of slices of bread in a day.

The more he eats, the more his marginal utility declines.

The table below shows Josephine's total and marginal utility from eating slices of cake. Use the table to answer questions 10 through 14.

Slices of Cake per Day	Marginal Utility	Total Utility
1	20	20
2	25	45
3	18	63
4	~~12~~	75
5	7	~~82~~
6	3	85
7	0	85
8	–4	81

10. Use your knowledge of the relationship between total and marginal utility to fill in the blanks in the table.

11. Eating which slice of cake causes Josephine to encounter diminishing marginal utility? _____ 3 RD.

12. Josephine gets disutility from which slice of cake? _____ 8 th

13. If Josephine could get all the cake she wanted for free, what's the largest number of slices of cake she would choose to eat in a day? _____ 7 (or 6)

14. Can you think of any circumstances in which Josephine would voluntarily choose to eat 8 slices of cake in a day? _____ as part of a consumer choice survey

Section 2: Utility and Choice

1. Stephanie is sitting in the cafeteria after lunch, thinking about having some more cake for dessert; cake costs $.25 a slice. To maximize her total utility, Stephanie should keep on buying more cake as long as
   a. her marginal utility from another slice of cake is greater than zero.
   b. her marginal utility from another slice of cake is greater than or equal to zero.
   c. her marginal utility from another slice of cake is greater than the marginal utility of anything else she could buy.
   d. her marginal utility from another slice of cake is greater than the marginal utility of anything else she could buy for $.25.

STOP HERE! If you didn't choose answer *d,* go back and review Section 2 of the chapter before you go on.

2. The equimarginal principle says, "In order to maximize utility, consumers must allocate their limited incomes among goods and services in such a way that the ___ utility ___ per ___ dollar ___ of expenditure on the ___ final ___ unit of each good ___ purchased ___ will be as nearly ___ equal ___ as possible."

3. The point at which the marginal utilities per dollar of expenditure on the last unit of each good purchased are equal is called ___ consumer equilibrium ___

4. Consumers are in equilibrium when they have no ~~desire~~ incentive to ___ reallocate ___ their limited budget or income.

5. For recreation, George likes to go to the video arcade and play some of the classic games: Donkey Kong®, Super Mario Bros.®, and Pac-Man®. Write the equation George should try to follow to make sure he gets the most utility from the money he spends on these video games. $\dfrac{MU_{SMB}}{P_{SMB}} = \dfrac{MU_{DK}}{P_{DK}} = \dfrac{MU_{PM}}{P_{PM}} = \dfrac{MU}{\$1}$

6. The table below gives George's marginal utilities for Donkey Kong, Super Mario Bros., and Pac-Man. Calculate the *MU/P* for each game, using the prices given.

Donkey Kong (P = $.50)			Super Mario Bros. (P = $2)			Pac-Man (P = $1)		
Games per Day	*MU*	*MU/P*	Games per Day	*MU*	*MU/P*	Games per Day	*MU*	*MU/P*
1	55	110	1	270	135	1	120	120
2	50	110	2	240	120	2	110	110
3	47	94	3	220	110	3	100	100
4	45	90	4	200	100	4	90	90
5	40	80	5	180	90	5	72	72
6	37	74	6	160	80	6	63	63
7	34	68	7	120	60	7	54	54
8	31	62	8	80	40	8	45	45

7. One afternoon, George strolls into the video arcade with $5 in his pocket. If he wants to spend the $5 on video games, which game should he play first to get the most utility for his money?

SMB₁

8. After he has played the first game of Super Mario Bros., how much money does he have left?

$3

9. After the first game of Super Mario Bros., what games should he play next? SMB₂
and PM₁

10. Can he play any more games? ~~yes~~ no Why? no money left

11. When George used up his $5, he had played 2 games of Super Mario Bros. and 1 game of Pac-Man. What is the *MU/P* for these games?

MU/P for second game of Super Mario Bros. 120

MU/P for first game of Pac-Man 120

12. Since the *MU/P* is the same, George must have attained Consumer equilibrium

13. Suppose that some other afternoon George had $12 to spend in the arcade. Use the method shown in Table 2 in your text to fill in the table below and to determine which combination of games gives George the most utility from his $12.

Step	Choices	Decision	Remaining Budget $
1ST purchase	DK 110	SMB	12-2 = 10
	SMB 135		
	RM 120		
2ND	DK 110	SMB	10-2 = 8
	SMB 120		
	P-M 120		
3RD	DK 110	P-M	8-1 = 7
	SMB 110		
	P-M 120		
4TH	DK 110	DK 110	7-.50 = 6.50
	SMB 110		
	P-M 110		
5TH	DK 110	DK 110	6.50-.50 = 6
	SMB 110		
	P-M 110		
6TH	DK 94	SMB 110	6-2 = 4
	SMB 110		
	RM 110		
7TH	DK 94	P-M 110	4-1 = 3
	SMB 100		
	P-M 110		
8TH	DK 94	SMB 100	3-2 = 1
	SMB 100		
	P-M 100		
9TH	DK 94	P-M 100	1-1 = 0
	SMB 90		
	P-M 100		

14. When she studies, Ashley likes to munch on either corn chips or potato chips. Last month she bought 24 bags of corn chips and 20 bags of potato chips. For the amounts she bought last month, her current *MU* for corn chips would be 40 and her current *MU* for potato chips would be 50. If corn chips cost $1 per bag and potato chips cost $2 per bag, would Ashley be at consumer equilibrium if she purchased the same amounts this month as she did last month? How do you know?

no   *MU / P corn chips = 40/$1 = 40*
        MU / P potato chips = 50/$2 = 25

15. To move toward consumer equilibrium while keeping her total spending on corn chips and potato chips the same, Ashley should buy _*more*_ (fewer or more) corn chips and

*fewer* (fewer or more) potato chips. Explain why.

_____

_____

Section 3: The Demand Curve Again

1. The demand curve shows that there is a(n) _*inverse*_ (direct or inverse) relationship between the _*price*_ of a product and the _*quantity demanded*_.

2. The two economic principles accounting for the inverse relationship between the price of a product and the quantity demanded are the principle of *diminishing marginal utility* and the _*equimarginal*_ principle.

3. A change in the price of a product affects consumers in two ways: these are called the _*substitution*_ effect and the _*income*_ effect.

4. Sam usually buys lots of videotapes every month. If the price of videotapes drops this month, videotapes will now give him _*more*_ (more or less) satisfaction per dollar than before, so that, relative to other goods he buys, he will buy _*more*_ (more or fewer) videotapes than before and _*less*_ (more or less) of some other things. This is known as the _*substitution*_ effect of a price change.

5. When the price of videotapes drops this month, Sam can now buy the same number of videotapes and everything else he bought last month with _*less*_ (more, less, or the same amount of) money than he spent last month. This change in his buying possibilities is known as the _*income*_ effect of a price change.

6. The difference between what a consumer is willing and able to pay and the market price of a good is known as the _*consumer surplus*_

7. Remember our friend Ashley, who likes to munch corn chips or potato chips while she studies? (If you don't remember, review questions 14 and 15 in Section 2 above.) She's been studying consumer choice in her economics class and thinking about her spending choices. This month, she bought 28 bags of corn chips and 18 bags of potato chips; for the amounts she bought this month, her *MU* for corn chips was 30

and her *MU* for potato chips was 60. If corn chips cost $1 per bag and potato chips cost $2 per bag, is Ashley at consumer equilibrium now? How do you know?

yes   MU/P   corn chips   30/$1 = 30

MU/P   potato chips   60/$2 = 30

8. How much money is she spending on corn chips and potato chips each month?

$64

9. When Ashley goes to the grocery store to buy next month's batch of chips, she finds that there's a sale on potato chips—they're only $1 a bag.

a. With the sale, how much would she spend if she bought the same amounts of chips as in question 7?

$46

b. If Ashley keeps spending $64 per month on chips, can she buy more or fewer chips than before?

more   This is an example of the *income* effect of a price change.

c. If Ashley keeps buying 28 bags of corn chips and 18 bags of potato chips after the price of potato chips drops, is she still in consumer equilibrium? *no*   How do you know?

MU/P   corn chips = 30   potato chips = 60

d. To move toward a new consumer equilibrium, should she buy more or fewer bags of potato chips?

yes more   Why?   *potato chips are now a better buy*

e. This change is an example of the *substitution* effect of a price change.

10. The table below gives Jim's demand for videotape rentals each week.

Price per Rental	Number of Rentals Each Week
$5	1
4	2
3	3
2	4
1	5

If the only video store in town charges $3 per rental, how many tapes will Jim rent each week? *3*

How much money will he spend on videotape rentals? *$9*

How much will Jim's consumer surplus be? *$6 $3*

11. Suppose the video store raises its prices to $4 per rental but offers a special "3 rentals for $11" bargain package rate. Would Jim be willing to rent 3 tapes at the bargain rate? *yes*   How much would his consumer surplus be now? *$1*

12. If you owned the video store and wanted people like Jim to rent 3 tapes per week, would you take in more money charging $3 per rental, or charging the "3 rentals for $11" package rate?

3 rentals for $11   Why?   *you decrease consumer surplus from $3 to $1.*

Section 4: Market Demand

1. Below are the demand curves for Jill and Jack for Perrier bottled water. Plot their individual demand curves on the graphs; then calculate and plot their market demand curve.

Price per Bottle	Quantities Demanded by		
	Jill	Jack	Market
$3.00	1	0	1
2.50	2	0	2
2.00	4	2	6
1.50	6	4	10
1.00	10	7	17
.50	20	12	32

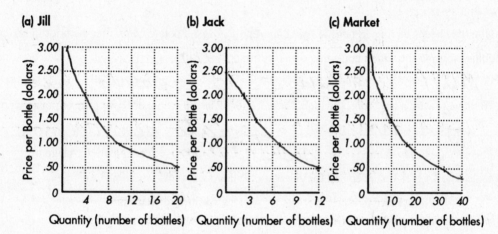

(a) Jill (b) Jack (c) Market

Quantity (number of bottles)   Quantity (number of bottles)   Quantity (number of bottles)

THINKING ABOUT AND APPLYING CONSUMER CHOICE

I. The Demand for Video Games

1. Remember George, the guy in Section 2 who spends his afternoons at the video arcade? The table below repeats George's marginal utilities for Donkey Kong, Super Mario Bros., and Pac-Man. Calculate the *MU/P* for each game, using the prices given.

Donkey Kong (P = $.50)			Super Mario Bros. (P = $2)			Pac-Man (various prices)					
Games per Day	MU	MU/P	Games per Day	MU	MU/P	Games per Day	MU	MU/P (P = $2)	MU/P (P = $1.50)	MU/P (P = $1)	MU/P (P = $.50)
1	55	___	1	270	___	1	120	___	___	___	___
2	50	___	2	240	___	2	110	___	___	___	___
3	47	___	3	220	___	3	100	___	___	___	___
4	45	___	4	200	___	4	90	___	___	___	___
5	40	___	5	180	___	5	72	___	___	___	___
6	37	___	6	160	___	6	63	___	___	___	___
7	34	___	7	120	___	7	54	___	___	___	___
8	31	___	8	80	___	8	45	___	___	___	___

2. Before we do anything with these numbers, let's look at some of the patterns and relationships in the Pac-Man sections of the table.

   a. As the price of Pac-Man games decreases from $2 down to $.50, does the added satisfaction (marginal utility) George gets from any game of Pac-Man change? _____

   b. As the price decreases, how does the added satisfaction *per dollar (MU/P)* change? _____

   _____

   c. What's the mathematical term for the relationship between the added satisfaction per dollar *(MU/P)* and the price? _____

   d. If the price is cut in half (say, from $2 to $1, or from $1 to $.50), what happens to the *MU/P*?

   _____

3. One evening George strolls into the video arcade with $16 that he plans to spend on video games that night. Using the prices of Donkey Kong and Super Mario Bros. given, figure out the number of games of Donkey Kong, Super Mario Bros., and Pac-Man George should play to reach consumer equilibrium for each of the prices for Pac-Man.

Price of Pac-Man	Games of Donkey Kong	Games of Super Mario Bros.	Games of Pac-Man
$2.00	_____	_____	_____
1.50	_____	_____	_____
1.00	_____	_____	_____
.50	_____	_____	_____

4. Draw George's demand curve for Pac-Man on the graph.

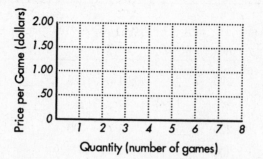

5. Use the income and substitution effects to explain why George plays more games of Pac-Man when the price of Pac-Man goes down.

_____

_____

_____

6. Use the income and substitution effects to explain why George plays fewer games of Donkey Kong and Super Mario Bros. when the price of Pac-Man goes down.

_____

_____

_____

II. Buying a Better Environment

The "Economically Speaking" section for this chapter deals with people's desire to promote a better-quality environment, even if that means paying more for other goods and services; surveys show that our willingness to pay more to protect the environment increased substantially between 1981 and 1990. Review that section in your text before starting on this problem.

Let's take a closer look at the idea of how we make trade-offs between environmental quality and other things we want. Suppose that we lump together all the goods and services we want (except environmental quality) and call this lump "other things." We get utility from these other things, and we get utility from environmental quality; both of these are subject to the law of diminishing marginal utility. The table below has hypothetical marginal utilities for "other things" and for environmental quality in 1981 and 1990. We'll assume that units of "other things" and units of environmental quality both cost $5,000 each.

"Other Things" (P = $5,000)			Environmental Quality (P = $5,000)				
Units	MU	MU/P	Units	MU (1981)	MU/P (1981)	MU (1990)	MU/P (1990)
1	50,000	____	1	30,000	____	40,000	____
2	45,000	____	2	26,000	____	35,000	____
3	40,000	____	3	22,000	____	30,000	____
4	35,000	____	4	18,000	____	26,000	____
5	30,000	____	5	15,000	____	23,000	____
6	25,000	____	6	12,000	____	21,000	____

1. Calculate the MU/P for "other things" and for environmental quality in 1981, and find this consumer's equilibrium consumption of "other things" and environmental quality if the consumer has $30,000 to spend.

   "Other things" _____ units (1981)

   Environmental quality _____ units (1981)

2. Surveys show that people in the United States think that the environment is in worse shape now than in the past. If so, people probably got more satisfaction (marginal utility) from additional units of environmental quality in 1990 than they did in 1981, as shown in the table. Using the same $30,000 spending as in 1981, find the consumer's 1990 consumer equilibrium.

   "Other things" _____ units (1990)

   Environmental quality _____ units (1990)

3. What can you conclude about how people's willingness to spend money on environmental improvements will be affected by increases in the utility to them of a better environment?

   _____

   _____

   _____

   _____

This analysis applies to other cases where changes in our tastes occur. If our tastes change so that we get more utility from potato chips, the marginal utility per dollar spent on potato chips will increase, leading us to increase our demand and buy more potato chips. On the other hand, if our tastes change so that we get less utility from videotape rentals, the marginal utility per dollar spent on videos will decrease, leading us to decrease our demand and rent fewer videos.

III. Fried Chicken and Consumer Surplus

"Smilin' Sam's Home-Style Fried Chicken" restaurant makes the best fried chicken in town—nobody makes it better. From experience and market research, Smilin' Sam knows that his average customer's demand looks like this:

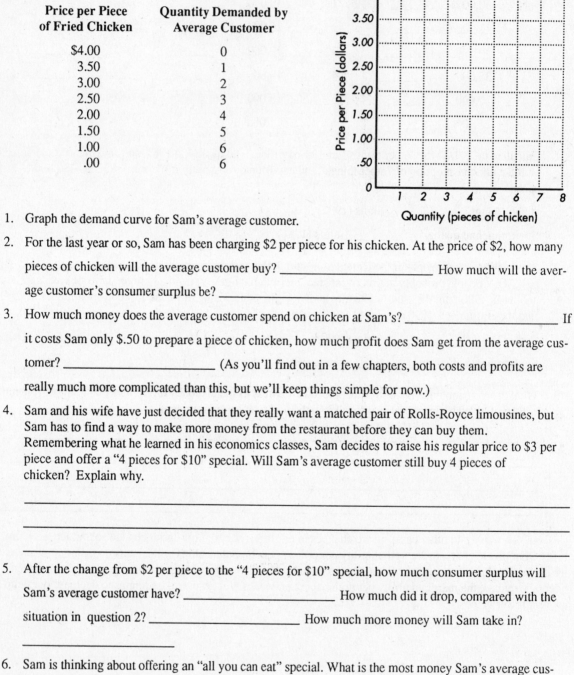

Price per Piece of Fried Chicken	Quantity Demanded by Average Customer
$4.00	0
3.50	1
3.00	2
2.50	3
2.00	4
1.50	5
1.00	6
.00	6

1. Graph the demand curve for Sam's average customer.

2. For the last year or so, Sam has been charging $2 per piece for his chicken. At the price of $2, how many

    pieces of chicken will the average customer buy? _____ How much will the aver-

    age customer's consumer surplus be? _____

3. How much money does the average customer spend on chicken at Sam's? _____ If

    it costs Sam only $.50 to prepare a piece of chicken, how much profit does Sam get from the average cus-

    tomer? _____ (As you'll find out in a few chapters, both costs and profits are

    really much more complicated than this, but we'll keep things simple for now.)

4. Sam and his wife have just decided that they really want a matched pair of Rolls-Royce limousines, but Sam has to find a way to make more money from the restaurant before they can buy them. Remembering what he learned in his economics classes, Sam decides to raise his regular price to $3 per piece and offer a "4 pieces for $10" special. Will Sam's average customer still buy 4 pieces of chicken? Explain why.

    _____

    _____

    _____

5. After the change from $2 per piece to the "4 pieces for $10" special, how much consumer surplus will

    Sam's average customer have? _____ How much did it drop, compared with the

    situation in question 2? _____ How much more money will Sam take in?

    _____

6. Sam is thinking about offering an "all you can eat" special. What is the most money Sam's average cus-

    tomer would be willing to spend for this special? _____

7. If Sam offers an "all you can eat for $13" special, explain why he would make more profit than he did on the "4 pieces for $10" special. _____

8. Most of his customers eat all their fried chicken at the restaurant now, but Sam lets people order more than they can eat for dinner and take the leftovers home to eat later. Explain why Sam needs to change this policy if he starts offering "all you can eat" specials.

_____

_____

_____

_____

ANSWERS

Quick Check Quiz

Section 1: Utility

1. b; 2. c; 3. b; 4. c; 5. c; 6. b
   If you missed any of these questions, you should go back and review pages 142–147 in Chapter 6 (pages 514–519 in *Economics*, Chapter 20).

Section 2: Utility and Choice

1. c; 2. d; 3. b; 4. a
   If you missed any of these questions, you should go back and review pages 147–151 in Chapter 6 (pages 519–523 in *Economics*, Chapter 20).

Section 3: The Demand Curve Again

1. a; 2. c; 3. a; 4. b; 5. b
   If you missed any of these questions, you should go back and review pages 151–158 in Chapter 6 (pages 523–530 in *Economics*, Chapter 20).

Section 4: Market Demand

1. a; 2. e
   If you missed any of these questions, you should go back and review pages 158–161 in Chapter 6 (pages 530–533 in *Economics*, Chapter 20).

Practice Questions and Problems

Section 1: Utility

1. Total; marginal
2. diminishing marginal utility
3. disutility

4. zero

    Look at Figures 1(a) and 1(b) in your text for help.

5. 5

    Total utility increases by 5 utils (from 30 to 35) after eating the fourth slice of cake.

6. 24

    Eating 3 slices gives him 20 utils; he gets an additional 4 utils from the fourth slice, so his total utility for 4 slices is 20 + 4 = 24.

7.

Slices of Bread per Day	Total Utility	Marginal Utility	Calculation
(0)	(0)	—	
1	4	4	Increased from 0 to 4; 4 – 0 = 4
2	14	10	Increased from 4 to 14; 14 – 4 = 10
3	20	6	Increased from 14 to 20; 20 – 14 = 6
4	24	4	Increased from 20 to 24; 24 – 20 = 4
5	24	0	Unchanged at 24; 24 – 24 = 0
6	21	–3	Decreased from 24 to 21; 21 – 24 = –3

8.

(b) Marginal Utility

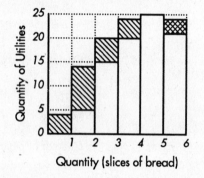

(a) Total and Marginal Utility

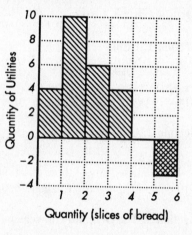

9. As Napolean eats more and more bread, his marginal utility starts to decline. The third slice has a smaller *MU* (6) than the second slice (10); the fourth slice is even smaller (4), and the fifth slice adds no utility at all.

10. The marginal utility of the fourth slice of cake is the total utility of 4 slices (75) minus the total utility of 3 slices (63); 75 – 63 = 12.

    The total utility of 5 slices is the total utility of 4 slices (75) plus the marginal utility of the fifth slice (7); 75 + 7 = 82.

11. third slice

    The second slice of cake's *MU* (25) is more than the first slice's *MU* (20), so marginal utility isn't diminishing yet. The third slice's *MU* (18) is lower than the second slice's, so marginal utility starts diminishing with the third slice.

    The eighth slice of cake is where *total* utility starts to diminish; this is where marginal utility becomes negative. *Marginal* utility can be diminishing while total utility is still increasing, as long as marginal utility is more than zero. Look at slices 3 through 6: marginal utility is getting smaller, while total utility is increasing.

12. The marginal utility of the *eighth* slice is negative, meaning that Josephine has less satisfaction after eating it than before. In other words, she is worse off.

13. 6 or 7

    She doesn't get any satisfaction from the seventh slice, but she isn't any worse off either: it doesn't matter to her whether she has the seventh slice or not. She definitely wouldn't eat the eighth slice. She has more utility from 7 slices, since the *MU* of the eighth slice is negative.

14. Someone would have to pay her enough money for eating the eighth slice of cake that the money (or what she could buy with it) would compensate for the loss of 3 units of satisfaction.

Section 2: Utility and Choice

1. d

    One of the key ideas in consumer choice is that people have only a limited amount of money to spend, so they look at the value of any purchase *relative to* other possible purchases—that is, they compare the marginal utility per dollar of different purchases and buy those goods and services with the highest *MU* per dollar.

2. marginal utility; dollar; last; consumed; equal

3. consumer equilibrium

4. incentive; reallocate

5. $$\frac{MU_{\text{Donkey Kong}}}{P_{\text{Donkey Kong}}} = \frac{MU_{\text{Super Mario Bros.}}}{P_{\text{Super Mario Bros.}}} = \frac{MU_{\text{Pac-Man}}}{P_{\text{Pac-Man}}} = \frac{MU}{\$1}$$

6.

Donkey Kong (P = $.50)			Super Mario Bros. (P = $2)			Pac-Man (P = $1)		
Games per Day	*MU*	*MU/P*	Games per Day	*MU*	*MU/P*	Games per Day	*MU*	*MU/P*
1	55	110	1	270	135	1	120	120
2	50	100	2	240	120	2	110	110
3	47	94	3	220	110	3	100	100
4	45	90	4	200	100	4	90	90
5	40	80	5	180	90	5	72	72
6	37	74	6	160	80	6	63	63
7	34	68	7	120	60	7	54	54
8	31	62	8	80	40	8	45	45

7. first game of Super Mario Bros.

8. $3

9. second game of Super Mario Bros.; first game of Pac-Man

    Since they have the same *MU/P*, which one George plays first doesn't matter.

10. no; he's used all his money

11. 120 for both

12. consumer equilibrium

13.

Step	Choices	Decision	Remaining Budget
1st purchase	1st Donkey Kong: $MU/P = 110$ 1st Super Mario: $MU/P = 135$ 1st Pac-Man: $MU/P = 120$	Super Mario	$12 − 2 = $10
2nd purchase	1st Donkey Kong: $MU/P = 110$ 2nd Super Mario: $MU/P = 120$ 1st Pac-Man: $MU/P = 120$	Super Mario	$10 − 2 = $8
3rd purchase	1st Donkey Kong: $MU/P = 110$ 3rd Super Mario: $MU/P = 110$ 1st Pac-Man: $MU/P = 120$	Pac-Man	$8 − 1 = $7
4th purchase	1st Donkey Kong: $MU/P = 110$ 3rd Super Mario: $MU/P = 110$ 2nd Pac-Man: $MU/P = 110$	Donkey Kong	$7 − .50 = $6.50
5th purchase	2nd Donkey Kong: $MU/P = 100$ 3rd Super Mario: $MU/P = 110$ 2nd Pac-Man: $MU/P = 110$	Super Mario	$6.50 − 2 = $4.50
6th purchase	2nd Donkey Kong: $MU/P = 100$ 4th Super Mario: $MU/P = 100$ 2nd Pac-Man: $MU/P = 110$	Pac-Man	$4.50 − 1 = $3.50
7th purchase	2nd Donkey Kong: $MU/P = 100$ 4th Super Mario: $MU/P = 100$ 3rd Pac-Man: $MU/P = 100$	Donkey Kong	$3.50 − .50 = $3
8th purchase	3rd Donkey Kong: $MU/P = 94$ 4th Super Mario: $MU/P = 100$ 3rd Pac-Man: $MU/P = 100$	Super Mario	$3 − 2 = $1
9th purchase	3rd Donkey Kong: $MU/P = 94$ 5th Super Mario: $MU/P = 90$ 3rd Pac-Man: $MU/P = 100$	Pac-Man	$1 − 1 = $0

14. no

The equimarginal principle says that the MU/P has to be equal, or almost equal, for Ashley to be at consumer equilibrium. Her MU/P for corn chips is 40/$1 = 40, and her MU/P for potato chips is 50/$2 = 25. Since 40 isn't equal to 25 (it's not even close), Ashley should reallocate her income.

15. more; fewer

At the amounts she bought last month, corn chips have a higher MU/P (40) than potato chips have (only 25). If Ashley spent $1 *less* on potato chips, she would have to give up 25 utils, but if she now spent $1 *more* on corn chips, she would get 40 utils from the additional corn chips. She would end up with 15 more utils of satisfaction for the same number of dollars.

Whenever the MU/P for one product is higher than the MU/P for a different product, you can gain by spending less on the product with the lower MU/P and more on the product with the higher MU/P.

Section 3: The Demand Curve Again

1. inverse; price; quantity demanded

If you aren't confident you understand about inverse and direct relationships, review the Appendix to Chapter 1, "Working with Graphs."

2. diminishing marginal utility; equimarginal
3. substitution; income
4. more; more; less; substitution

If the price of videotapes decreases, the marginal utility of videotapes won't change, so the *MU/P* of videotapes must be higher than before; *per dollar spent* on videotapes, Sam now gets more utility. Videotapes are now a "better buy" than before, so Sam will reallocate some of his income, buying more videotapes and less of something else.

5. less; income
6. consumer surplus
7. yes

Her *MU/Ps* for corn chips and potato chips are now equal: $30/1 = 60/2 = 30$.

8. $64—$28 for 28 bags of corn chips at $1 per bag, and $36 for 18 bags of potato chips at $2.
9. a. $46—$28 for the corn chips and $18 for the potato chips, now that they are both $1 per bag.

  b. more; income

  c. no

  The *MU/P* for corn chips is still $30/1 = 30$, but the *MU/P* for potato chips has increased to $60/1 = 60$. She still gets the same utility from potato chips, but she doesn't have to give up as many dollars to get it.

  d. more

  Potato chips are now a "better buy" since the price went down: Ashley gets more utils per dollar from potato chips than from corn chips. When Ashley starts buying more potato chips, the principle of diminishing marginal utility says that the *MU* of potato chips will fall. Eventually, the *MU* of potato chips will decrease enough so that the *MU/P* of potato chips will be equal to the *MU/P* of corn chips. At that point, Ashley will have reached consumer equilibrium again.

  e. substitution

10. 3; $9; $3

He will spend $3 each on 3 rentals; $3 × 3 = $9.

  His consumer surplus on the first rental is $2 (the $5 Jim would be willing to pay minus the $3 he actually paid), and his consumer surplus on the second rental is $1 (the $4 he would be willing to pay minus $3), so his total consumer surplus is $2 + $1 = $3.

11. yes; $1

The value of the first, second, and third rental to Jim is $12 ($5 for the first, $4 for the second, and $3 for the third). Since he gets $12 worth of value from the $11 rental of three tapes, he would be willing to rent the tapes.

12. "3 rentals for $11" package rate

You take in more money using the "3 for $11" package rate for providing the same service. What you have really done is found a way to put some of the consumer surplus Jim got at the $3 per rental price into your bank account.

Section 4: Market Demand

1.

Price per Bottle	Quantities Demanded by		
	Jill	Jack	Market
$3.00	1	0	1
2.50	2	0	2
2.00	4	2	6
1.50	6	4	10
1.00	10	7	17
.50	20	12	32

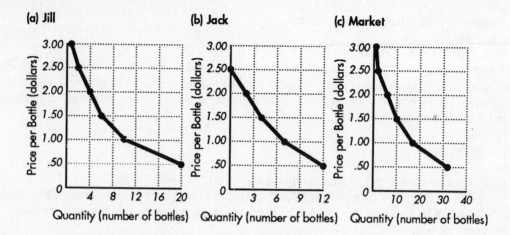

(a) Jill **(b) Jack** **(c) Market**

Thinking About and Applying Consumer Choice

I. The Demand for Video Games

1.

Donkey Kong (P = $.50)			Super Mario Bros. (P = $2)			Pac-Man (various prices)					
Games per Day	MU	MU/P	Games per Day	MU	MU/P	Games per Day	MU	MU/P (P = $2)	MU/P (P = $1.50)	MU/P (P = $1)	MU/P (P = $.50)
1	55	110	1	270	135	1	120	60	80	120	240
2	50	100	2	240	120	2	110	55	73.3	110	220
3	47	94	3	220	110	3	100	50	66.7	100	200
4	45	90	4	200	100	4	90	45	60	90	180
5	40	80	5	180	90	5	72	36	48	72	144
6	37	74	6	160	80	6	63	31.5	42	63	126
7	34	68	7	120	60	7	54	27	36	54	108
8	31	62	8	80	40	8	45	22.5	30	45	90

2. a. no

   b. Since the *MU* isn't changed by a change in the price, the *MU/P* will increase when the price decreases, and the *MU/P* will decrease when the price increases.

   c. inverse

   Review the Appendix to Chapter 1 if you didn't get this right.

   d. When the price is cut in half (divided by 2), the *MU/P* doubles (multiplied by 2). If the price were multiplied by 3, the *MU/P* would be divided by 3. The price and the *MU/P* are inversely proportional.

3.

Price of Pac-Man	Games of Donkey Kong	Games of Super Mario Bros.	Games of Pac-Man
$2.00	8	6	0
1.50	5	6	1
1.00	4	5	4
.50	4	5	8

4.

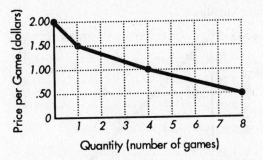

5. Income effect: When the price of Pac-Man decreases, George can buy the same number of games of Pac-Man (and other games) for less money. He has some money left that he can spend on more games of Pac-Man.

    Substitution effect: When the price of Pac-Man decreases, the *MU/P* increases, and Pac-Man becomes a better buy than other games. George will reallocate his income to buy more games of Pac-Man.

6. Income effect: When the price of Pac-Man decreases, George can buy the same number of games of Donkey Kong, Super Mario Bros., and Pac-Man for less money, since he has some money left that he could spend on more games of Donkey Kong and Super Mario Bros. Since he ended up buying fewer games of Donkey Kong and Super Mario Bros., the income effect didn't have much effect in this case.

    Substitution effect: When the price of Pac-Man decreases, the *MU/P* increases, and Pac-Man becomes a better buy than Donkey Kong and Super Mario Bros. George will reallocate his income to buy more games of Pac-Man and fewer games of Donkey Kong and Super Mario Bros.

II. Buying a Better Environment

1.

"Other Things" (P = $5,000)			Environmental Quality (P = $5,000)					
Units	*MU*	*MU/P*	Units	*MU* (1981)	*MU/P* (1981)	*MU* (1990)	*MU/P* (1990)
1	50,000	10	1	30,000	6	40,000	8
2	45,000	9	2	26,000	5.2	35,000	7
3	40,000	8	3	22,000	4.4	30,000	6
4	35,000	7	4	18,000	3.6	26,000	5.2
5	30,000	6	5	15,000	3	23,000	4.6
6	25,000	5	6	12,000	2.4	21,000	4.2

"Other things" 5 units
Environmental quality 1 unit

2. "Other things" 4 units
    Environmental quality 2 units

3. When the utility of environmental improvements (or anything else) goes up, our willingness to spend money on that will increase. Increases in utility increase the *MU/P*, making that a "better buy" relative to other things we also want.

III. Fried Chicken and Consumer Surplus

1.

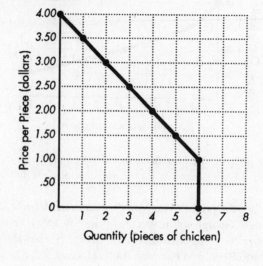

2. 4; $3

    At $2 per piece, Sam's customer gets a consumer surplus of $1.50 on the first piece ($3.50 − $2.00), plus $1.00 on the second piece ($3.00 − $2.00), plus $.50 on the third piece ($2.50 − $2.00), for a total consumer surplus of $1.50 + $1.00 + $.50 = $3.00.

3. $8; $6

    Sam's income per customer is $8 ($2 per piece times 4 pieces), and his costs are $2 ($.50 per piece times 4 pieces), giving him a profit (income minus costs) of $6.

4. yes

    The 4 pieces of chicken are worth $11 to Sam's customers ($3.50 + $3.00 + $2.50 + $2.00), so they would be willing to pay $10 for 4 pieces.

5. $1; $2; $2

    The customer would be willing to pay $11 ($3.50 + $3.00 + $2.50 + $2.00) for the 4 pieces of chicken, but only has to pay $10, leaving a consumer surplus of $1. In question 2, the consumer surplus was $3, so it dropped by $2. In fact, it dropped from the consumer into Sam's wallet.

6. $13.50

    The maximum amount is the sum of the prices the customer is willing to pay for each of the 6 pieces the customer is willing to buy: $3.50 + $3.00 + $2.50 + $2.00 + $1.50 + $1.00 = $13.50.

7. Sam's average customer would eat 6 pieces of chicken instead of 4 and would pay $13 instead of $10. Sam takes in an additional $3 in income and only has an additional $1 in costs (2 more pieces times $.50 cost per piece), so Sam ends up with an additional $2 in profit. Remember the discussion of Disneyland's pricing in the text? Disneyland's pricing system is about the same as Sam's "all you can eat for $13" special.

8. The principle of diminishing marginal utility explains why Sam's average customers won't eat more than 6 pieces of fried chicken for a meal: after 6 pieces, they're completely full of chicken, and their marginal utility from more has diminished so much that it is negative. After they've had time to digest the chicken and get hungry again, they'll be happy to eat more of Sam's delicious chicken. If Sam lets his customers take home chicken to eat later, the principle of diminishing marginal utility won't apply in the same way. There's still a limit to how much free fried chicken someone would eat in a year, but it's a lot more than 6 pieces.

APPENDIX TO CHAPTER 6
Indifference Analysis

SUMMARY

Indifference analysis is an alternative, graphical way to look at the way consumers make choices and reach consumer equilibrium. Instead of looking at tables of marginal utilities, we look at **indifference curves,** each of which represents all combinations of two goods that give a consumer equal satisfaction: since a consumer gets the same utility from any combination on the curve, the consumer will be **indifferent** (won't care) about which combination is chosen. There are different indifference curves for different amounts of satisfaction; the complete set of all indifference curves is called the **indifference map.**

Instead of calculating the marginal utility per dollar (*MU/P*) to find consumer equilibrium, indifference analysis uses a **budget line** that is derived from the prices of the two goods and the amount of income the consumer has to spend on those goods. Together, the budget line and the indifference map determine consumer equilibrium. The consumer gets the most satisfaction from the available income at the point where an indifference curve just touches, or is tangent to, the budget line.

KEY TERMS

indifferent
indifference curves
indifference map
budget line

PRACTICE QUESTIONS AND PROBLEMS

1. Indifference curves show all combinations of _____ goods that make the consumer

    equally _____ .

2. An indifference _____ is a complete set of indifference curves filling up the

    _____ quadrant of a graph.

3. The budget line shows the combinations of two goods that a consumer is _____ .

4. Referring to the budget line and indifference curves, where does consumer equilibrium occur?

    _____

    _____

5. Which labeled point on the indifference map below gives this consumer the most utility? _____

   Which gives the least utility? _____

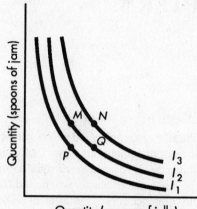

6. Let's use our friend George (Remember George? He plays video games at the arcade.) to explore indifference analysis. This time, we'll make George's problem simpler. The Super Mario Bros. game is broken, so he only wants to play Donkey Kong or Pac-Man. Let's suppose that George has $6 to spend on video games and that both Donkey Kong and Pac-Man each cost $2 today.

   a. If George spends all his money on Donkey Kong, how many games can he play today? _____

   b. If George spends all his money on Pac-Man, how many games can he play today? _____

   c. You just figured out the two endpoints on George's budget line. Plot the two endpoints on the graph below. Label the one with only games of Donkey Kong as point A and the one with only games of Pac-Man as point B. If you connect points A and B with a straight line (use a ruler or straightedge), you'll have George's budget line.

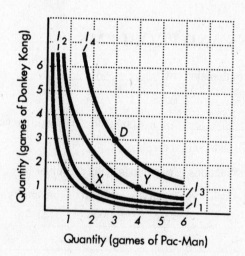

d. What combination of Donkey Kong and Pac-Man gives George the highest utility for his $6?

_____ game(s) of Donkey Kong and _____ game(s) of

Pac-Man. Mark this combination on the graph as point *C*.

e. Why doesn't George choose the combination shown as point *D*?

_____

_____

_____

7. Suppose that the price of Pac-Man had been only $1 per game instead of $2 per game. Draw George's new budget line on the graph above, and figure out how many games of Donkey Kong and Pac-Man give George the most satisfaction now.

_____ game(s) of Donkey Kong and _____ game(s) of Pac-Man

8. You just figured out two points on George's demand curve for Pac-Man. Plot these two points on the graph below.

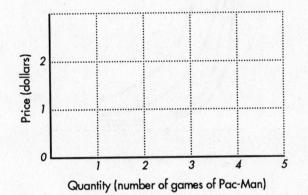

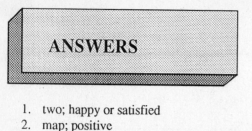

ANSWERS

1. two; happy or satisfied
2. map; positive
3. able to buy
4. at the point where an indifference curve is just touching the budget line
5. *N; P*
6. a. 3

   George has $6 to spend. If Donkey Kong costs $2 per game, he can only buy $6/$2 = 3 games.

   b. 3

   c.

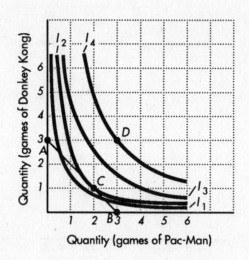

   d. 1; 2

   This is the point where George's budget line is just touching an indifference curve.

   e. At $2 per game for Donkey Kong and Pac-Man, it would cost George $12 to play 3 games of Donkey Kong and 3 games of Pac-Man; he has only $6 to spend. Either he has to get some more money, or else the prices of Donkey Kong and Pac-Man have to come down, before he can reach point *D*.

7. 1; 4

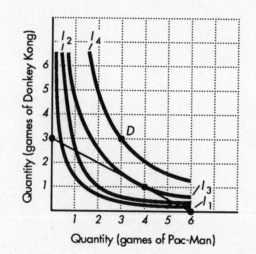

8.

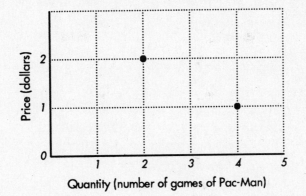

CHAPTER 7*
Elasticities of Demand and Supply

1. How do we measure whether and how much consumers alter their purchases in response to a price change?

   When your favorite clothing store has a sale on jeans, do you go out and buy some? When the bookstore raised the price of required textbooks, did you buy fewer textbooks? We know from our study of demand that people usually respond to prices and price changes by changing the quantity they buy, but how big is the response? Most people respond more to changes in the price of jeans than they do to changes in the price of required textbooks. Is there any way to measure how much more?

   Elasticity gives us a way to measure how such people react to price changes or to changes in other variables. Specifically, the **price elasticity of demand** measures how much consumers respond to changes in price by changing the quantity demanded, ceteris paribus. Price elasticity of demand is calculated using this formula:

   $$e_d = \frac{\text{percentage change in quantity demanded}}{\text{percentage change in price}}$$

   Because price and quantity demanded are inversely related, the price elasticity of demand is always a negative number; for convenience, we usually leave off the negative sign.

   For most products, the price elasticity of demand is different at different prices. If Pepsi® usually cost five cents a can, you would pay much less attention to a sale on Pepsi than you would if Pepsi cost five dollars a can. If we follow along a straight-line demand curve, we find that demand is *elastic* at high prices (e_d more than 1), *inelastic* at low prices (e_d less than 1), and *unit elastic* (e_d equal to 1) in the middle.

2. How does a business determine whether to increase or decrease the price of the product it sells?

   When your favorite store has a sale on jeans, they sell more jeans but take in less money per pair. Did they gain or lose revenue from the sale? That depends on the price elasticity of demand for their jeans. If the demand for their jeans is elastic, the percentage change in quantity is bigger than the percentage change in price, so a sale on jeans increases their **total revenue.** But if the demand for their jeans is inelastic, the percentage change in price is bigger than the percentage change in quantity, so a sale on jeans would decrease their *total revenue;* when demand is inelastic, increasing the price increases total revenue.

3. Why might senior citizens or children receive price discounts relative to the rest of the population?

   Senior citizens and children receive discounts because they usually have more elastic demands than the rest of the population. If children's demand for movies is elastic, giving them a discount lowers the

*Economics Chapter 21.

price they pay and increases the theater's total revenue. The rest of us aren't so responsive to the price of movies, so the theater doesn't gain by giving us a discount. Whenever different groups of customers have different price elasticities of demand, firms can increase their total revenue by using **price discrimination.**

4. What will determine whether consumers alter their purchases a little or a lot in response to a price change?

Three factors help determine how elastic the demand for a particular product is. First, the greater the number of close *substitutes* there are, the more elastic demand will be. If the price of Kellogg's Corn Flakes goes up, you can find lots of other things to eat. If the price of required economics textbooks goes up, you can't just buy a cheaper anthropology text instead—not if you expect to pass economics.

Second, the greater the proportion of a household's budget a good constitutes, the more elastic demand will be. As Table 1 in your text shows, the demand for salt is very inelastic. We only spend pennies a week on salt, so we don't respond much to price changes. For most of us, though, a trip to Europe or the Far East would take a large chunk of our incomes; we're much more sensitive to the price of foreign travel.

Third, the longer the time period under consideration, the more elastic demand will be. When the price of gasoline went up sharply in the 1970s, people didn't reduce their purchases very much at first; the demand was very inelastic. The response to the higher prices took a while to show up because it took people time to change their driving habits, to buy more fuel-efficient cars, and so on. Over longer periods of time, the demand for gasoline becomes more elastic.

5. How do we measure whether income changes or changes in the prices of related goods affect consumer purchases?

The **income elasticity of demand,** the percentage change in quantity demanded divided by the percentage change in income, measures how much changes in income affect consumer purchases. The **cross-price elasticity of demand,** the percentage change in the quantity demanded of one good divided by the percentage change in the price of a related good, measures how much changes in the price of related goods affect consumer purchases.

6. How do we measure whether producers respond to a price change?

We do this in the same basic way we measure whether consumers respond to a price change: we calculate the **price elasticity of supply.** Like the price elasticity of demand, the price elasticity of supply is the percentage change in quantity divided by the percentage change in price. The price elasticity of supply depends primarily on the length of time producers have to vary their output in response to changes in price.

KEY TERMS

price elasticity of demand	total revenue	inferior goods
arc elasticity	price discrimination	price elasticity of supply
perfectly elastic demand curve	cross-price elasticity of demand	short run
perfectly inelastic demand curve	income elasticity of demand	long run
	normal goods	

QUICK CHECK QUIZ

Section 1: The Price Elasticity of Demand

1. The price elasticity of demand is a measure of the degree to which
    a. consumers will alter the prices they pay for a product they purchase in response to changes in the quantities they buy of that product.
    b. sellers will alter the quantities of a product they offer for sale in response to changes in the price of that product.
    c. consumers will alter the quantities of a product they purchase in response to changes in their family income.
    d. consumers will alter the quantities of a product they purchase in response to changes in the price of that product.
    e. sellers will alter the quantities of a product they offer for sale in response to changes in the incomes of buyers.

2. The price elasticity of demand is always a
    a. positive number, and economists always include the plus sign.
    b. negative number, but economists usually ignore the minus sign.
    c. negative number, and economists always include the minus sign.
    d. positive number, but economists usually ignore the plus sign.

3. Mathematically, the price elasticity of demand is a
    a. ratio.
    b. graph.
    c. sum.
    d. straight line.
    e. curved line.

4. Which of the following is the equation for price elasticity of demand?

    a. $e_d = \dfrac{\text{change in quantity demanded}}{\text{change in price}}$

    b. $e_d = \dfrac{\text{change in price}}{\text{change in quantity demanded}}$

    c. $e_d = \dfrac{\text{percentage change in quantity demanded}}{\text{percentage change in price}}$

    d. $e_d = \dfrac{\text{percentage change in price}}{\text{percentage change in quantity demanded}}$

    e. $e_d = \dfrac{\text{change in price}}{\text{percentage change in quantity demanded}}$

5. When the price elasticity of demand is greater than 1, demand is called
    a. elastic.
    b. unit-elastic.
    c. inelastic.
    d. nonelastic.
    e. perfectly inelastic.

6. When the price elasticity of demand is less than 1, demand is called
   a. elastic.
   b. unit-elastic.
   c. inelastic.
   d. nonelastic.
   e. perfectly elastic.

7. When the price elasticity of demand is equal to 1, demand is called
   a. elastic.
   b. unit-elastic.
   c. inelastic.
   d. nonelastic.
   e. perfectly inelastic.

Section 2: The Use of Price Elasticity of Demand

1. The total expenditures made on a product by a group of buyers is found by multiplying
   a. price times elasticity.
   b. price times quantity bought.
   c. elasticity times quantity bought.
   d. quantity bought divided by price.
   e. elasticity divided by price.

2. Price times quantity is also the way to calculate
   a. total revenue.
   b. the foreign exchange rate.
   c. the price elasticity of demand.
   d. price discrimination.
   e. the price elasticity of supply.

3. If elasticity is greater than 1, total revenue will increase if price is
   a. decreased.
   b. increased.
   c. held constant.

4. If elasticity is less than 1, total revenue will increase if price is
   a. decreased.
   b. increased.
   c. held constant.

5. Charging different customers different prices for the same product is called
   a. foreign exchange exploitation.
   b. labor exploitation.
   c. perfect elasticity.
   d. price discrimination.
   e. pure price competition.

6. A business knows that it has two sets of customers, with one set of customers having a much more elastic demand than the other set. If the business uses price discrimination, which set of customers will receive a lower price?
   a. Both sets will receive the same price.
   b. Both sets will receive a higher price.
   c. It doesn't matter to the business which set gets a lower price.
   d. The set with the more elastic demand will receive a lower price.
   e. The set with the less elastic demand will receive a lower price.

7. Compared with people addicted to narcotics, potential narcotics users have a price elasticity of demand for narcotics that is
   a. the same as addicts' demand because it is based on the same factors.
   b. the same as addicts' demand but based on different factors.
   c. less elastic than addicts' demand.
   d. more elastic than addicts' demand.
   e. more perfectly elastic than addicts' demand.

Section 3: Determinants of the Price Elasticity of Demand

1. The price elasticity of demand depends primarily on
   a. how elastic the budgets of consumers are.
   b. the total revenues taken in by sellers of a particular product.
   c. how readily and easily consumers can switch their purchases from one product to another.
   d. the amount of taxes paid by consumers.
   e. the number of consumers in the market.

2. The price elasticity of demand for a product will be largest when
   a. there are no good substitutes for the product.
   b. there is only one good substitute for the product.
   c. there are two or three good substitutes for the product.
   d. there are many good substitutes for the product.

3. The price elasticity of demand for a product will be largest when
   a. the product constitutes a large proportion of the consumer's budget.
   b. the product constitutes a small proportion of the consumer's budget.
   c. the time period under consideration is very short.

4. The price elasticity of demand for a product will be largest when
   a. the time period under consideration is long.
   b. the time period under consideration is very short.
   c. the product constitutes a small proportion of the consumer's budget.

Section 4: Other Elasticities: Cross, Income, and Supply

1. The percentage change in quantity demanded of one product that results from a 1 percent change in the price of a related product is called the
   a. cross-price elasticity of demand.
   b. price elasticity of demand.
   c. income elasticity of demand.
   d. straight-line demand curve.
   e. price elasticity of supply.

2. Two goods that have a positive cross-price elasticity of demand are called
   a. substitutes.
   b. complements.
   c. luxuries.
   d. necessities.
   e. supply-oriented goods.

3. Two goods that have a negative cross-price elasticity of demand are called
   a. substitutes.
   b. complements.
   c. luxuries.
   d. necessities.
   e. demand-oriented goods.

4. The percentage change in demand that results from a 1 percent change in income is called the
   a. cross-price elasticity of demand.
   b. price elasticity of demand.
   c. income elasticity of demand.
   d. straight-line demand curve.
   e. price elasticity of supply.

5. Luxuries have a larger income elasticity of demand than do
   a. necessities.
   b. substitutes.
   c. complements.
   d. independents.

6. Which of the following is the equation for price elasticity of supply?

a. $e = \dfrac{\text{change in quantity supplied}}{\text{change in price}}$

b. $e = \dfrac{\text{change in price}}{\text{change in quantity supplied}}$

c. $e = \dfrac{\text{percentage change in quantity supplied}}{\text{percentage change in price}}$ *(circled)*

d. $e = \dfrac{\text{percentage change in price}}{\text{percentage change in quantity supplied}}$

e. $e = \dfrac{\text{change in price}}{\text{percentage change in quantity supplied}}$

7. The price elasticity of supply depends mainly on
   a. the length of time producers have to vary their output in response to price changes. *(circled)*
   b. how willing consumers are to buy additional units of output at the current price.
   c. the number of buyers in the market.
   d. the price elasticity of demand.
   e. whether a good is a complement or a substitute.

8. Which of the following statements is correct?
   a. The short run is less than two weeks; the long run is more than two weeks.
   b. The short run is less than two months; the long run is more than two months.
   c. The short run is less than two years; the long run is more than two years.
   d. The short run is just short enough that the quantities of all resources cannot be varied; the long run is just long enough that the quantities of all resources can be varied. *(circled)*
   e. The short run is just short enough that the quantities of all resources can be varied; the long run is just long enough that the quantities of all resources cannot be varied.

PRACTICE QUESTIONS AND PROBLEMS

Section 1: The Price Elasticity of Demand

1. Elasticity is a way to measure the _responsiveness_ of consumers or producers to a _change_ in some variable.

2. The price elasticity of demand measures the degree to which consumers alter their _~~purchase~~ ~~quantity demanded~~_ in response to a _price_ change, ceteris paribus.

3. The equation used to calculate the price elasticity of demand is
   $$e_d = \dfrac{\text{percentage change in } \textit{quantity demanded}}{\text{percentage change in } \textit{price}}$$

4. If e_d is less than 1, demand is _inelastic_.

5. If e_d is greater than 1, demand is _elastic_.

6. If e_d is equal to 1, demand is _unit elastic_

7. If e_d is equal to infinity, demand is _perfectly elastic_.

8. If e_d is equal to zero, demand is _perfectly inelastic_.

9. As you move down a straight-line demand curve, the price elasticity of demand
   decreases (increases or decreases).

10. If a 5 percent change in the price of movies causes a 10 percent change in the number of movie tickets
    sold, $e_d =$ _2_ and demand is _elastic_.

11. If a 6 percent change in the price of coffee causes a 3 percent change in the quantity of coffee bought,
    $e_d =$ _.5_ and demand is _inelastic_.

12. If a 2 percent change in the price of wine causes a 2 percent change in the number of bottles of wine
    bought, $e_d =$ _1_ and demand is _unit elastic_.

13. If a 5 percent change in the price of heroin causes no change (0 percent change) in the amount of
    heroin bought, $e_d =$ _0_ and demand is _perfectly inelastic_.

14. Below is a hypothetical demand for box seats at a baseball game. Fill in the blanks to calculate the elastici-
    ties for the different price ranges. Refer to Section 1.d, "Average or Arc Elasticity," on pages 177–178 in
    Chapter 7 (pages 549–550 in *Economics,* Chapter 21) if you need help.

Quantity Demanded	Change in Quantity Demanded	Price	Change in Price	Average Quantity $(Q_1+Q_2)/2$	Average Price $(P_1+P_2)/2$	Percent Change in Q	Percent Change in P	Elasticity
400		$100						
	100		$10	450	$95	22	11	2.11
500		90						
	100		$10	550	$85	18	12	1.55
600		80						
	0		$10	600	$75	0	13	0
600		70						
	100		$10	650	$65	15	15	1.00
700		60						

15. Suppose that a movie theater knows that it will sell 450 tickets per day if it charges $4.50 per ticket; if the
    ticket price goes up to $5.50, the theater will only sell 350 tickets per day. What is the theater's price elas-
    ticity of demand for this price range?

    a. 1.00
    b. 1.57
    c. 0.80
    d. 1.25
    e. 1.22

16. Suppose that an airline knows that it will have 90 passengers per day on a particular route if it charges $200 per ticket; if the fare goes down to $180, the airline will sell 110 tickets per day. What is the airline's price elasticity of demand for this price range?
    a. 1.90
    b. 0.53
    c. 2.22
    d. 1.64
    e. 2.00

(handwritten: 20/100, $20/$190)

Section 2: The Use of Price Elasticity of Demand

1. Total revenue is found by multiplying ___*price*___ by ___*quantity bought*___.

2. a. When demand is elastic, the percentage change in ___*quantity*___ (quantity or price) is larger than the percentage change in ___*price*___ (quantity or price).

   b. If the price decreases, quantity will increase. Will total revenue then increase or decrease?

   ___*increase*___

3. a. When demand is inelastic, the percentage change in ___*price*___ (quantity or price) is larger than the percentage change in ___*quantity*___ (quantity or price).

   b. If the price decreases, quantity will increase. Will total revenue then increase or decrease?

   ___*decrease*___

4. Complete the table below.

Demand Elasticity	Price Change	Effect on Total Revenue (increase, decrease, unchanged)
Elastic	Increase	~~increase~~ *decrease*
Elastic	Decrease	~~decrease~~ *increase*
Inelastic	Increase	~~decrease~~ *increase*
Inelastic	Decrease	*decrease*
Unit-elastic	Increase	*unchanged*
Unit-elastic	Decrease	*"*

For questions 5 through 7, suppose that you are the president of the Wonderful Widget Works, Inc. Widgets are a hypothetical product that you produce in many different colors.

5. Your marketing manager tells you that you can increase total revenue for blue widgets if you lower their price from $2.00 to $1.80. You know that the demand for blue widgets in this price range is
   a. elastic.
   b. inelastic.
   c. unit-elastic.

6. Next, your marketing manager tells you that if you lower the price of red widgets from $1.20 to $1.00 you will decrease total revenue for red widgets. You know that the demand for red widgets in this price range is
   a. elastic.
   b. inelastic.
   c. unit-elastic.

7. Your marketing manager admits that he can't figure out what's happening with orange widgets. When he lowers the price from $1.60 to $1.40, total revenue stays the same. Because you understand elasticity, you know that the demand for orange widgets in this price range is
   a. elastic.
   b. inelastic.
   c. unit-elastic.

8. Suppose you are the city manager of a small midwestern city. Your city-owned bus system is losing money, and you have to find a way to take in more revenues. Your staff recommends raising the bus fare to take in more money, but bus riders argue that reducing bus fares to attract new riders would increase revenues. You conclude that
   a. your staff thinks that the demand for bus service is elastic, whereas the bus riders think that demand is inelastic.
   b. your staff thinks that the demand for bus service is inelastic, whereas the bus riders think that demand is elastic.
   c. both your staff and the bus riders think that the demand for bus service is elastic.
   d. both your staff and the bus riders think that the demand for bus service is inelastic.
   e. both your staff and the bus riders think that the demand for bus service is unit-elastic.

9. Airlines know from experience that vacation travelers have an elastic demand for air travel, whereas business travelers have an inelastic demand for air travel. If an airline wants to increase its total revenues, it should
   a. decrease fares for both business and vacation travelers.
   b. increase fares for both business and vacation travelers.
   c. increase fares for business travelers and decrease fares for vacation travelers.
   d. decrease fares for business travelers and increase fares for vacation travelers.
   e. leave fares the same for both groups.

For questions 10 through 13, assume you are the owner of the only movie theater in a small town. From past experience, you have calculated that the price elasticity of demand for movie tickets varies with the age of the customer. At your current prices, senior citizens have a demand elasticity of 2.0, younger adults have a demand elasticity of 1.0, and teenagers have a demand elasticity of 0.5. You want to adjust your prices to increase your total revenue.

10. Should you change the ticket price for senior citizens to increase your revenues?
    a. No. You should leave the price where it is.
    b. Yes. You should increase the price for senior citizens.
    c. Yes. You should decrease the price for senior citizens.

11. Should you change the ticket price for younger adults to increase your revenues?
    a. No. You should leave the price where it is.
    b. Yes. You should increase the price for younger adults.
    c. Yes. You should decrease the price for younger adults.

12. Should you change the ticket price for teenagers to increase your revenues?
    a. No. You should leave the price where it is.
    b. Yes. You should increase the price for teenagers.
    c. Yes. You should decrease the price for teenagers.

13. Suppose you decided (correctly) to lower the ticket price for senior citizens. To get the most revenue from this set of customers, how far should you lower the ticket price?
    a. You should let the senior citizens in for free.
    b. You should charge only a very low price.
    c. You should keep cutting the price as long as each price cut increases ticket sales.
    d. You should keep cutting the price as long as demand is still elastic.

Section 3: Determinants of the Price Elasticity of Demand

1. List the three determinants of the price elasticity of demand.
   existence amount of substitutes
   importance of the product in consumer's Total budget
   time period under consideration.

2. A product with ___more many___ (many or few) good substitutes will have a more elastic demand than a product with ___few___ (many or few) good substitutes.

3. Which would you expect to be more elastic, the demand for new cars or the demand for new Chevrolet cars? ___Chevys___

4. Which would you expect to be more elastic, the demand for paperback novels or the demand for required college textbooks? ___paperback novels___.

5. A product that takes a ___large___ (large or small) portion of a consumer's budget will have a more elastic demand than a product that takes a ___small___ (large or small) portion.

6. Which would you expect to be more elastic, the demand for European vacations or the demand for video-cassette tapes? ___European vacations___

7. When consumers have a ___long___ (long or short) period of time to react to price changes, demand will be more elastic than when consumers have a ___short___ (long or short) period of time to react.

8. Figure 3 in your text shows that the price elasticity of demand for gasoline in the short run is 0.2, whereas the price elasticity of demand for gasoline in the long run is substantially higher. Explain why the elasticity values are so different.

   Alternatives can be found over a
   long period of time.

Section 4: Other Elasticities: Cross, Income, and Supply

1. The _cross-price_ elasticity of demand measures how consumers adjust their purchases of a product when the price of some other product changes.

2. The _income_ elasticity of demand measures how much demand for a product changes when consumers' incomes change.

3. If the cross-price elasticity of demand is positive, the two goods are ~~Compliments~~ _substitutes_. If the cross-price elasticity of demand is negative, the two goods are ~~Substitute~~ _Compliments_

4. _Luxuries_ (Luxuries or Necessities) have a higher income elasticity of demand than do _necessities_ (luxuries or necessities).

5. When the price of Kellogg's Corn Flakes increases 5 percent, the quantity demanded of Post Corn Flakes increases 20 percent. The cross-price elasticity of Post Corn Flakes with respect to Kellogg's Corn Flakes is _4_. These two products are _Substitutes_.

6. When the price of milk increases 4 percent, the quantity demanded of corn flakes decreases 2 percent. The cross-price elasticity of milk with respect to corn flakes is _-.5_. These two products are _complements_.

7. The income elasticity of demand is the percentage change in ~~Quantity demanded~~ _demand_ divided by the percentage change in ~~price~~ _income_. Economists classify goods whose income elasticity of demand is positive as ~~confusing~~ _normal_ goods, and goods whose income elasticity of demand is negative as ~~necessary~~ _inferior_ goods.

8. Suppose that the demand for Mercedes-Benz automobiles goes up 15 percent when people's incomes go up by 10 percent. The income elasticity of demand for Mercedes-Benz autos is _positive (+1.5)_ these autos are _normal_ (normal or inferior) goods.

9. Suppose that the demand for ten-year-old used cars goes down 10 percent when people's incomes go up by 10 percent. The income elasticity of demand for these old used cars is _negative_; they are _inferior (-1)_ (normal or inferior) goods.

10. The price elasticity of supply is the percentage change in *quantity supplied* divided by the percentage change in _*price*_ . The price elasticity of supply depends on the _*time*_ producers have to vary their output in response to price changes.

11. Sketch a perfectly inelastic supply curve on graph a, a typical short-run supply curve on graph b, and a typical long-run supply curve on graph c. For prices P_1 and P_2, mark the quantities supplied on the graphs.

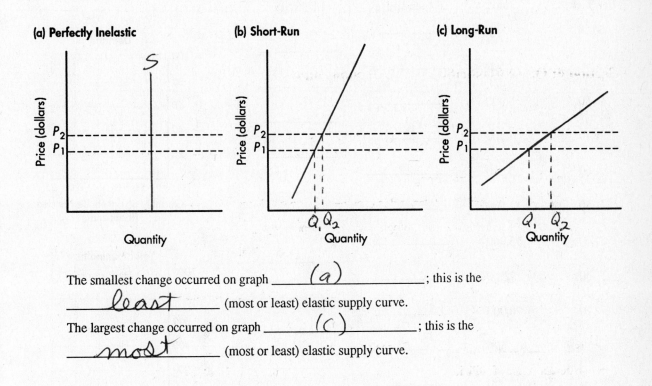

(a) Perfectly Inelastic   **(b) Short-Run**   **(c) Long-Run**

The smallest change occurred on graph _*(a)*_ ; this is the _*least*_ (most or least) elastic supply curve.

The largest change occurred on graph _*(c)*_ ; this is the _*most*_ (most or least) elastic supply curve.

THINKING ABOUT AND APPLYING ELASTICITY

I. Elasticity and Bruce Springsteen

Great news! Bruce Springsteen is going to give a concert at your convention center. The table below gives the demand for concert tickets.

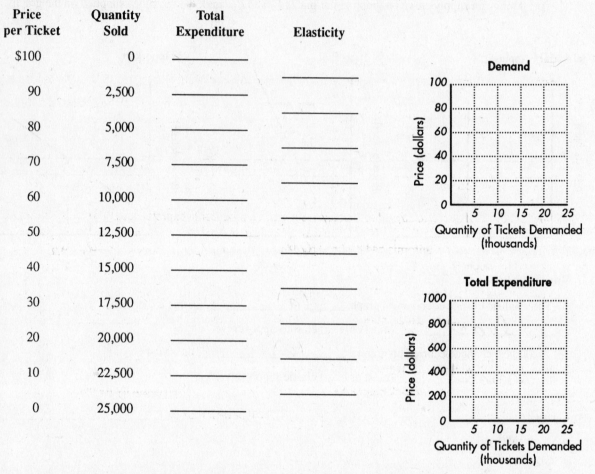

Price per Ticket	Quantity Sold	Total Expenditure	Elasticity
$100	0	_____	
			_____
90	2,500	_____	
			_____
80	5,000	_____	
			_____
70	7,500	_____	
			_____
60	10,000	_____	
			_____
50	12,500	_____	
			_____
40	15,000	_____	
			_____
30	17,500	_____	
			_____
20	20,000	_____	
			_____
10	22,500	_____	
			_____
0	25,000	_____	

1. Calculate the total expenditure ($P \times Q$) at each ticket price, calculate the demand elasticity for each of the price changes listed, draw the demand curve and the total expenditure curve on the appropriate graphs, and mark the segments of the demand curve that are elastic, inelastic, and unit-elastic.
2. Because you decided to donate $10,000 to a certain charity organization, the convention center asked you to organize the concert. Under the agreement, you can keep all the profits for yourself. Renting the convention center will cost you $5,000, you must pay Bruce Springsteen $100,000 for the concert, and you have $35,000 in miscellaneous expenses. If the convention center seats 22,500 customers, what price should you charge for tickets to get the maximum profit (total revenue minus all costs)?

My price would be _____ per ticket.

I would sell _____ tickets.

My profit would be _____ .

3. Would your ticket price be any different if you had to pay Bruce $200,000? _____.
    Explain. _____
    _____
    _____
    _____

4. Assuming you have to pay Bruce $100,000, is there anything you could do to increase your total revenues
    and profits even more? _____

5. Suppose you decided to sell 2,500 seats at each of the prices listed between $90 and $10, with the seats
    getting better as the price goes up. How much revenue will you take in if you sell all those seats?

    _____

II. Taxing Tobacco

According to the law of demand, taxes that increase the price of a product are expected (ceteris paribus) to reduce
consumption of the product. In 1988, California increased its cigarette tax by 25 cents a pack; by the middle of
1989, cigarette purchases in California had declined by 10 percent. Use this information to answer the questions
below.

1. How much was the increase in California's cigarette tax? _____ cents a pack
    How much was the reported decrease in cigarette sales in California in 1989? _____ percent
    For simplicity, assume that all of this decrease was caused by the price of cigarettes increasing in price by
    $.25 as a result of the tax increase.

2. If cigarettes cost $1.00 per pack before the tax increase, what is the demand elasticity for cigarettes over
    this price range? _____. Is it elastic or inelastic? _____

3. Use the determinants of demand elasticity discussed in Section 3 of the chapter to explain why you would
    expect the demand for cigarettes to be inelastic.
    _____
    _____

4. If there were 1 billion (1,000,000,000) packs of cigarettes sold in California before the tax, how many
    packs were sold after the tax went into effect, and how much tax revenue did California take in from the
    tax of 25 cents per pack? _____ packs sold; _____ in tax
    revenue

5. What do you think will happen if California raises the tax on cigarettes by 25 cents *every year* from now
    until the year 2000? Will California's tax revenue from the cigarette tax keep increasing for the whole
    time? _____

ANSWERS

Quick Check Quiz

Section 1: The Price Elasticity of Demand

1. d; 2. b; 3. a; 4. c; 5. a; 6. c; 7. b
   If you missed any of these questions, you should go back and review pages 176–180 in Chapter 7 (pages 548–552 in *Economics*, Chapter 21).

Section 2: The Use of Price Elasticity of Demand

1. b; 2. a; 3. a; 4. b; 5. d; 6. d; 7. d
   If you missed any of these questions, you should go back and review pages 180–185 in Chapter 7 (pages 552–557 in *Economics*, Chapter 21).

Section 3: Determinants of the Price Elasticity of Demand

1. c; 2. d; 3. a; 4. a
   If you missed any of these questions, you should go back and review pages 185–187 in Chapter 7 (pages 557–559 in *Economics*, Chapter 21).

Section 4: Other Elasticities: Cross, Income, and Supply

1. a; 2. a; 3. b; 4. c; 5. a; 6. c; 7. a; 8. d
   If you missed any of these questions, you should go back and review pages 187–192 in Chapter 7 (pages 559–564 in *Economics*, Chapter 21).

Practice Questions and Problems

Section 1: The Price Elasticity of Demand

1. responsiveness; change
2. purchases; price
3. quantity demanded; price
4. inelastic
5. elastic
6. unit-elastic
7. perfectly elastic
8. perfectly inelastic
9. decreases
10. 2; elastic
    Remember the equation for the price elasticity of demand:

$$e_d = \frac{\text{percentage change in quantity demanded}}{\text{percentage change in price}}$$

The percentage change in quantity demanded is 10 percent, and the percentage change in price is 5 percent, so $e_d = 10/5 = 2$. This is more than 1, so demand must be elastic.

11. 0.5; inelastic

    Refer to the equation for the price elasticity of demand above. In this problem, the percentage change in quantity demanded is 3 percent, and the percentage change in price is 6 percent, so $e_d = 3/6 = 0.5$. This is less than 1.0, so demand must be inelastic.

12. 1; unit-elastic

    Refer to the equation for the price elasticity of demand above. In this problem, the percentage change in quantity demanded is 2 percent, and the percentage change in price is 2 percent, so $e_d = 2/2 = 1$; therefore, demand must be unit-elastic.

13. 0; perfectly inelastic

    Refer to the equation for the price elasticity of demand above. In this problem, the percentage change in quantity demanded is 0 percent, and the percentage change in price is 5 percent, so $e_d = 0/5 = 0$; therefore, demand must be perfectly inelastic.

14.

Quantity Demanded	Change in Quantity Demanded	Price	Change in Price	Average Quantity $(Q_1+Q_2)/2$	Average Price $(P_1+P_2)/2$	Percent Change in Q	Percent Change in P	Elasticity
400		$100						
	100		$10	450	$95	.2222	.1053	2.11
500		90						
	100		10	550	85	.1818	.1176	1.55
600		80						
	100		10	650	75	.1538	.1333	1.15
600		70						
	100		10	750	65	.1333	.1538	0.87
700		60						

For help, refer to Section 1.d, "Average or Arc Elasticity," on pages 177–178 in Chapter 7 (pages 549–550 in *Economics*, Chapter 21).

15. Answer *d* is correct. If you don't know how to do this problem, use the same process you went through in question 14 above.

    If you chose answer *a, b,* or *e,* you didn't remember to use the *average* quantity and *average* price. Reread pages 177–178 in Chapter 7 (pages 549–550 in *Economics*, Chapter 21); then try it again.

    If you chose answer *c,* you had the equation upside down: the percentage change in *quantity* is on top, and the percentage change in *price* is on the bottom. Reread pages 177–178 in Chapter 7 (pages 549–550 in *Economics*, Chapter 21); then try it again.

16. Answer *a* is correct. If you don't know how to do this problem, use the same process you went through in question 14 above.

    If you chose answer *b,* you had the equation upside down: the percentage change in *quantity* is on top, and the percentage change in *price* is on the bottom. Reread pages 177–178 in Chapter 7 (pages 549–550 in *Economics*, Chapter 21); then try it again.

    If you chose answer *c, d,* or *e,* you didn't remember to use the *average* quantity and *average* price. Reread pages 177–178 in Chapter 7 (pages 549–550 in *Economics*, Chapter 21); then try it again.

Section 2: The Use of Price Elasticity of Demand

1. price; quantity
2. a. quantity; price
   b. increase
3. a. price; quantity
   b. decrease

4.

Demand Elasticity	Price Change	Effect on Total Revenue (increase, decrease, unchanged)
Elastic	Increase	Decrease
Elastic	Decrease	Increase
Inelastic	Increase	Increase
Inelastic	Decrease	Decrease
Unit-elastic	Increase	Unchanged
Unit-elastic	Decrease	Unchanged

5. Answer *a* is correct. Decreasing the price increases total revenue; since price and revenue move in opposite directions, the quantity change must be larger than the price change, so demand must be elastic.

6. Answer *b* is correct. Decreasing the price decreases total revenue; since price and revenue move in the same direction, the price change must be larger than the quantity change, so demand must be inelastic.

7. Answer *c* is correct. If total revenue is unchanged, the percentage change in quantity must be the same size as the percentage change in price, so the price elasticity of demand must be 1, or unit-elastic.

8. Answer *b* is correct. Your staff thinks that increasing the price will increase total revenue; this will only happen if demand is inelastic. The bus riders think that decreasing the price will increase total revenue; this will only happen if demand is elastic.

9. Answer *c* is correct. When demand is elastic (vacationers), reducing the price increases total revenue. When demand is inelastic (business travelers), increasing the price increases total revenue.

10. Answer *c* is correct. Senior citizens have an elastic demand ($e_d = 2$: greater than 1), so decreasing the price increases total revenue.

11. Answer *a* is correct. With unit-elastic demand, total revenue is as high as possible.

12. Answer *b* is correct. Teenagers have an inelastic demand ($e_d = 0.5$: less than 1), so increasing the price increases total revenue.

13. Answer *d* is correct. As price decreases, demand usually becomes less elastic. As long as the senior citizens' demand is still elastic, decreases in price will increase total revenue. When demand becomes unit-elastic, you have reached the maximum total revenue and shouldn't reduce price any further. See Figure 2 in the text for further help.

   Answer *a* can't be correct. If tickets are free, total revenue from senior citizens will be zero.

   Answer *b* isn't likely to be correct. If the ticket price is very low, demand is probably inelastic, and you should raise the price some to increase total revenue.

   Answer *c* isn't correct. Even when prices are very low, a further cut will usually increase sales, but since demand is usually inelastic at low prices, further price cuts would reduce total revenue.

Section 3: Determinants of the Price Elasticity of Demand

1. existence of substitutes; importance of the product in the consumer's total budget; the time period under consideration

2. many; few

3. Chevrolets
   For most people, there are many good substitutes for Chevrolets: Fords, Plymouths, Toyotas, Volkswagens, and so on. The demand for a particular brand of a product is usually more elastic than the demand for the product itself.

4. novels
   There are few, if any, good substitutes for required texts, but many other forms of literature, and entertainment in general, are available as substitutes for paperback novels.

5. large; small

6. vacations
   Videocassettes are inexpensive; for most of us, a European vacation would take a large share of our budgets.

7. long; short
8. It is difficult to change your gasoline consumption in a short period of time. The number of miles you drive depends on where you live relative to where you must go to attend class, go to work, and go to shop, and the miles per gallon depend on your car's efficiency. None of these factors are easy to change quickly. Over a longer period of time, you can take gasoline prices into account when deciding what kind of car to buy and where to live and work.

Section 4: Other Elasticities: Cross, Income, and Supply

1. cross-price
2. income
3. substitutes; complements
4. Luxuries; necessities
5. +4; substitutes
   Cross-price elasticity is the percentage change in the quantity demanded of one good divided by the percentage change in the price of another good. The quantity demanded of Post Corn Flakes increases 20 percent when the price of Kellogg's Corn Flakes increases by 5 percent, so the cross-price elasticity is +20%/+5% = +4. Since Post's quantity increases when Kellogg's price increases, the two goods are substitutes: people will switch from Kellogg's to Post's when the price of Kellogg's goes up.
6. −0.5; complements
   The cross-price elasticity is −2%/+4% = −0.5. Milk and corn flakes are complements (most people put milk on their corn flakes), so an increase in the price of milk makes corn flakes with milk more expensive, reducing the amount of corn flakes bought.
7. demand; income; normal; inferior
8. +1.5; normal
   The income elasticity of demand is +15%/+10% = +1.5. Since demand increases when income increases, the income elasticity of demand is positive (greater than zero), so Mercedes-Benz autos are normal goods.
9. −1; inferior
   The income elasticity of demand is −10%/+10% = −1. Since demand decreases when income increases, the income elasticity of demand is negative (less than zero), so ten-year-old used cars are inferior goods. If you could afford it, wouldn't you buy a Mercedes rather than an old used car? The higher your income is, the more likely it is that you will buy a Mercedes and the less likely it is that you will buy an old used car.
10. quantity supplied; price; length of time
11.

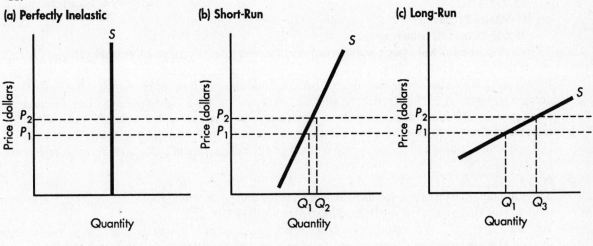

(a) Perfectly Inelastic   (b) Short-Run   (c) Long-Run

a; least
c; most

Thinking About and Applying Elasticity

I. Elasticity and Bruce Springsteen

1. If you had problems with the graphs or the calculation, refer to Section 1.d, "Average or Arc Elasticity," on pages 177–178 in Chapter 7 (pages 549–550 in *Economics,* Chapter 21).

Price per Ticket	Quantity Sold	Total Expenditure	Elasticity
$100	0	$ 0	
			19.00
90	2,500	225,000	
			5.67
80	5,000	400,000	
			3.00
70	7,500	525,000	
			1.86
60	10,000	600,000	
			1.22
50	12,500	625,000	
			0.82
40	15,000	600,000	
			0.54
30	17,500	525,000	
			0.33
20	20,000	400,000	
			0.18
10	22,500	225,000	
			0.05
0	25,000	0	

Demand

Total Expenditure

2. price = $50; tickets = 12,500; profit = $475,000
   Your costs for putting on the concert are $150,000:
   $ 10,000 for donation
      5,000 for rent
    100,000 for Bruce
     35,000 for miscellaneous expenses
   None of these costs will change with the number of tickets sold, so your problem is simple: you want to set the ticket price where it will give you the maximum total revenue. Of course, you could find that price from looking at the total expenditure figures, but you could also find it by looking at the elasticities. If demand is elastic (as it is for all prices above $50), you know that lowering the price will increase total revenue. If demand is inelastic (as it is for all prices below $50), you know that raising the price will increase total revenue. At the price where demand is unit-elastic, total revenue is at its maximum.
   If you set the price at $50 per ticket, you will sell 12,500 tickets, take in $625,000 in revenue, and have a profit of $475,000 ($625,000 revenue minus $150,000 costs).
3. no
   $50 is still the price that gives you the maximum revenue and profit. Your profit would of course be lower (only $375,000) if you had to pay Bruce $200,000 rather than $100,000.
4. You could try price discrimination. If you raise the price of the seats closest to the stage, the people willing to pay $90 might buy them at those prices; if you set a low price for seats farther away, people who wouldn't pay $50 for a seat might come if the price were, say, $30.

5. Each set of 2,500 seats will be a separate set of consumers, and each set of consumers will have its own separate price. The calculation looks like this:

Price per Seat	Quantity Sold at That Price	Revenue from Those Seats
$90	2,500	$225,000
80	2,500	200,000
70	2,500	175,000
60	2,500	150,000
50	2,500	125,000
40	2,500	100,000
30	2,500	75,000
20	2,500	50,000
10	2,500	25,000

Total revenue = $1,125,000

Whenever market conditions allow price discrimination to be used, you can increase total revenue by discriminating.

II. Taxing Tobacco

1. 25; 10
2. 0.45; inelastic

   If cigarette prices increased from $1.00 to $1.25 per pack, this would be about a 22 percent increase relative to the average price. Since the quantity demanded decreased only 10 percent when the price increased 22 percent, the price elasticity of demand for cigarettes is 10%/22% = 0.45; this is inelastic. You should note that this calculation isn't exactly accurate. The 10 percent decrease in quantity was probably determined relative to the starting quantity rather than the average quantity.

3. To people who smoke cigarettes, there are few, if any, good substitutes; many cigarette smokers consider cigarettes to be a necessity.

4. 900,000,000 (a 10 percent decrease from 1 billion); $225,000,000 (900,000,000 packs times $.25)

5. Each tax increase will be reflected in an increase in the price paid by buyers. As the price paid increases, demand usually becomes more elastic. At high enough prices (and taxes), demand will become elastic; further tax increases beyond that point will decrease sales enough that tax revenues will eventually begin to decline.

CHAPTER 8*
The Costs of Doing Business

1. What is the law of diminishing marginal returns?

    The **law of diminishing marginal returns** is a description of the relationship between the amount of resources used in production and the amount of output produced when the amount of some resources cannot be changed (the short run). For example, the law describes how many hamburgers Joe's Gourmet Burger Stand can produce with different numbers of workers when the size of the hamburger grill stays the same.

    Starting with only one worker, as Joe adds more workers the total number of hamburgers that can be produced (the **total physical product**, or **TPP**) will go up, as each worker adds more output (the **marginal physical product**, or **MPP**) to the total. With only one worker, total output (TPP) will be pretty low: Joe's has a big grill, and one worker can't flip burgers fast enough to use all of it. As Joe adds more workers, for a while both total output (TPP) and the output added by each additional worker (MPP) will increase because the additional workers will make more efficient use of the grill. Eventually, though, there will be so many workers that the area around the grill will get crowded and workers will start to get in each other's way. At this point, the MPP will start going down. Each additional worker adds smaller numbers of hamburgers to the total product. Even though adding one more worker still increases TPP, the MPP declines.

    The law of diminishing marginal returns says that all short-run production processes in the world work the same way Joe's Burger Stand does: as you add more and more workers (variable resources) to use the grill (a fixed resource), eventually the workers' MPP will start to get smaller. More formally, the law of diminishing returns states that when successive equal amounts of a variable resource are combined with a fixed amount of another resource, there will be a point beyond which the extra or marginal product that can be attributed to each additional unit of the variable resource will decline.

2. How do economic costs and profit differ from accounting costs and profit?

    Economic costs and **economic profit** differ from accounting costs and accounting profit because economists and accountants are interested in different things. Accountants are interested in keeping track of *money*, and economists are interested in keeping track of *resources*. Both accountants and economists include as costs the resources bought by the firm; these are called explicit costs. Resources already owned by the owner of the business and used in the business are not normally counted as costs by accountants, but they are by economists because these resources have alternative uses elsewhere in the economy.

    The difference between the accounting and economics approach leads to the following definitions:

    Accounting profit = total revenue minus explicit costs

    Economic profit = total revenue minus explicit costs and the opportunity costs
    of the resources already owned by the producer

Economics Chapter 22.

3. What accounts for the shapes of the cost curves?

Average- and marginal-cost curves are usually U-shaped: they start out at relatively high values, decrease for a while as output increases, reach a minimum, and eventually begin increasing as output continues to increase. Short-run average-cost curves are U-shaped because of the law of diminishing marginal returns. In the case of Joe's Gourmet Burger Stand, the size of the hamburger grill is fixed. If Joe produces only a few hamburgers, Joe's workers can't make efficient use of the grill: it's too big for those few people to use all of it. These one or two workers have to spend much of their time running from one end of the grill to another to flip all the burgers, not to mention having to run around putting lettuce, tomato, and all of Joe's special gourmet ingredients on the burgers.

Hiring more people will let Joe increase the number of hamburgers produced at a lower cost per burger. Some people can stand in one place at the grill flipping burgers while others work at putting the burgers together; in this way, both sets of workers can work more efficiently, lowering the costs. As Joe keeps increasing the number of workers so he can produce more burgers, eventually the workers will start to get in each other's way, fighting to use the grill or trying to find a place to put together more burgers. Some of their time will be spent waiting to use the fixed resource, which will reduce their efficiency and increase the costs per burger.

In the short run, Joe can't do anything to increase the size of his grill to let his many workers be more efficient. Although he could buy a larger grill in the long run, his cost curves could still be U-shaped because of **economies of scale** and **diseconomies of scale**. Small businesses are often less efficient and have higher average costs than larger businesses. Some businesses get so big that they can't be managed efficiently, and their average costs are higher than those of businesses that aren't quite so large.

4. Is large always better than small?

Large is not always better than small, but neither is small always better than large. In industries with a U-shaped average-cost curve, very small firms have relatively high costs. As they grow, economies of scale cause their average costs to decrease until they reach the **minimum efficient scale (MES)**, where the **long-run average total cost (LRAC)** is at its minimum. As a firm continues to grow, eventually it will encounter diseconomies of scale, and its long-run average total cost will then begin to rise. The best size depends on the structure of costs and the extent of the market.

KEY TERMS

total physical product (TPP)
marginal physical product
  (MPP)
law of diminishing marginal
  returns
average physical product
economic profit
opportunity cost of capital

economic costs
total fixed costs (TFC)
average fixed costs (AFC)
total variable costs (TVC)
total costs
average total costs (ATC)
marginal costs (MC)
average variable costs (AVC)

short-run average total cost
  (SRAC)
long-run average total cost
  (LRAC)
economies of scale
diseconomies of scale
constant returns to scale
minimum efficient scale (MES)

QUICK CHECK QUIZ

Section 1: Firms and Business

1. Which term do economists use to refer to all types of businesses?
   a. sole proprietorship
   b. partnership
   c. firm
   d. corporation
   e. entrepreneurship

2. The total physical product is
   a. the maximum output that can be produced when successive units of a variable resource are added to fixed amounts of other resources.
   b. the additional quantity that is produced when one additional unit of a resource is used in combination with the same quantities of all other resources.
   c. the lowest-cost combination of resources that can produce a specified level of output.
   d. the output per unit of resource.
   e. the value of the output that can be produced from a combination of resources.

3. The marginal physical product is
   a. the maximum output that can be produced when successive units of a variable resource are added to fixed amounts of other resources.
   b. the additional quantity that is produced when one additional unit of a resource is used in combination with the same quantities of all other resources.
   c. the lowest-cost combination of resources that can produce a specified level of output.
   d. the output per unit of resource.
   e. the value of the output that can be produced from a combination of inputs.

4. The average physical product is
   a. the maximum output that can be produced when successive units of a variable resource are added to fixed amounts of other resources.
   b. the additional quantity that is produced when one additional unit of a resource is used in combination with the same quantities of all other resources.
   c. the lowest-cost combination of resources that can produce a specified level of output.
   d. the output per unit of resource.
   e. the value of the output that can be produced from a combination of resources.

5. The law of diminishing returns says that when successive equal amounts of
   a. a fixed resource are combined with a given amount of a variable resource, the MPP of the fixed resource will eventually decline.
   b. a variable resource are combined with a fixed amount of another resource, the MPP of the variable resource will eventually decline.
   c. a good are consumed, the marginal utility of the good will eventually decline.
   d. a good are consumed, the MPP of the good will eventually decline.
   e. all resources are increased, eventually the unit costs will begin to increase.

Section 2: Revenue, Costs, and Profit

1. The difference between accounting costs and economic costs is that
    a. accountants include the opportunity costs of the owner's resources used in the business, and economists don't.
    b. economists include the opportunity costs of the owner's resources used in the business, and accountants don't.
    c. accountants include the explicit costs, and economists don't.
    d. economists include the explicit costs, and accountants don't.
    e. economists include only money costs, and accountants include all resources.

2. Which of the following equations is false?
    a. Accounting profit = total revenues minus explicit costs
    b. Economic profit = total revenues minus explicit costs and the opportunity costs of resources already owned by the producer
    c. Economic profit = accounting profit minus the opportunity costs of resources already owned by the producer
    d. Economic profit plus the opportunity costs of resources already owned by the producer = accounting profit
    e. Economic profit plus accounting profit = the opportunity costs of resources already owned by the producer

3. The opportunity cost of capital provided by the owner of a business is
    a. zero.
    b. the amount of capital provided.
    c. the amount of capital provided divided by the opportunity cost of the owner's time.
    d. the forgone return on funds used in a business.
    e. the amount of capital divided by the interest rate.

Section 3: Cost Schedules and Cost Curves

1. Total costs are the sum of
    a. average fixed and average variable costs.
    b. total fixed and total variable costs.
    c. total variable and marginal costs.
    d. average variable and marginal costs.
    e. total fixed and average marginal costs.

2. Fixed costs are those costs that
    a. never vary.
    b. can't be varied during the time period under consideration.
    c. occur only in the short run.
    d. match both a and c above.
    e. match both b and c above.

3. The average-fixed-cost curve
    a. always decreases as output increases.
    b. always increases as output increases.
    c. first decreases, then reaches a minimum, and then increases as output increases.
    d. first increases, then reaches a maximum, and then decreases as output increases.
    e. is always a horizontal line.

4. The average-variable-cost curve
   a. always decreases as output increases.
   b. always increases as output increases.
   c. first decreases, then reaches a minimum, and then increases as output increases.
   d. first increases, then reaches a maximum, and then decreases as output increases.
   e. is always a horizontal line.

5. Short-run cost curves are U-shaped because of
   a. economies and diseconomies of scale.
   b. the law of diminishing marginal utility.
   c. the law of diminishing marginal returns.
   d. taxes.
   e. constant returns to scale.

6. Which of the following statements is false?
   a. $ATC = AFC + AVC$
   b. MC crosses ATC at the low point on the ATC curve.
   c. MC crosses AVC at the low point on the AVC curve.
   d. ATC crosses AVC at the low point on the MC curve.
   e. $TC = TFC + TVC$

Section 4: The Long Run

1. The long-run average-total-cost curve is
   a. the lowest-cost combination of resources with which each level of output is produced when all resources are variable.
   b. the lowest-cost combination of resources with which each level of output is produced when all resources are fixed.
   c. the output level at which the cost per unit of output is the lowest.
   d. the average of the explicit cost curves.
   e. the sum of the short-run average-cost curves.

2. Economies of scale exist
   a. when unit costs decrease as the quantity of production increases and all resources are variable.
   b. at the minimum point of the long-run average-cost curve.
   c. when unit costs increase as the quantity of production increases and all resources are variable.
   d. at the output level at which the cost per unit is the lowest.
   e. when unit costs remain constant as the quantity of production increases and all resources are variable.

3. Diseconomies of scale exist
   a. when unit costs decrease as the quantity of production increases and all resources are variable.
   b. at the minimum point of the long-run average-cost curve.
   c. when unit costs increase as the quantity of production increases and all resources are variable.
   d. at the output level at which the cost per unit is the lowest.
   e. when unit costs remain constant as the quantity of production increases and all resources are variable.

4. Constant returns to scale exist
   a. when unit costs decrease as the quantity of production increases and all resources are variable.
   b. at the minimum point of the long-run average-cost curve.
   c. when unit costs increase as the quantity of production increases and all resources are variable.
   d. at the output level at which the cost per unit is the lowest.
   (e.) when unit costs remain constant as the quantity of production increases and all resources are variable.

5. The minimum efficient scale is
   a. when unit costs decrease as the quantity of production increases and all resources are variable.
   b. the minimum point of the long-run average-cost curve.
   c. when unit costs increase as the quantity of production increases and all resources are variable.
   d. the output level at which the cost per unit is the lowest.
   (e.) both b and d above.

PRACTICE QUESTIONS AND PROBLEMS

Section 1: Firms and Business

1. Economists use the word _firm_ to refer to any of these three types of businesses: _Sole proprietorships_, _partnerships_, and _Corporation_.

2. What terms match the definitions below?

   a. ___MPP___ : the additional quantity that is produced when one additional unit of a resource is used in combination with the same quantities of all other resources

   b. ___TPP___ : the maximum output that can be produced when successive units of a variable resource are added to fixed amounts of other resources

   c. ___APP___ : the output per unit of resource

3. The _short-run_ is a period of time just short enough that the quantity of at least one of the resources cannot be altered.

4. The law of diminishing marginal returns applies
   a. only in the immediate period.
   b. only in the short run.
   c. only in the long run.
   d. in both the short run and the long run, but not in the immediate period.
   e. in the immediate period, in the short run, and in the long run.

5. The table below gives the number of hamburgers produced per hour at Joe's Gourmet Burger Stand with different numbers of workers.

   a. Find the *TPP*, *MPP*, and *APP* at each number of workers, plot the *TPP* curve on the left graph, and plot the *MPP* and *APP* curves on the right graph.

Number of Workers	Number of Burgers	TPP	MPP	APP
1	5	5	~~5~~ 5	5
2	23	23	~~17~~ 17	11.5
3	50	50	~~27~~ 27	16.7
4	80	80	~~30~~ 30	20
5	100	100	~~20~~ 20	20
6	110	110	10	18.3
7	110	110	0	15.7
8	100	100	-10	12.5

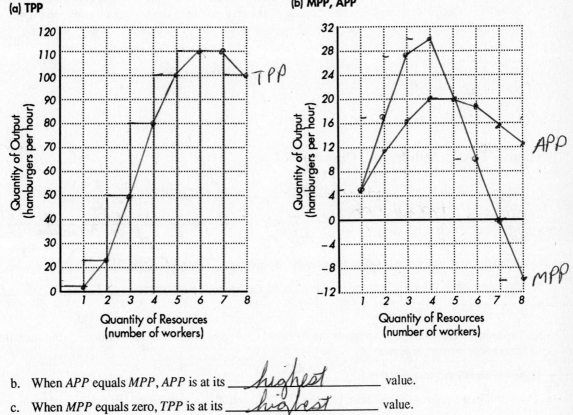

(a) TPP

(b) MPP, APP

b. When *APP* equals *MPP*, *APP* is at its _____highest_____ value.

c. When *MPP* equals zero, *TPP* is at its _____highest_____ value.

6. Use the law of diminishing returns to explain why you can't grow enough wheat in a small flowerpot to feed the entire world.

_____

_____

_____

_____

Section 2: Revenue, Costs, and Profit

1. If a business has a choice of different resource combinations that can produce the same amount of output, the business should choose the _lowest – cost_ combination.

2. What do economists include as costs that accountants don't include?
   opportunity costs of resources already owned

3. What already owned resources does the producer usually provide to a business? _personal funds_ _capital_
   and _owner's labor_.

4. You currently work as a donut-hole maker, at a salary of $25,000. You also have $50,000 in the bank earning 10 percent interest per year. If you decide to quit your job, invest your $50,000 in buying your own donut-hole shop, and spend your time running your own donut-hole shop, what are your opportunity costs for a year?
   a. zero
   b. $5,000
   c. $25,000
   d. $30,000
   e. $75,000

Section 3: Cost Schedules and Cost Curves

1. Total costs include both _total fixed_ and _total variable_ costs.
2. ATC = _total costs divided by output quantity_
3. MC = _the additional cost of producing one more unit of output_
4. When the marginal value is below the average, the average _falls_ (falls, rises, stays the same). When the marginal value is above the average, the average _rises_ (falls, rises, stays the same).

5. The table on the following page gives the short-run total costs of Joe's Gourmet Burger Stand for different amounts of output per minute.
   a. What is Joe's total fixed cost? _5.5_
   b. Fill in the columns in the table, plot the TC, TFC, and TVC curves on the left graph on the following page, and plot the ATC, AVC, AFC, and MC curves on the right graph on the following page.

Burgers	TC	TFC	TVC	AFC	AVC	ATC	MC
0	$ 5.50	$5.50	$ 0				
1	9.00		3.50	$2.75 5.50	$3.56	$9.00	$3.50
2	10.00		4.50	1.83 2.75	2.25	5.00	1.00
3	10.50		5.00	1.38 1.83	1.67	3.50	.50
4	11.50		6.00	1.38	1.50	2.88	1.00
5	13.00		7.50	1.10	1.50	2.60	1.50
6	15.00		9.50	.92	1.58	2.50	2.00
7	17.50		12.00	.79	1.71	2.50	2.50
8	20.50		15.00	.69	1.88	2.56	3.00
9	24.00		18.50	.61	2.06	2.67	3.50
10	28.00		22.50	.55	2.25	2.80	4.00

(a) Total Costs   **(b) Unit Costs**

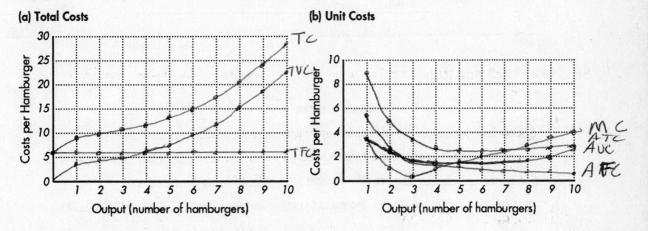

6. a. Where does the *MC* curve cross the *AVC* curve?

   output of 1 and 5.

   b. Where does the *MC* curve cross the *ATC* curve?

   output of 7

7. Explain why the following curves are shaped the way they are.

   a. *AFC*

_____

_____

_____

_____

b. *MC*

_____

_____

_____

_____

c. *AVC*

_____

_____

_____

_____

d. *ATC*

_____

_____

_____

_____

Section 4: The Long Run

1. Economies of scale result when increases in output lead to __*decreases*__ in unit __*costs*__ when all resources are __*variable*__ .

2. Diseconomies of scale result when increases in output lead to __*increases*__ in unit __*costs*__ when all resources are __*variable*__ .

3. Constant returns to scale result when increases in output lead to __*no change*__ in unit __*costs*__ when all resources are __*variable*__ .

4. The table below contains the short-run average total costs (*SRAC*) of Joe's Gourmet Burger Stand for four different sizes of burger stands.

Number of Burgers	Size #1 SRAC	Size #2 SRAC	Size #3 SRAC	Size #4 SRAC	LRAC
1	$3.45	$4.40	$6.00	$14.00	$ 3.45
2	3.20	3.70	4.70	9.50	3.20
3	3.00	3.20	4.10	6.90	3.00
4	3.20	2.80	3.65	5.70	2.80
5	3.50	2.50	3.30	5.10	2.50
6	3.90	2.75	3.00	4.65	2.75
7	4.40	3.00	2.75	4.30	2.75
8	5.00	3.50	2.50	4.00	2.50
9	5.70	4.00	3.00	3.50	3.00
10	6.50	4.75	3.50	3.25	3.25
11	8.00	5.75	4.00	3.50	3.50
12	9.90	7.25	4.50	4.20	4.20

a. Graph the four *SRAC* curves on the graph below.

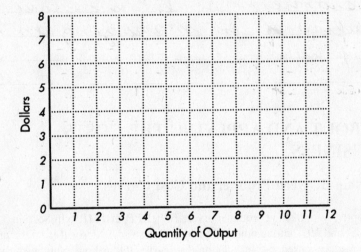

b. If we assume that these are the only possible sizes for Joe's stand, fill in the table for the long-run average-total-cost (*LRAC*) curve for Joe's Gourmet Burgers and graph the *LRAC* curve. (Hint: If Joe wants to get the most profit for a particular level of output, what size stand will he want to choose for that output level?)

5. The graph on the following page shows the long-run average-cost curve for Joe's Gourmet Burger Stand, taking into account all possible sizes for the burger stand. On the graph, what range of output levels shows

a. economies of scale? _____0 – 5_____

b. constant returns to scale? _____5 – 8_____

c. diseconomies of scale? _____8 – 12_____

d. What is the minimum efficient scale? _____5 burgers_____

Long-Run Average Cost

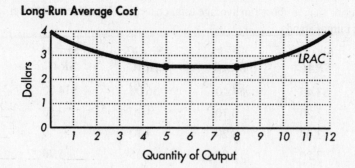

6. Give some reasons that might explain why Joe's Gourmet Burger Stand shows economies of scale at small levels of output.

> *At small levels of output, there are not enough workers to take advantage of specialization, and small-scale machinery is usually less efficient than larger machines.*

7. Give some reasons that might explain why Joe's Gourmet Burger Stand shows diseconomies of scale at large levels of output.

> *Diseconomies of scale can result from difficulties of in managing large enterprises.*

THINKING ABOUT AND APPLYING THE COSTS OF DOING BUSINESS

I. The Relationship Between Product and Cost Curves

In Section 1 of the chapter, we looked at product curves: *TPP, APP,* and *MPP.* In Section 3, we looked at cost curves: *ATC, AFC, AVC,* and *MC,* among others. The cost curves can be derived from the product curves if we know the prices of the resources used, because the product curves tell us how many resources are needed to produce different amounts of output. The table below shows basically the same product curves for Joe's Gourmet Burger Stand that you calculated in Section 1; also given are the wage Joe pays his workers and his fixed costs (to keep things simple, we'll leave out all other costs).

Wage = $10.00 per worker
Total fixed cost (TFC) = $500.00

Number of Workers	Number of Burgers	TPP	MPP	MC	APP	AVC	AFC	ATC
1	5	5	5	$2.00	5.00	$ 2.00	$100.00	$102.00
2	23	23	18	.56	11.50	.87	21.74	22.61
3	50	50	27	_____	16.67	_____	_____	_____
4	80	80	30	_____	20.00	_____	_____	_____
5	100	100	20	_____	20.00	_____	_____	_____
6	110	110	10	_____	18.33	_____	_____	_____
7	111	111	1	_____	15.86	_____	_____	_____

Let's look at the relationship between the product and cost curves. The *MPP* curve shows how many more burgers one more worker can produce: the marginal costs of each of those burgers are the added costs paid to the additional worker (the wage of $10.00) divided by the number of burgers that person produced. For example, hiring the first worker costs Joe an additional $10, and the worker produces 5 more burgers, so each of those 5 burgers adds $2 ($10/5 burgers) to Joe's costs. The second worker produces an additional 18 burgers for an additional cost of $10, so each of those burgers adds $.56 ($10/18) to Joe's costs.

The *AVC* curve is derived from the *APP* curve in a similar way. *APP* shows the average number of burgers produced per worker. Since we're assuming that labor is the only variable resource, the average variable cost is the labor cost per burger: the cost of an average worker (the wage) divided by the number of burgers produced by the average worker (*APP*). When Joe is hiring two workers, total output is 23 burgers, or 11.5 burgers per worker on average. Each worker costs Joe $10, so the *AVC* is $.87 per burger ($10/11.5 burgers) when two workers are used.

The *AFC* and *ATC* curves are calculated the same way as in Section 3: *AFC* = *TFC/Q* (*Q* is the number of burgers), and *ATC* = *AFC* + *AVC*.

1. Fill in the blanks in the table; then graph the product curves on the top left graph below and the cost curves on the bottom left and right graphs. Be careful: the cost curve graph on the left has the number of *workers* on the horizontal axis, and the cost curve graph on the right has the number of *burgers* on the horizontal axis.

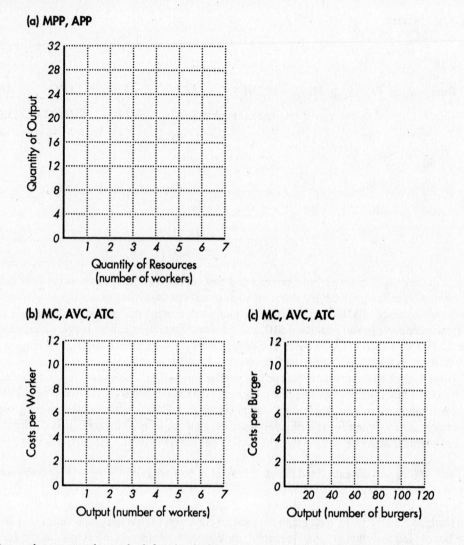

(a) MPP, APP

(b) MC, AVC, ATC

(c) MC, AVC, ATC

2. Looking at the two graphs on the left, what is the relationship between the maximum *MPP* and the minimum *MC*? Why do the curves have this relationship?

_____

_____

_____

_____

3. On the left graphs, what is the relationship between the maximum *APP* and the minimum *AVC*? Why do the curves have this relationship?

_____

_____

_____

_____

II. Production Functions for Wine and Gourmet Burgers

Underlying all the product curves and cost curves we've been looking at in this chapter is the production function: the mathematical relationship between the amount of resources used and the amount of output produced. The "Economically Speaking" section of the chapter examines one production function that relates resources (rainfall, timing of rainfall, and temperature) to an output (the quality of wine). Orley Ashenfelter, an economist at Princeton University, used statistical techniques to calculate the production function for wine quality. Many other real-world studies of costs and production have been done it the same way. We can't do complex statistics here, but let's take a look at some of the factors that would determine the production function for Joe's Gourmet Burger Stand.

1. Start by listing the resources that Joe needs to make and sell his gourmet burgers. (You can decide what all goes into a gourmet burger.)

    _____

    _____

    _____

    _____

2. Some of these resources will be variable in the short run, and some of them only in the long run. Mark your list of resources to show those that are variable in the short run.

3. Some of these resources will be used in fixed proportions; for example, for each hamburger, you need exactly one hamburger roll. Some of the resources will be used in variable proportions: you know from problem 5 in Section 1, where you calculated Joe's *APP* for labor, that the amount of labor per hamburger can have different values, depending on how many hamburgers Joe is making. Mark your list of resources to show those that are used in fixed proportions.

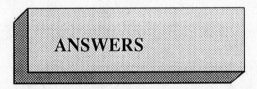

ANSWERS

Quick Check Quiz

Section 1: Firms and Business

1. c; 2. a; 3. b; 4. d; 5. b
   If you missed any of these questions, you should go back and review pages 201–206 in Chapter 8 (pages 573–578 in *Economics*, Chapter 22).

Section 2: Revenue, Costs, and Profit

1. b; 2. e; 3. d
   If you missed any of these questions, you should go back and review pages 206–208 in Chapter 8 (pages 578–580 in *Economics*, Chapter 22).

Section 3: Cost Schedules and Cost Curves

1. b; 2. e; 3. a; 4. c; 5. c; 6. d

If you missed any of these questions, you should go back and review pages 208–213 in Chapter 8 (pages 580–585 in *Economics*, Chapter 22).

Section 4: The Long Run

1. a; 2. a; 3. c; 4. e; 5. e

If you missed any of these questions, you should go back and review pages 208–219 in Chapter 8 (pages 585–591 in *Economics*, Chapter 22).

Practice Questions and Problems

Section 1: Firms and Business

1. firm; sole proprietorships; partnerships; corporations
2. a. marginal physical product
   b. total physical product
   c. average physical product
3. short run
4. b
5. a.

Number of Workers	Number of Burgers	TPP	MPP	APP
1	5	5	5	5.00
2	23	23	18	11.50
3	50	50	27	16.67
4	80	80	30	20.00
5	100	100	20	20.00
6	110	110	10	18.33
7	110	110	0	15.71
8	100	100	-10	12.50

TPP is the same as the number of burgers.
MPP is the change in *TPP* from using one more worker.
APP is *TPP* divided by the number of workers.

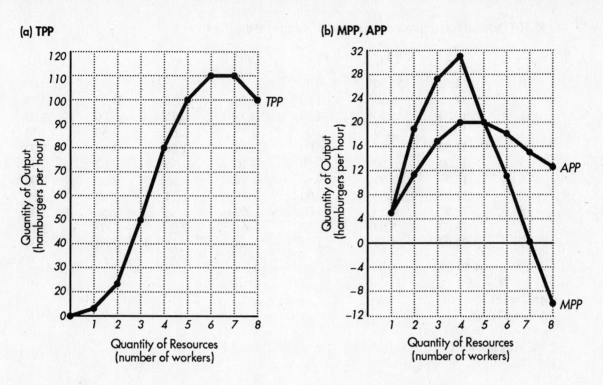

(a) TPP

(b) MPP, APP

b. highest
c. highest
6. As you add more seed, fertilizer, and water (variable resources) to the dirt in the flowerpot (the fixed resource), the added output gets smaller and smaller. Eventually, the wheat is drowned or burned and the *TPP* actually declines. The fixed resource, the space in which to grow wheat, limits the quantity of wheat that can be produced.

Section 2: Revenue, Costs, and Profit

1. lowest-cost
2. resources already owned by the producer
3. labor; capital
4. d
   Answer a is wrong—your time and capital have other valuable uses. Answer b is wrong—you didn't count the salary from your current job as an opportunity cost. Answer c is wrong—you didn't count the forgone interest from your capital as an opportunity cost. Answer e is wrong—the opportunity cost of using your capital is the interest forgone, not the whole amount of the capital.

Section 3: Cost Schedules and Cost Curves

1. fixed; variable
2. *TC/Q* (total cost divided by output quantity)
3. change in *TC* from producing one more unit of output
4. falls; rises

5. a. $5.50 (The total cost of producing zero units of output is the fixed cost.)

    b.
Burgers	TC	TFC	TVC	AFC	AVC	ATC	MC
0	$ 5.50	$5.50	$ 0.00				
1	9.00	5.50	3.50	$5.50	$3.50	$9.00	$3.50
2	10.00	5.50	4.50	2.75	2.25	5.00	1.00
3	10.50	5.50	5.00	1.83	1.67	3.50	.50
4	11.50	5.50	6.00	1.38	1.50	2.88	1.00
5	13.00	5.50	7.50	1.10	1.50	2.60	1.50
6	15.00	5.50	9.50	.92	1.58	2.50	2.00
7	17.50	5.50	12.00	.79	1.71	2.50	2.50
8	20.50	5.50	15.00	.69	1.88	2.56	3.00
9	24.00	5.50	18.50	.61	2.06	2.67	3.50
10	28.00	5.50	22.50	.55	2.25	2.80	4.00

TFC is always $5.50.
TVC = TC − TFC
AFC = TFC/Q
AVC = TVC/Q
ATC = TC/Q = AFC + AVC
MC = change in TC

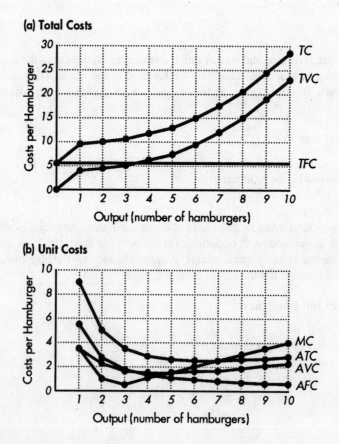

6. a. at 5 units—the low point on the AVC curve
    b. at 7 units—the low point on the ATC curve

7. a. *AFC* always decreases as Q increases because *TFC* is fixed: as Q increases, the same amount of costs is spread over more and more units of output.

b. *MC* is U-shaped because in the short run some resource is fixed in amount. At very low amounts of output, there are not enough variable resources to use the fixed resource efficiently. As output increases, the fixed resources can be used more efficiently, so *MPP* increases and *MC* decreases. As you keep expanding output by adding more variable resources, eventually you have so many variable resources used that they cannot all use the fixed resource efficiently. *MPP* starts to fall, and *MC* increases.

Look back to question 5 for Section 1 above. As Joe's Gourmet Burgers increased its output from zero, marginal physical product (added output per worker) increased at first. The second worker added more hamburgers (18) to the total than did the first worker (5): having 2 workers let both of them use Joe's hamburger grill more efficiently. Each worker is paid the same amount of money per hour, so the marginal cost of the second worker's hamburgers is lower than the marginal cost of the hamburgers produced by the first worker. If the workers are paid $5 each and labor is the only variable resource, the marginal cost of the 5 hamburgers produced by the first worker is $1 each ($5 for the worker divided by the 5 hamburgers produced). The marginal cost of the hamburgers produced by the second worker is only about $.28 ($5/18 burgers) because adding the second worker increased efficiency. As Joe adds more and more workers, the *MPP* eventually starts to decrease (the law of diminishing marginal returns) as each worker gets to use a smaller fraction of the hamburger grill. When *MPP* starts going down, *MC* will increase.

c. *AVC* is also U-shaped for similar reasons. At low levels of output, the average output per worker (*APP*) is low because there are not enough workers to use the fixed resources efficiently. As more variable resources are added and output increases, the fixed resource is used more efficiently, *APP* increases, and *AVC* decreases. Eventually there are more than enough variable resources, and output per worker starts to fall, causing *AVC* to increase.

Looking at Joe's Gourmet Burger Stand again, when Joe is using 2 workers and producing 23 burgers, the average output per worker (*APP*) is 11.5. If each worker costs Joe $5, the labor cost per burger is about $.43 ($5 per worker/11.5 burgers per worker). If Joe hires 4 workers and produces 80 burgers, the *APP* is 20, so the labor cost per burger is only about $.25 ($5/20 burgers). If labor is the only variable resource, the labor cost per burger is the *AVC*.

d. *ATC* is the sum of *AFC* and *AVC*. At low levels of output, both *AFC* and *AVC* are falling, so *ATC* must also be falling. As output expands, *AFC* keeps going down, but at a slower and slower rate, while *AVC* increases. Eventually the increase in *AVC* becomes larger than the fall in *AFC*, and *ATC* begins to increase.

If you want further information on the shape of cost curves, review Sections 1.b and 3.c in the text, and the discussion of Fundamental Questions 1 and 3 above. Problem I in the section on "Thinking About and Applying the Costs of Doing Business" also deals with the shape of cost curves and the relationship between cost and product curves.

Section 4: The Long Run

1. decreases; unit costs; variable
2. increases; unit costs; variable
3. no change; unit costs; variable

4. a.

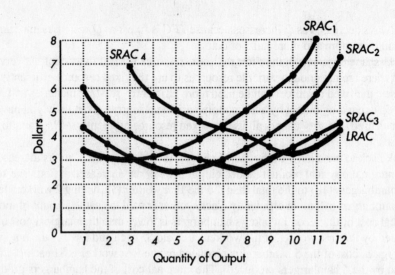

b.

Number of Burgers	Size #1 SRAC	Size #2 SRAC	Size #3 SRAC	Size #4 SRAC	LRAC	Stand Size
1	$3.45	$4.40	$6.00	$14.00	$3.45	#1
2	3.20	3.70	4.70	9.50	3.20	#1
3	3.00	3.20	4.10	6.90	3.00	#1
4	3.20	2.80	3.65	5.70	2.80	#2
5	3.50	2.50	3.30	5.10	2.50	#2
6	3.90	2.75	3.00	4.65	2.75	#2
7	4.40	3.00	2.75	4.30	2.75	#3
8	5.00	3.50	2.50	4.00	2.50	#3
9	5.70	4.00	3.00	3.50	3.00	#3
10	6.50	4.75	3.50	3.25	3.25	#4
11	8.00	5.75	4.00	3.50	3.50	#4
12	9.90	7.25	4.50	4.20	4.20	#4

In the long run, Joe can choose whatever size stand he wants, based on the number of burgers he expects to be able to sell. For each output level from 1 burger through 12 burgers, Joe will choose the stand size with the lowest *SRAC*. The *SRAC* figures for the stands chosen make up the *LRAC* curve (also shown in Figure 8). The stands with the lowest *SRAC* are listed in the table above.

5. a. up to 5 burgers (where *LRAC* is falling)
   b. from 5 to 8 burgers (where *LRAC* is level)
   c. beyond 8 burgers (where *LRAC* is rising)
   d. 5 burgers (the smallest output where *LRAC* is at its minimum value)

6. At small levels of output, there are not enough workers to take advantage of specialization, and small-scale machinery usually is less efficient than larger machines.

7. Diseconomies of scale can result from difficulties in managing large enterprises.

Thinking About and Applying the Costs of Doing Business

I. Relationships Between Product and Cost Curves

1.

Number of Workers	Number of Burgers	TPP	MPP	MC	APP	AVC	AFC	ATC
1	5	5	5	$ 2.00	5.00	$2.00	$100.00	$102.00
2	23	23	18	.56	11.50	.87	21.74	22.61
3	50	50	27	.37	16.67	.60	10.00	10.60
4	80	80	30	.33	20.00	.50	6.25	6.75
5	100	100	20	.50	20.00	.50	5.00	5.50
6	110	110	10	1.00	18.33	.55	4.55	5.09
7	111	111	1	10.00	15.86	.63	4.50	5.14

(a) MPP, APP

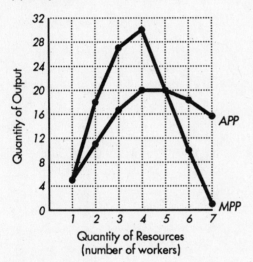

Quantity of Output

Quantity of Resources
(number of workers)

(b) MC, AVC, ATC

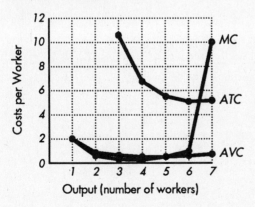

Costs per Worker

Output (number of workers)

(c) MC, AVC, ATC

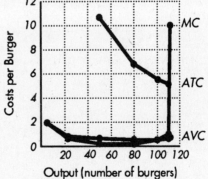

Costs per Burger

Output (number of burgers)

2. When *MPP* is at its highest value, *MC* is at its lowest value. The larger the additional output per worker (*MPP*), the more units of output the cost of that worker can be spread over, so each additional unit of output takes less labor time and labor cost.

3. When *APP* is at its highest value, *AVC* is at its lowest value. The larger the average output per worker (*APP*), the more units of output the cost of the average worker can be spread over, so each unit of output takes less labor time and labor cost.

II. Production Functions for Wine and Gourmet Burgers

1. The list could include hamburger, roll, ketchup, mustard, lettuce, tomato, onion, salt, steak sauce, labor, grill, burger stand, land, and entrepreneurship. You should have included some ingredients for the hamburgers, plus labor, capital, land, and entrepreneurship—resources needed for any business.

2. Burger ingredients and labor can be changed much faster than capital, land, and entrepreneurship.

3. The hamburger ingredients are used in fixed proportions; the rest are in variable proportions.

CHAPTER 9*
An Overview of Product Markets

1. What is a market structure?

To economists (and to you as a student of economics), a market structure is a model of the way business firms behave, based on several characteristics of the firms involved, and implying that firms will pursue particular business strategies in the marketplace.

First, a market structure is a model—a simplified way to represent reality. By concentrating on only a few important characteristics of businesses, we can look at some of the similarities and differences between types of business behavior without getting bogged down in a lot of detail. No business in the real world exactly matches any of our models of market structure, but almost all are close enough to one of the market-structure models that understanding the market structure can help us understand the behavior of a real-world business.

We use three characteristics of businesses to define the market-structure models:

1. the number of firms directly competing with each other in the market
2. how easy or difficult it is for a new firm to enter the industry and successfully compete with older firms
3. the type of product being produced

In looking at market structures, we classify products as either differentiated or standardized (nondifferentiated). **Standardized products** are perceived by buyers as identical; **differentiated products** are perceived as having characteristics that other sellers' products do not have. The key idea here is people's perceptions. Regardless of whether or not there are any chemical differences among brands of gasoline, if you think some brands are better than others, then gasoline is a differentiated product *to you*. If you think all brands of gasoline are the same, then it's a standardized product *to you*.

2. What distinguishes perfect competition, monopoly, monopolistic competition, and oligopoly?

Each of these four market-structure models is defined by different combinations of the three characteristics listed above. The differences among market structures are summarized in the following table:

Market Structure	Number of Firms	Entry Condition	Product type
Perfect competition	Very large number	Easy	Standardized
Monopoly	One	No entry possible	Only one product
Monopolistic competition	Large number	Easy	Differentiated
Oligopoly	Few	Impeded	Standardized or differentiated

*Economics Chapter 23.

3. What are price takers?

Price takers are business firms that are forced to take the market price for their products: individually, there is nothing they can do to change the market price. Firms in perfectly competitive markets are price takers. If a single firm tries to raise its price even a little bit, buyers will immediately switch to other sellers.

4. What are price makers?

Price makers are firms that can choose the selling price of their product, although their choice is affected by the demand curve for their product. Firms in a monopoly market, an oligopolistic market, or a monopolistically competitive market are price makers.

5. What is competition?

Competition between firms can take many forms besides price competition. In addition to competing for buyers by charging low prices, firms can compete by changing product characteristics (remember "new" Coca-Cola?), improving product quality, developing new products, and so on. The recently developed **theory of contestable markets** shows that the possibility of future competition can have an effect on a firm's behavior, even if the firm is the only one in the market.

6. Do firms maximize profit?

The assumption that firms maximize profit is part of the economist's model of business behavior. Like all models, it is a simplification of reality that helps us understand how the real world works. Most business firms try to come close to profit maximization most of the time, although there are some organizations—such as governments and charities, that have other objectives.

Economists usually talk about profit maximization in terms of firms' decisions about their output level—how many units of output they will produce. From that viewpoint, profit maximization can be looked at in two equivalent ways:

1. finding the output level where total revenue exceeds total cost by the greatest amount
2. finding the output level where **marginal revenue** equals marginal cost

These two rules always give the same answer.

7. When do firms go out of business?

Firms go out of business when that's their best available alternative. A temporary shutdown will happen when revenues are not enough to cover variable costs, when the firm loses less money by shutting down than it would if it kept running. In the long run, a firm will permanently shut down and exit the industry when revenues do not cover all costs and the situation is not expected to improve.

KEY TERMS

differentiated products	price maker
standardized or nondifferentiated products	theory of contestable markets
natural monopoly	marginal revenue
price taker	

QUICK CHECK QUIZ

Section 1: Market Structure

1. Which of the market characteristics listed below is NOT used to help define market structures?
    a. the number of firms in the market
    b. the ease of entry into the market by new firms
    c. the percentage of the firms' incomes that are paid in taxes
    d. the type of product produced (standardized or differentiated)
    e. All of the above characteristics are used to help define market structures.

2. Which of the following is NOT one of the market structures defined in the chapter?
    a. perfect competition
    b. monopoly
    c. monopolistic competition
    d. oligopoly
    e. All of the above are market structures defined in the chapter.

3. In which of the following market structures does only one firm supply the product and entry cannot occur?
    a. perfect competition
    b. monopolistic competition
    c. oligopoly
    d. monopoly
    e. None of these market structures matches the definition.

4. In which of the following market structures do a few firms produce either a standardized or differentiated product, with entry being possible but not easy?
    a. perfect competition
    b. monopolistic competition
    c. oligopoly
    d. monopoly
    e. None of these market structures matches the definition.

5. Which of the following market structures is defined as having very many firms producing a standardized product and easy entry?
    a. perfect competition
    b. monopolistic competition
    c. oligopoly
    d. monopoly
    e. None of these market structures matches the definition.

6. Which of the following market structures is defined as having many firms producing differentiated products and easy entry?
    a. perfect competition
    b. monopolistic competition
    c. oligopoly
    d. monopoly
    e. None of these market structures matches the definition.

7. In which of the following market structures are firms interdependent?
   a. perfect competition
   b. monopolistic competition
   c. oligopoly
   d. monopoly
   e. Firms in all of the above market structures are interdependent.

8. A natural monopoly is caused by
   a. economies of scale.
   b. government intervention.
   c. anticompetitive practices by large firms.
   d. control over natural resource supplies.
   e. patent laws.

Section 2: Profit Maximization

1. Economists' models of the behavior of business firms assume that firms try to maximize
   a. total revenue.
   b. marginal revenue.
   c. profit.
   d. market share.
   e. political influence.

2. Marginal revenue is the
   a. revenue gained from selling all the output produced by a firm.
   b. cost incurred from making all the output produced by a firm.
   c. additional revenue gained from selling one more unit of output.
   d. additional cost incurred from making an additional unit of output.
   e. the difference between total revenue and total cost.

3. The demand curve facing a perfectly competitive firm is
   a. a vertical line at the market price.
   b. a horizontal line at the market price.
   c. downward sloping.
   d. upward sloping.
   e. dependent on other firms' decisions.

4. The demand curve facing firms in all types of markets except perfect competition is
   a. a vertical line at the market price.
   b. a horizontal line at the market price.
   c. downward sloping.
   d. upward sloping.
   e. dependent on other firms' decisions.

5. Profit is maximized when
   a. total revenues are at their maximum value.
   b. total revenues exceed total costs by the greatest amount.
   c. marginal revenue equals marginal cost.
   d. Both a and b are correct.
   e. Both b and c are correct.

PRACTICE QUESTIONS AND PROBLEMS

Section 1: Market Structure

1. The four market structures are *perfect competition* ; *monopolistic competition* *oligopoly* ; and *monopoly* .

2. Perfect competition is a market structure in which *very many* firms are producing a *standardized* product and entry is *easy* .

3. Monopolistic competition is a market structure in which *many* firms are producing a *differentiated* product and entry is *easy* .

4. Oligopoly is a market structure in which *few* firms are producing a *standardized or differentiated* product and entry is *impeded* .

5. Monopoly is a market structure in which *one* firm supplies a product and entry *is not possible*.

6. Oligopoly is the only market structure in which firms are *interdependent*.

7. When there are large economies of scale, a *natural* monopoly can occur.

8. When buyers perceive different sellers' products to be identical, we say the products are *standardized*; when buyers perceive different sellers' products to be different, we say the products are *differentiated*.

9. The idea that potential competition can force even monopoly firms to behave as if they were perfectly competitive is called the theory of *contestable markets*.

10. Firms that are price makers are found in which market structures? *monopoly + monopolistic competition + oligopoly*

11. On the graph below, sketch the shape of a demand curve for the product sold by a firm that is a price maker.

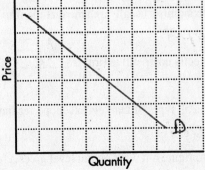

12. Firms that are price takers are found in which market structure? *perfect competition*.

13. The left-hand graph below shows the market demand and supply for a market. On the right-hand graph below, sketch the demand curve for a price taker firm selling in that market.

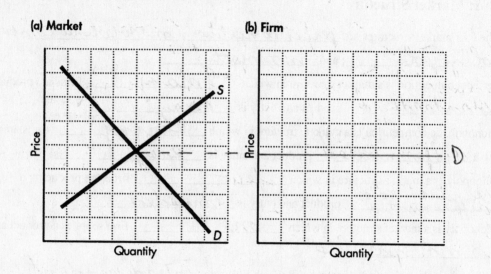

(a) Market (b) Firm

14. For the three market structures listed below, describe how much advertising an individual seller is likely to use.

Perfect competition _____ *none* _____

Monopolistic competition _____ *much* _____

Monopoly _____ *none* _____

15. Explain what factor is most likely to determine whether a firm selling in an oligopoly does a lot of advertising. (Hint: Look at the list of key terms covered in this section.)

_____ *Whether its product is differentiated or not.* _____

Section 2: Profit Maximization

1. In analyzing business behavior, economists usually assume that the firm's objective is to

maximize profit

2. The demand curve facing the perfectly competitive firm is *horizontal* at the

market price

3. The demand curves facing firms in all types of markets except perfect competition

slope downward

4. List the two criteria you can use to figure out what output level gives a firm the most profit.

when total revenue exceeds total cost by the greatest amount

when marginal revenue equals marginal cost.

5. The Kilroy Manufacturing Company makes and sells a computer game called "Kilroy Was Here." The company knows from experience that it can sell 10 games per day when it charges a price of $50. If it wants to sell 11 games per day, it has to cut the price to $49.

   a. Does Kilroy sell its game in a perfectly competitive market? __*no*__

   b. What is the marginal revenue of the eleventh game it sells per day? __*$39.*__

6. Sally Smith is a world-famous artist who carves exquisitely beautiful models of birds out of rare, expensive woods. Sally knows that if she carves only 1 bird per month, her customers will pay a high price for it because of its rarity. If she makes more birds per month, people will only be willing to pay lower prices. Moreover, when she carves more birds per month, her hands get very sore and she has to spend more money having them massaged.

   The table below gives the price Sally can charge for different numbers of birds sold per month and her total costs of making different numbers of birds per month. Calculate Sally's total revenue, marginal revenue, marginal cost, and profit for each output level.

Q	P	TR	TC	MR	MC	Profit
0	–	$0	$ 500	–	–	*-500*
1	$2,000	*2000*	700	*2000*	*200*	*1300*
2	1,800	*3600*	1,100	*1600*	*400*	*2500*
3	1,600	*4800*	1,700	*1200*	*600*	*3100*
4	1,400	*5600*	2,500	*800*	*800*	*3100*
5	1,200	*6000*	3,500	*400*	*1000*	*2500*
6	1,000	*6000*	4,700	*0*	*1200*	*1300*

   a. At what output level is Sally's profit at its maximum? __*3 or 4 birds*__

   b. At what output level does Sally's marginal revenue equal her marginal cost?
   __*4 birds ($800)*__

   c. On the left graph on the following page, plot Sally's profit at each output level. On the right graph on the following page, plot Sally's marginal cost and marginal revenue. As you can see, profit is maximized at the same output level where $MR = MC$, isn't it?

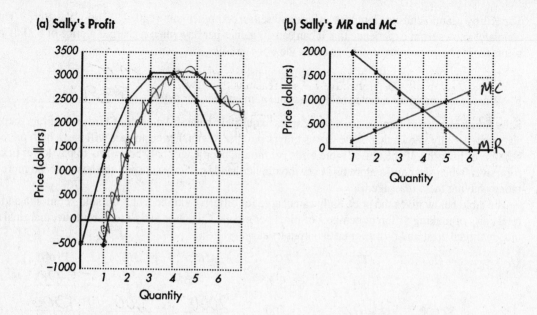

(a) Sally's Profit

(b) Sally's *MR* and *MC*

THINKING ABOUT AND APPLYING MARKET STRUCTURE AND PROFIT MAXIMIZATION

I.   The Market Structures of Aspirin

The next time you're in the grocery store or drug store, walk by the aspirin displays and take a look at the different brands of plain aspirin and their prices. Chances are you'll find several different brands: one or more nationally advertised brands (Bayer, for example), the store's own brand name, maybe some aspirin with no brand name on it at all, and probably some other local or regional brands. If you look in other stores, you'll find many other brands of aspirin. When you read the labels, you'll find that all regular-strength aspirin has the same active ingredient: 325 mg of aspirin (or acetylsalicylic acid, the chemical name for aspirin); extra-strength aspirin has 500 mg of aspirin.

1.   Since there seem to be a large number of sellers of an identical product, what kind of market structure would aspirin fit into? _____

2.   If aspirin is sold in a perfectly competitive market, would you predict that all sellers would charge the same price, or different prices? _____

3.   When you check the prices, you'll find that they are quite different rather than the same. The prices will probably follow a predictable pattern: the national brands will be most expensive, followed by other regional and local brands; the store's own brand will be least expensive unless there's generic, no-brand aspirin available. Use what you have learned in this chapter to explain how this could come about.

_____

_____

_____

_____

II. Profit Maximization and Pollution Reduction

The ideas of profit maximization and of comparing marginal revenue and marginal cost to find the profit-maximizing output level can be useful even for organizations that aren't involved in profit maximization, because all organizations need to find the most effective ways of reaching their goals.

Suppose you are the head of the Environmental Protection Agency (EPA), and you have to decide how much, if any, pollution a particular water treatment plant should be allowed to produce. Right now, the plant produces 4 tons of pollutants per day. The plant is owned by the federal government, so any cleanup costs will be paid for through taxes. Let's assume that the EPA knows what the benefits and cost (in dollars) are from reducing pollution by various amounts. Using the benefits and costs in the table below, find the amount of pollution reduction that gives people the biggest "profit." "Profit" in this case would be the net value people get from pollution reduction: the total benefits minus the total costs.

Pollution Improvement: Tons Reduced per Day	Marginal Benefits	Marginal Costs
1	$10 million	$ 1 million
2	5 million	4 million
3	2 million	10 million
4	1 million	30 million

Amount of reduction: _____

Explain why you chose this amount:

_____

_____

_____

_____

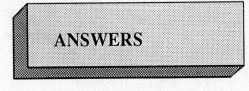

ANSWERS

Quick Check Quiz

Section 1: Market Structure

1. c; 2. e; 3. d; 4. c; 5. a; 6. b; 7. c; 8. a

If you missed any of these questions, you should go back and review pages 228–238 in Chapter 9 (pages 600–610 in *Economics*, Chapter 23).

Section 2: Profit Maximization

1. c; 2. c; 3. b; 4. c; 5. e

If you missed any of these questions, you should go back and review pages 239–243 in Chapter 9 (pages 611–615 in *Economics*, Chapter 23).

PRACTICE QUESTIONS AND PROBLEMS

Section 1: Market Structure

1. perfect competition; monopoly; monopolistic competition; oligopoly
2. very many; standardized (or nondifferentiated); easy
3. many; differentiated; easy
4. few; standardized or differentiated; possible but not easy
5. one; cannot occur
6. interdependent
7. natural
8. standardized (or nondifferentiated); differentiated
9. contestable markets
10. monopoly and monopolistic competition

11.

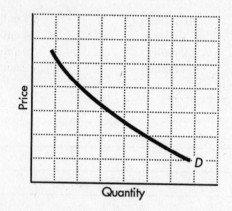

The demand curve for a price maker firm slopes downward.

12. perfect competition

13.

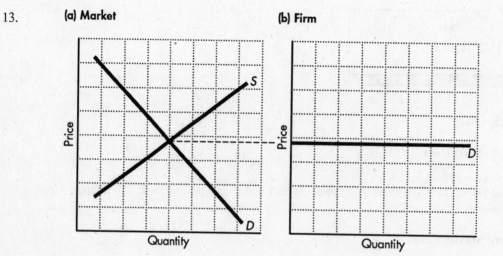

14. none; lots; not much

15. Whether its product is differentiated or not is the key factor in determining whether an oligopoly will do much advertising. In oligopolies with differentiated products (automobiles, for example), firms do a lot of advertising; in oligopolies with standardized products (steel, for example), they do little advertising.

Section 2: Profit Maximization

1. maximize profit
2. horizontal (or perfectly elastic); market price
3. slope downward
4. when total revenue exceeds total cost by the greatest amount; when marginal revenue equals marginal cost
5. a. no

    If Kilroy sold its game in a perfectly competitive market, it could sell more without reducing market price. A downward-sloping demand curve (when increasing quantity sold requires reducing price) is characteristic of all market structures except perfect competition.

   b. $39

    At $50, Kilroy's total revenue is $500 (price of $50 times quantity of 10 games); at $49, total revenue is $539. Marginal revenue is the additional revenue obtained by selling an additional unit of output, or $539 – $500 = $39.

6.

Q	P	TR	TC	MR	MC	Profit
0	–	$ 0	$ 500	–	–	$ –500
1	$2,000	2,000	700	$2,000	$ 200	1,300
2	1,800	3,600	1,100	1,600	400	2,500
3	1,600	4,800	1,700	1,200	600	3,100
4	1,400	5,600	2,500	800	800	3,100
5	1,200	6,000	3,500	400	1,000	2,500
6	1,000	6,000	4,700	0	1,200	1,300

$TR = P \times Q$.
MR is the change in TR from selling 1 more bird per month.
MC is the change in TC from making 1 more bird per month.
Profit = $TR - TC$.

   a. Both 3 birds and 4 birds give Sally $3,100 profit per month.
   b. $MR = MC = \$800$ at 4 birds per month.

c.

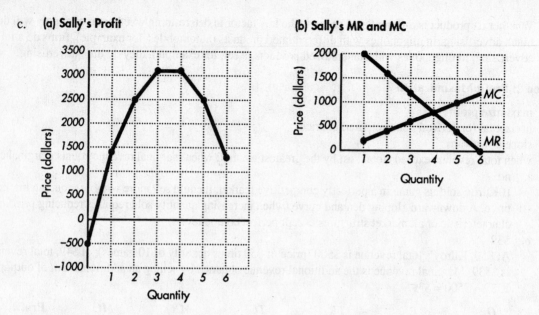

(a) Sally's Profit

(b) Sally's MR and MC

THINKING ABOUT AND APPLYING MARKET STRUCTURES AND PROFIT MAXIMIZATION

I. The Market Structures of Aspirin

1. perfect competition
Perfect competition is the only market structure with many sellers selling a standardized product.
2. same price
3. At least some aspirin buyers must perceive aspirin as a differentiated product. If everyone perceived aspirin as a standardized product, no one would pay more for specific brands. Even though all aspirin has the same active ingredients, the packaging can be different: the size and shape of the tablet, how the aspirin is held in the tablet, what the tablet is made of besides aspirin, and so on. Whether these differences are significant enough to justify the price differences can be argued both ways, but it is clear that some buyers behave as though the differences are significant to them.

II. Profit Maximization and Pollution Reduction

2 tons of reduction
For the first 1-ton reduction, people gain $10 million in benefits at a cost of $1 million in costs; the "profit" is $9 million from the first 1-ton reduction.
The second 1-ton reduction gives us $5 million in benefits at a cost of $4 million; we gain an additional $1 million "profit" from the second 1-ton reduction. After reducing pollution by 2 tons, we have total benefits of $15 million ($10 + $5 million) and total costs of $5 million ($1 + $4 million), for a total net gain or "profit" of $10 million.
If we made the third 1-ton reduction, we would gain $2 million in benefits at a cost of $10 million; we'd "lose" $8 million on the third 1-ton reduction. If we reduced pollution by a total of 3 tons, our total benefits would be $17 million ($10 + $5 + $2 million), and our total costs would be $15 million ($1 + $4 + $10 million), for a total net gain of $2 million. By the criterion specified for this example, we would be better off with only 2 tons of pollution reduction; we would get more value from spending $10 million on other things than on the third 1-ton reduction of pollution.
Although making decisions about pollution reduction is much more complex than this simple example, this problem does illustrate the basic concepts involved, including some of the economic principles we've

been studying in the last few chapters. The principle of diminishing marginal utility applies to pollution reduction as well as to other desirable results; the marginal benefits in the example decrease as we get more pollution reductions. The law of diminishing marginal returns explains why the marginal costs of pollution reduction increase as more pollution is eliminated. We'll look further at the economics of the environment and environmental protection in a later chapter.

CHAPTER 10*
Perfect Competition

1. What is perfect competition?

   Perfect competition is a market structure in which many small firms are producing an identical product and entry and exit are easy. Very few, if any, real-world markets fit this definition exactly; agriculture, illegal drugs, the scrap metal market, and video rentals come closest. In fact, although these are not perfect illustrations, they come close enough for the perfectly competitive model to be useful in explaining how they work. Perfect competition is also worth studying because, to the economist's way of thinking, perfectly competitive markets work better than other market structures.

2. What does the demand curve facing the individual firm look like and why?

   Put yourself in the shoes of an average wheat farmer: you produce and sell a product that is identical to the product sold by thousands of other wheat farmers. The market price for wheat is set by the overall market demand and supply. If you try to charge more than the market price, buyers can find so many other farmers to buy from that they won't be willing to deal with you. All you can do is take the market price or leave it.

   That wheat farmer is typical of an individual firm in perfect competition. The firm's demand curve is a horizontal line at the market price. The firm is a price taker: the only thing it can control is how much it chooses to sell.

3. How does the firm maximize profit in the short run?

   The firm chooses the output level that maximizes its profits. That output level can be found by looking for the output level where the difference between total revenue and total cost is largest, or by finding the output level where marginal revenue equals marginal cost. Both methods give the same answer.

4. At what point does a firm decide to suspend operations?

   A firm will shut down temporarily if the market price is below its **shutdown price,** which is equal to the minimum point of the average-variable-cost curve. The firm has to be able to pay all its variable costs if it is to remain in operation. If the price is below this level, the firm will lose less money if it shuts down than if it keeps on producing.

5. When will a firm shut down permanently?

   A firm will shut down permanently if it can't cover all of its costs in the long run. If the market price is below the minimum point of the firm's average-total-cost curve and is expected to stay there, the firm will shut down permanently. The firm is not producing enough revenue to pay the opportunity costs of

*Economics Chapter 24.

the resources provided by its owner, so the owner could do better by taking his or her resources elsewhere in the economy.

6. What is the break-even price?

The firm **breaks even** when economic profits are zero—that is, when the demand curve (the market price) just equals the minimum point of the average-total-cost curve. At this point, the firm is covering all of its costs, including the opportunity costs of resources provided by the owner.

7. What is the firm's supply curve in the short run?

If the firm is producing (is not shut down), it will produce the output level where $MR = MC$. As the market price rises above the short-run shutdown price, the output level the firm produces will be determined by the market price (the firm's MR) and the MC curve. The firm's supply curve in the short run is therefore the portion of the marginal-cost curve that lies above the minimum point of the average-variable-cost curve.

8. What is the firm's supply curve in the long run?

The logic of the firm's long-run supply curve is the same as for the short-run supply curve, except for the shutdown price. Since in the long run the firm will shut down permanently if price is below the minimum point of the average-total-cost curve, the firm's long-run supply curve is the portion of the marginal-cost curve that lies above the minimum point of the average-total-cost curve.

9. What is the long-run market supply curve?

To get the short-run market supply curve, we just add (horizontally sum) the supply curves of all firms currently in the market. Finding the long-run supply curve is a little more complex, because more things can happen in the long run: firms can expand or contract, new firms can enter the industry, and existing firms can exit. If firms currently in the industry are receiving economic profits, entrepreneurs will move into the industry to try to gain a share of the profits. On the other hand, if firms currently in the industry are taking economic losses, some entrepreneurs in the industry will take their resources elsewhere in the economy, where they can get a better return. Only when existing firms are just breaking even is there no incentive to enter or exit the industry. The long-run market supply curve shows the amounts supplied at various prices after all entry and exit have taken place.

In a **constant-cost industry,** the long-run supply curve is a horizontal line. In an **increasing-cost industry,** the long-run supply curve slopes upward, and in a **decreasing-cost industry,** the long-run supply curve slopes downward.

10. What are the long-run equilibrium results of a perfectly competitive market?

As long as there are no **external costs** or **external benefits,** long-run equilibrium in a perfectly competitive market provides **allocative efficiency.** All firms earn a normal rate of return by producing at the lowest possible cost (economic efficiency), and all consumers buy the goods at a price equal to the marginal cost of producing them (consumer efficiency).

KEY TERMS

shutdown price
break-even price
constant-cost industry
increasing-cost industry
decreasing-cost industry
allocative efficiency

external costs
external benefits
social costs
marginal social cost
social benefits
marginal social benefit

QUICK CHECK QUIZ

Section 1: The Perfectly Competitive Firm in the Short Run

1. Which of the following is NOT part of the definition of a perfectly competitive market structure?
   a. many small firms
   b. standardized or identical product
   c. many individual brand names
   d. buyers and sellers with perfect information
   e. easy entry and exit

2. The demand curve facing an individual firm in perfect competition is a
   a. vertical line at the market price.
   b. vertical line at the market quantity.
   c. downward-sloping line.
   d. horizontal line at the market price.
   e. horizontal line at the market quantity.

3. The individual firm in perfect competition is
   a. a price taker.
   b. a price maker.
   c. a price reviser.
   d. a quantity taker.
   e. a cost maker.

4. If not shut down, firms maximize profits by producing the output quantity where
   a. $P = MR$.
   b. $MR = AVC$.
   c. $MC = AVC$.
   d. $MR = MC$.
   e. $P = AFC$.

5. What is a perfectly competitive firm's temporary (short-run) shutdown price?
   a. the price that is just equal to the minimum point on the average-fixed-cost curve
   b. the price that is just equal to the minimum point on the average-variable-cost curve
   c. the price that is just equal to the minimum point on the average-total-cost curve
   d. the price that is just equal to the maximum point on the average-variable-cost curve
   e. the price that is just equal to the maximum point on the marginal-cost curve

6. What is a perfectly competitive firm's permanent (long-run) shutdown price?
   a. the price that is just equal to the minimum point on the average-fixed-cost curve
   b. the price that is just equal to the minimum point on the average-variable-cost curve
   c. the price that is just equal to the minimum point on the average-total-cost curve
   d. the price that is just equal to the maximum point on the average-variable-cost curve
   e. the price that is just equal to the maximum point on the marginal-cost curve

7. What is a perfectly competitive firm's break-even price?
   a. the price that is just equal to the minimum point on the average-fixed-cost curve
   b. the price that is just equal to the minimum point on the average-variable-cost curve
   c. the price that is just equal to the minimum point on the average-total-cost curve
   d. the price that is just equal to the maximum point on the average-variable-cost curve
   e. the price that is just equal to the maximum point on the marginal-cost curve

8. What is a perfectly competitive firm's supply curve in the short run?
   a. its marginal-cost curve above the minimum point on the total-variable-cost curve
   b. its marginal-cost curve above the minimum point on the total-cost curve
   c. its marginal-cost curve above the minimum point on the average-fixed-cost curve
   d. its marginal-cost curve above the minimum point on the average-variable-cost curve
   e. its marginal-cost curve above the minimum point on the average-total-cost curve

9. What is a perfectly competitive firm's supply curve in the long run?
   a. its marginal-cost curve above the minimum point on the total-variable-cost curve
   b. its marginal-cost curve above the minimum point on the total-cost curve
   c. its marginal-cost curve above the minimum point on the average-fixed-cost curve
   d. its marginal-cost curve above the minimum point on the average-variable-cost curve
   e. its marginal-cost curve above the minimum point on the average-total-cost curve

Section 2: The Long Run

1. The short-run market supply curve is
   a. the firm's marginal-cost curve above the minimum point on the average-variable-cost curve.
   b. the firm's marginal-cost curve above the minimum point on the average-total-cost curve.
   c. the vertical sum of the short-run supply curves of all firms currently in the industry.
   d. the horizontal sum of the short-run supply curves of all firms currently in the industry.
   e. the quantities supplied at each price by all firms in the industry after exit and entry occur.

2. The long-run market supply curve is
   a. the firm's marginal-cost curve above the minimum point on the average-variable-cost curve.
   b. the firm's marginal-cost curve above the minimum point on the average-total-cost curve.
   c. the vertical sum of the short-run supply curves of all firms currently in the industry.
   d. the horizontal sum of the short-run supply curves of all firms currently in the industry.
   e. the quantities supplied at each price by all firms in the industry after exit and entry occur.

3. There will be no entry nor exit of firms in a perfectly competitive industry in the long run only when
   a. barriers to entry and exit are sufficiently high.
   b. individual firms receive economic profits.
   c. individual firms take economic losses.
   d. individual firms receive a normal rate of return.
   e. all firms have shut down.

4. In an increasing-cost industry, the long-run supply curve
   a. is a horizontal line, because changes in the size of the industry don't affect resource prices.
   b. slopes upward, because changes in the size of the industry increase resource prices.
   c. slopes upward, because changes in the size of the industry decrease resource prices.
   d. slopes downward, because changes in the size of the industry increase resource prices.
   e. slopes downward, because changes in the size of the industry decrease resource prices.

5. In a decreasing-cost industry, the long-run supply curve
   a. is a horizontal line, because changes in the size of the industry don't affect resource prices.
   b. slopes upward, because changes in the size of the industry increase resource prices.
   c. slopes upward, because changes in the size of the industry decrease resource prices.
   d. slopes downward, because changes in the size of the industry increase resource prices.
   e. slopes downward, because changes in the size of the industry decrease resource prices.

6. In a constant-cost industry, the long-run supply curve
   a. is a horizontal line, because changes in the size of the industry don't affect resource prices.
   b. slopes upward, because changes in the size of the industry increase resource prices.
   c. slopes upward, because changes in the size of the industry decrease resource prices.
   d. slopes downward, because changes in the size of the industry increase resource prices.
   e. slopes downward, because changes in the size of the industry decrease resource prices.

7. Which of the following is NOT true of allocative efficiency?
   a. Allocative efficiency requires economic efficiency.
   b. Allocative efficiency requires consumer efficiency.
   c. Allocative efficiency requires equality of marginal social costs and marginal social benefits.
   d. Allocative efficiency may not occur if there are external costs or benefits.
   e. Allocative efficiency may not occur if there are private costs or benefits.

PRACTICE QUESTIONS AND PROBLEMS

Section 1: The Perfectly Competitive Firm in the Short Run

1. List the four characteristics of the perfectly competitive market structure.

   _____

   _____

   _____

   _____

2. The individual firm in perfect competition is a price _____ (maker, taker), and its

   demand curve is a _____ line at the _____ .

3. What equation determines the profit-maximizing output level? _____

4. What is the firm's short-run shutdown price?

   _____

5. What is the firm's long-run shutdown price?

   _____

6. What is the firm's break-even price?

_____

7. The table below shows some of the cost curves for Joe's Gourmet Burger Stand that you calculated in the chapter on the costs of doing business. Let's assume that burger stands are a perfectly competitive industry. (Actually, they're probably monopolistically competitive, but we won't worry about that now.)

Burgers	TC	TR	MR	AFC	AVC	ATC	MC
0	$ 5.50	$____					
1	9.00	____	$____	$5.50	$3.50	$9.00	$3.50
2	10.00	____	____	2.75	2.25	5.00	1.00
3	10.50	____	____	1.83	1.67	3.50	.50
4	11.50	____	____	1.38	1.50	2.88	1.00
5	13.00	____	____	1.10	1.50	2.60	1.50
6	15.00	____	____	.92	1.58	2.50	2.00
7	17.50	____	____	.79	1.71	2.50	2.50
8	20.50	____	____	.69	1.88	2.56	3.00
9	24.00	____	____	.61	2.06	2.67	3.50
10	28.00	____	____	.55	2.25	2.80	4.00

a. How high does the market price of burgers have to be before it's worth it to Joe to hire some workers and start selling burgers, at least in the short run? _____

b. How high does the market price of burgers have to be to make it worthwhile for Joe to stay in the burger stand business? _____

c. Let's say that the market price for burgers is $3.00. Fill in Joe's total-revenue and marginal-revenue columns, plot total revenue and total costs on the top graph on the following page, plot the amount of profit on the middle graph, and plot marginal cost and marginal revenue on the bottom graph. Then find the number of burgers that gives Joe the most profit, and how much profit Joe is making at that price.

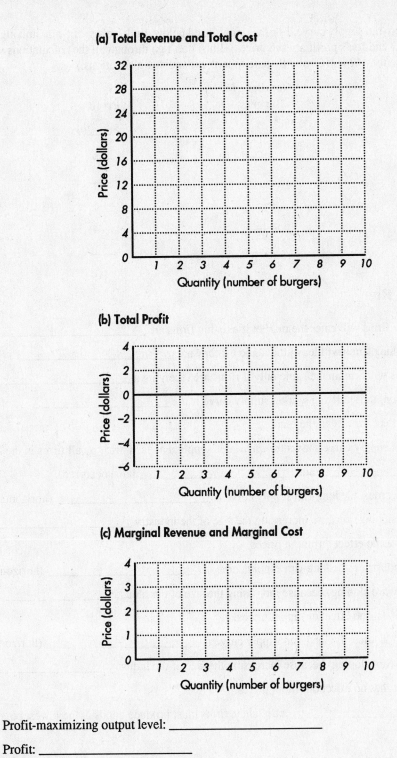

(a) Total Revenue and Total Cost

(b) Total Profit

(c) Marginal Revenue and Marginal Cost

Profit-maximizing output level: _____

Profit: _____

8. Let's find Joe's short-run supply curve. For the prices listed below, find Joe's profit-maximizing output (number of burgers) and Joe's profit at each price. (Hints: don't go through all the calculations you did in problem 7—just use the *MR = MC* rule. Be sure to look for shutdown situations.)

Market Price	Number of Burgers	Profit
$3.50	____	$____
3.00	____	____
2.50	____	____
2.00	____	____
1.50	____	____
1.00	____	____

Section 2: The Long Run

1. In the long run, new firms will enter the market if existing firms are _____.

2. In the long run, existing firms will leave the market if they are _____.

3. The number of firms will remain the same only if firms are receiving a _____.

4. In perfect competition, the short-run market supply curve is the _____ of the supply curves of the firms currently in the market.

5. The long-run market supply curve shows the quantities supplied at each price by all firms in the industry after _____ and _____ have occurred.

6. In constant-cost industries, the long-run supply curve is _____ (horizontal, upward sloping, downward sloping) because increasing the size of the industry _____ (increases, decreases, has no effect on) input prices.

7. In increasing-cost industries, the long-run supply curve is _____ (horizontal, upward sloping, downward sloping) because increasing the size of the industry _____ (increases, decreases, has no effect on) input prices.

8. In decreasing-cost industries, the long-run supply curve is _____ (horizontal, upward sloping, downward sloping) because increasing the size of the industry _____ (increases, decreases, has no effect on) input prices.

9. To achieve _____ efficiency, firms must produce goods at the lowest possible costs.

10. To achieve _____ efficiency, consumers must be purchasing goods at their marginal cost.

11. Allocative efficiency requires _____ efficiency and _____ efficiency, and also requires that _____ equals _____.

12. External costs and benefits are borne not by the producer or consumer, but by

    _____ .

13. Social costs equal _____ costs plus _____ costs; social

    benefits equal _____ benefits plus _____ benefits.

14. The graph below shows the cost curves for a typical perfectly competitive firm.

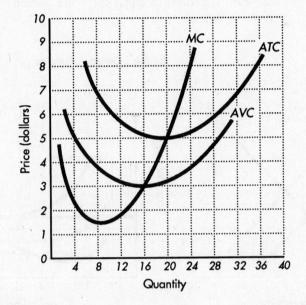

a. The long-run equilibrium price is _____ , and the long-run equilibrium quantity

   is _____ .

b. Explain why that quantity is economically efficient.

   _____

   _____

   _____

   _____

c. Explain why that quantity allows consumer efficiency.

   _____

   _____

   _____

   _____

THINKING ABOUT AND APPLYING PERFECT COMPETITION

I. Effects of Entry on Video Stores and Burger Stands

The "Economically Speaking" section in this chapter looks at video stores and the effects on profits of the entry of new firms into the market. Let's take those ideas a little further, looking at the burger stand industry again.

Let's start out with Joe's Gourmet Burger Stand and the rest of the perfectly competitive burger stand industry in long-run equilibrium, and see how they react to changes. The graph on the left below shows the current market equilibrium, determined by demand curve D_1 and short-run supply curve SRS_1, which determine Joe's demand curve and MR curve at $2.50, Joe's break-even price.

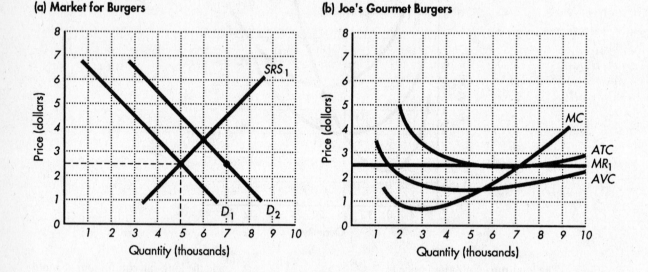

(a) Market for Burgers

(b) Joe's Gourmet Burgers

1. Let's suppose that a new scientific study shows that eating burgers is much better for your health than eating oat bran or similar stuff. The demand for burgers jumps overnight to D_2, raising the price to $3.50. How is Joe going to respond to the higher price in the short run? Will he do anything different in the long run?

_____

_____

_____

_____

2. In the short run, Joe can enjoy his economic profits, since there isn't time for anyone new to enter the burger stand industry. In the long run, new entrants will certainly be attracted into the industry. The burger stand industry is a constant-cost industry. Explain why.

_____

_____

_____

_____

3. As new firms enter, the short-run market supply curve will shift to the right as more and more firms start selling burgers. Knowing that this is a constant-cost industry, draw in the long-run supply curve on the left graph and sketch in what the new short-run market supply curve must look like after long-run equilibrium has been restored.

4. Why did the price have to go up in the short run to restore market equilibrium, but did not have to go up in the long run?

_____

_____

_____

_____

ANSWERS

Quick Check Quiz

Section 1: The Perfectly Competitive Firm in the Short Run

1. c; 2. d; 3. a; 4. d; 5. b; 6. c; 7. c; 8. d; 9. e

   If you missed any of these questions, you should go back and review pages 251–262 in Chapter 10 (pages 623–634 in *Economics*, Chapter 24).

Section 2: The Long Run

1. d; 2. e; 3. d; 4. b; 5. e; 6. a; 7. d

   If you missed any of these questions, you should go back and review pages 263–272 in Chapter 10 (pages 635–644 in *Economics*, Chapter 24).

Practice Questions and Problems

Section 1: The Perfectly Competitive Firm in the Short Run

1. many firms
   identical or standardized product
   easy entry and exit
   perfect information
2. taker; horizontal; market price
3. *MR = MC*
4. the minimum point of the average-variable-cost curve
5. the minimum point of the average-total-cost curve
6. the minimum point of the average-total-cost curve

7. a. $1.50

   When the market price is at or above the short-run shutdown price, it is worth producing burgers. The shutdown price is the lowest value on the *AVC* curve. The table shows that value as $1.50.

   b. $2.50

   At the break-even price, it is just barely worthwhile to remain in the burger stand business rather than do something else. The break-even price is the lowest value on the *ATC* curve. The table shows that value as $2.50.

   c.

Burgers	TC	TR	MR	AFC	AVC	ATC	MC
0	$ 5.50	$ 0.00					
1	9.00	3.00	$3.00	$5.50	$3.50	$9.00	$3.50
2	10.00	6.00	3.00	2.75	2.25	5.00	1.00
3	10.50	9.00	3.00	1.83	1.67	3.50	.50
4	11.50	12.00	3.00	1.38	1.50	2.88	1.00
5	13.00	15.00	3.00	1.10	1.50	2.60	1.50
6	15.00	18.00	3.00	.92	1.58	2.50	2.00
7	17.50	21.00	3.00	.79	1.71	2.50	2.50
8	20.50	24.00	3.00	.69	1.88	2.56	3.00
9	24.00	27.00	3.00	.61	2.06	2.67	3.50
10	28.00	30.00	3.00	.55	2.25	2.80	4.00

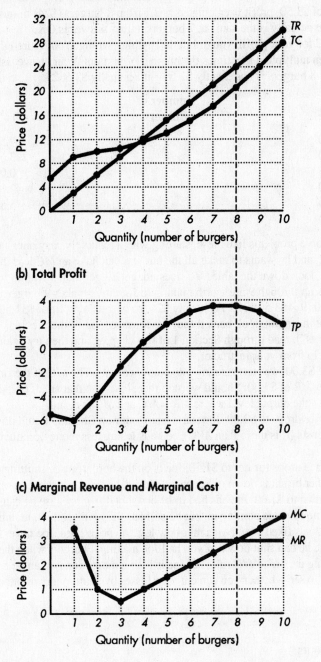

(a) Total Revenue and Total Cost

(b) Total Profit

(c) Marginal Revenue and Marginal Cost

TR is calculated as price ($3.00) times quantity; *MR* is the change in *TR* from selling 1 more burger. Since this is a perfectly competitive market, you can always sell another burger at the market price, so *MR* always equals price.

Profit = maximizing output level: 8
Profit: $3.50

All three graphs showing ways of finding the profit-maximizing output level come up with 8 burgers, with a profit of $3.50; profit is calculated as *TR* from 8 burgers ($24) minus the *TC* of 8 burgers ($3.50). The profit actually is the same at 7 burgers; either answer is OK.

If you got $3.52 for your profit, you didn't do anything wrong. You figured the profit per burger (price – *ATC*), then multiplied that times the number of burgers. Your answer is a little different because the *ATC* for 8 burgers is not exactly $2.56—it's actually $2.5625.

8.

Market Price	Number of Burgers	Profit
$3.50	9	$7.50
3.00	8	3.50
2.50	7	0.00
2.00	6	–3.00
1.50	5	–5.50
1.00	0	–5.50

Let's look at how to solve problems like these, starting with a relatively easy one: a market price of $3.50. This price is Joe's *MR,* and he wants to make all the burgers that have an *MC* less than or equal to *MR*. Starting with 1 burger, look down the table. *MC* does not get bigger than *MR* until you get to the tenth burger. All the burgers up through 9 are worth making to Joe. If he makes 9 burgers when the price is $3.50, his *TR* is $31.50 (9 × $3.50). His *TC* is only $24, so he gets a profit of $31.50 – $24 = $7.50. If you are having problems at this point, look back through the last section of the previous chapter ("An Overview of Product Markets"), read through Section 1 of this chapter, and then try again. If it still doesn't make sense, ask for help from your instructor.

At a market price of $3.00, we start running into complications. The *MC* of the first burger is $3.50, which is more than our *MR* of $3.00. Should we stop there? No—at that small output level, *MC* is still falling. We want to find the output level where *MR* = *MC* and *MC* is rising.

When the market price drops to $2.00, Joe starts losing money. Should he shut down? Not yet. He is still covering his variable costs (*P* is more than *AVC*), so he is losing less money producing than he would be if he shut down.

When the market price drops further to $1.50, Joe is on the borderline of shutting down: $1.50 is his shutdown price. Whether he shuts down or keeps producing, he loses the same amount of money.

When the price is down to $1.00, Joe has had it: he has shut down because he can no longer cover his variable costs. He has no revenue coming in, but he still has $5.50 in costs. Remember from the chapter on costs that the $5.50 is Joe's fixed cost. No matter how low the price goes, Joe never has to lose more than his fixed costs, because he can shut down. If you had Joe making 4 burgers when the price was $1.00, you did a good job following the *MR* = *MC* rule, but Joe is losing more money than he has to. Whenever profits are negative, check to see whether you can cut your losses by shutting down rather than by following the *MR* = *MC* rule.

Section 2: The Long Run

1. receiving economic profits
2. taking economic losses
3. normal rate of return
4. horizontal sum
5. entry; exit
6. horizontal; has no effect on
7. upward sloping; increases
8. downward sloping; decreases
9. economic
10. consumer

11.   economic; consumer; marginal social benefit; marginal social cost
12.   society as a whole
13.   private; external; private; external
14.   a. $5.00; 20
        Long-run equilibrium requires that $P = ATC$, so the firm is just breaking even. Profit maximization
        requires that $MR = MC$. Since $P = MR$ all the time in perfect competition, for long-run equilibrium you
        must have $P = MR = MC = ATC$. $MC = ATC$ at $5.00 and 20 units of output. When P is $5.00, the firm
        is both profit-maximizing and breaking even.
    b.   Twenty units is economically efficient because that is the lowest-cost output—ATC is at its low point.
    c.   Twenty units is consumer efficient because consumers pay a price equal to marginal cost.

Thinking About and Applying Perfect Competition

I.   Effects of Entry on Video Stores and Burger Stands

1.   Joe can increase his output from 7 burgers to 9 burgers; at the higher price, it is profitable for him to make
     more burgers in his current burger stand. He probably will not do anything different in the long run. Even
     though he could expand his burger stand, if Joe is a good businessman he is already using the lowest-cost
     combination of inputs and producing at the low point on his long-run average-cost curve. A larger burger
     stand might cause him to run into diseconomies of scale.
2.   Constant-cost industries are those that do not use large amounts of their input: they can expand or contract
     without affecting the prices of their inputs. Burger stands fit that definition: they are only a small part of
     the market for beef, rolls, labor, and so on.

3.

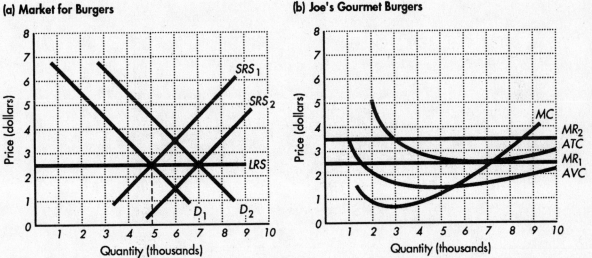

(a) Market for Burgers

(b) Joe's Gourmet Burgers

The long-run supply curve *(LRS)* is a horizontal line. Since the market was in equilibrium to start with at a
price of $2.50, the *LRS* must be at that level. For the market to be in equilibrium after the demand shift, the
price must go back to $2.50, so there are no economic profits or losses, and no entry or exit. The new
short-run supply curve SRS_2 intersects the new demand curve at that price, as shown on the graph.

4. The price had to go up in the short run to encourage Joe and the other burger stand owners to expand output from their current stands; otherwise, they would lose money expanding output, since expanding output from their current stands increased their costs. At 9 burgers, Joe's stand is not running as efficiently as possible, even though it is more profitable for Joe.

In the long run, as new stands entered the market, the output from existing stands shrank back toward 7 burgers, their efficient output level. Their costs went back down, and so did the price. In the new equilibrium, Joe is back making 7 burgers, selling them for $2.50, and just breaking even again.

CHAPTER 11*
Monopoly

1. What is monopoly?

    Monopoly is the market structure at the other extreme from perfect competition. Instead of many firms, there is only one supplier of a product for which there are no close substitutes. The U.S. Post Office is a **monopolist** in the market for letter mail; your electricity, water, natural gas, and cable TV are probably provided by monopolists.

2. How is a monopoly created?

    For a monopoly to be able to stay a monopoly, there usually has to be something that serves as a **barrier to entry**—something that keeps potential competitors out of the monopolist's market. Three types of barriers exist: natural barriers, such as economies of scale; actions taken by firms that create barriers, such as ownership of an essential resource; and actions taken by governments that create barriers, such as patents and licenses.

3. What does the demand curve for a monopoly firm look like and why?

    Because the monopolist is the only producer of a good or service, the monopolist's demand curve is the entire industry demand curve. Like market demand curves in general, the monopolist's demand curve is downward sloping, meaning that the monopolist must lower prices to increase sales. In turn, this means that the monopolist's marginal-revenue curve lies below the demand curve.

4. Why would someone want to have a monopoly in some business or activity?

    In some ways, monopolies are like the perfectly competitive firms we looked at in the last chapter: they can receive a normal rate of return, make economic profits, or take economic losses. Just having a monopoly on a process to make ordinary rocks at a cost of $5 million a pound does not mean that you will get rich. In perfect competition, economic profits are only temporary because new entrants will soon eliminate economic profits. If you are fortunate enough to have a profitable monopoly, barriers to entry let you keep making profits for a long time.

5. Under what conditions will a monopolist charge different customers different prices for the same product?

    The simple answer is that a monopolist will use **price discrimination** whenever it will add to the monopolist's profits. There are some conditions that are necessary for price discrimination to be profitable for a monopolist: buyers must have different elasticities, the firm must be able to separate buyers according to their price elasticities, and the firm must be able to prevent resale of the product.

*Economics Chapter 25.

Price discrimination does not work for many products. Although buyers usually have different elasticities, frequently they either cannot be separated or they cannot be kept separate. Suppose that your local grocery store knows that some buyers really like Crest toothpaste and are willing to pay a high price to get that brand but that other buyers will only choose Crest if it is on sale. Can the grocery store put out some tubes of Crest priced at $3.00 for buyers who really like Crest and another batch of tubes of Crest priced at $1.00 for the people who don't care that much? Obviously not—everybody will take the $1.00 tubes. The store might place discount coupons for Crest in the newspaper. This strategy price-discriminates by separating those people who have the time and desire to clip the coupons from those who do not.

It is easier for electric companies and telephone companies to discriminate among different groups of buyers. They can just look and see whether it's a large business, a small business, or a family using the electricity or the telephone line, and set the price accordingly.

6. How do the predictions of the models of perfect competition and monopoly differ?

A comparison of monopoly and perfect competition leads to the conclusion that monopoly is inefficient and imposes costs on society. These costs include less output being produced and sold at a higher price.

KEY TERMS

monopoly	regulated monopoly	deadweight loss
monopoly firm (monopolist)	monopoly power	potential competition
barrier to entry	price discrimination	X-inefficiency
natural monopoly	dumping	rent seeking
local monopoly	predatory dumping	

QUICK CHECK QUIZ

Section 1: The Market Structure of Monopoly

1. Which of the following is NOT characteristic of a monopoly?
   a. It is a market structure.
   b. A monopolist is the sole supplier of a product.
   c. The monopolist's product has no close substitutes.
   d. To remain a monopoly, there must be barriers to entry.
   e. Monopolists are price takers.

2. Which of the following is NOT a barrier to entry?
   a. large economies of scale
   b. ownership of an essential resource
   c. large profits
   d. patents
   e. government licenses

3. Monopoly power is
   a. the common way to provide electricity and gasoline in the United States.
   b. the ability to set prices.
   c. the ability to control the political process.
   d. the common way to avoid regulation.
   e. the same as regulation.

Section 2: The Demand Curve Facing a Monopoly Firm

1. The monopolist's demand curve is
   a. horizontal at the market price.
   b. vertical at the market price.
   c. horizontal at the market quantity.
   d. vertical at the market quantity.
   e. the same as the industry demand curve.

2. The monopolist's marginal-revenue curve
   a. is horizontal at the market price.
   b. is horizontal at half the market price.
   c. is identical to the monopolist's demand curve.
   d. lies below the demand curve.
   e. lies above the demand curve.

3. A monopolist can sell 20 units of output at a price of $50. To sell 21 units, the monopolist must cut the price of all units to $49. What is the monopolist's marginal revenue from the twenty-first unit sold?
   a. $29
   b. $50
   c. $49
   d. $1
   e. –$1

Section 3: Profit Maximization

1. A monopoly maximizes profit by producing the output level where
   a. $MR = MC$.
   b. $P = MC$.
   c. $P = MR$.
   d. $P = ATC$.
   e. $MC = ATC$.

2. A monopolist's price will be
   a. the prevailing market price determined by demand and supply.
   b. the value on the vertical axis where $MR = MC$.
   c. the point on the demand curve corresponding to the quantity where $MR = MC$.
   d. the point on the demand curve corresponding to the quantity where $P = MC$.
   e. the point on the supply curve corresponding to the quantity where $MR = MC$.

3. In the long run, economic profits
   a. will be competed away from a monopolist by new entrants.
   b. can continue for a monopolist.
   c. are inevitable for a monopolist.
   d. will cause a monopolist to shut down.
   e. will result in higher prices for the monopolist's inputs.

Section 4: Price Discrimination

1. Price discrimination is
   a. refusing to serve certain groups of people.
   b. providing different customers different products.
   c. charging different customers different prices for different products.
   d. providing different customers the same products.
   e. charging different customers different prices for the same products.

2. Which of the following conditions is NOT required for successful price discrimination?
   a. The firm must be a monopolist.
   b. The firm must be able to separate customers according to price elasticity.
   c. The buyers must have different elasticities.
   d. The firm cannot be a price taker.
   e. The firm must be able to prevent resale of the product.

3. Dumping is
   a. setting a higher price on goods sold domestically than on goods sold in foreign markets.
   b. setting a higher price on goods sold in foreign markets than on goods sold domestically.
   c. selling inferior-quality products in foreign markets for the same price as domestic goods.
   d. selling inferior-quality products in domestic markets for the same price as foreign goods.
   e. selling superior-quality products in foreign markets for the same price as domestic goods.

Section 5: Comparison of Perfect Competition and Monopoly

1. Compared with a perfectly competitive industry, a monopolist
   a. produces more output at a lower price.
   b. produces more output at a higher price.
   c. produces less output at a higher price.
   d. produces more output at a higher price.
   e. produces the same output at a higher price.

2. X-inefficiency is
   a. the reduction in consumer surplus without a corresponding increase in monopoly profit when a perfectly competitive firm is monopolized.
   b. the outcome of threatened entry by possible rival firms.
   c. the tendency of firms not faced with competition to become inefficient.
   d. the use of resources to transfer existing wealth without increasing production.
   e. charging higher prices in domestic markets than in foreign markets.

3. Deadweight loss is
   a. the reduction in consumer surplus without a corresponding increase in monopoly profit when a perfectly competitive firm is monopolized.
   b. the outcome of threatened entry by possible rival firms.
   c. the tendency of firms not faced with competition to become inefficient.
   d. the use of resources to transfer existing wealth without increasing production.
   e. charging higher prices in domestic markets than in foreign markets.

PRACTICE QUESTIONS AND PROBLEMS

Section 1: The Market Structure of Monopoly

1. A monopoly firm is the _____ supplier of a product for which there are _____ substitutes.

2. A monopoly remains that way because of _____.

3. Barriers to entry are anything that _____ the ability of firms to enter a market in which existing firms are earning _____.

4. Monopoly power is the ability to _____.

5. Name the kinds of monopolies described below.

   a. _____ monopoly: a firm that has a monopoly within a limited geographic area

   b. _____ monopoly: a firm whose behavior is monitored and prescribed by a government entity

   c. _____ monopoly: a monopoly that results from large economies of scale

Section 2: The Demand Curve Facing a Monopoly Firm

1. The demand curve facing a monopoly is the same as the _____ demand curve.

2. As price declines, total revenue increases in the _____ portion of the demand curve, reaches a maximum at the _____ point, and declines in the _____ portion.

3. The table below gives the demand curve for a monopolist.

Price	Quantity	TR	MR
$6	0	$_____	
5	1	_____	$_____
4	2	_____	_____
3	3	_____	_____
2	4	_____	_____
1	5	_____	_____
0	6	_____	_____

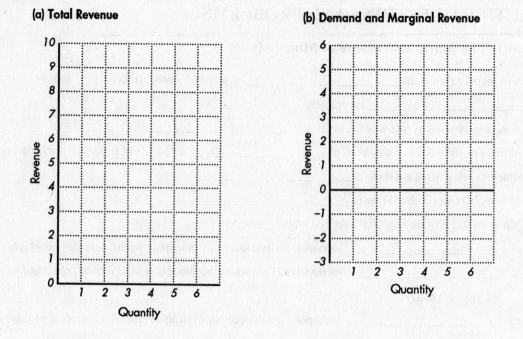

(a) Total Revenue

(b) Demand and Marginal Revenue

a. Calculate the monopolist's total revenue *(TR)* and marginal revenue *(MR)*, plot the total-revenue curve on the left graph, and plot the demand curve and marginal-revenue curve on the right graph.

b. Over what price range is demand elastic? _____

c. Over what price range is demand inelastic? _____

d. At what price is demand unit-elastic? _____

4. In monopoly, price is _____ (less than, more than, equal to) marginal revenue, whereas in perfect competition, price is _____ (less than, more than, equal to) marginal revenue.

Section 3: Profit Maximization

1. A monopolist maximizes profit by choosing the output level where _____ = _____ and then charging the price on the _____ at the quantity produced.

2. Below are the cost curves for our old friend, Joe's Gourmet Burger Stand, along with a demand curve for burgers. Because new nutritional evidence has convinced most people that burgers are not healthy, Joe's is the only burger stand left in town; he now has a monopoly. Calculate Joe's *TR* and *MR*, and figure out how many burgers Joe should make to maximize his profits, what price he should charge, and how much profit he will get.

Burgers	TC	Price	TR	MR	AFC	AVC	ATC	MC
1	$ 9.00	$6.00	$____	$____	$5.50	$3.50	$9.00	$3.50
2	10.00	5.50	____	____	2.75	2.25	5.00	1.00
3	10.50	5.00	____	____	1.83	1.67	3.50	.50
4	11.50	4.50	____	____	1.38	1.50	2.88	1.00
5	13.00	4.00	____	____	1.10	1.50	2.60	1.50
6	15.00	3.50	____	____	.92	1.58	2.50	2.00
7	17.50	3.00	____	____	.79	1.71	2.50	2.50
8	20.50	2.50	____	____	.69	1.88	2.56	3.00
9	24.00	2.00	____	____	.61	2.06	2.67	3.50
10	28.00	1.50	____	____	.55	2.25	2.80	4.00

Quantity: _____

Price: _____

Profit: _____

Section 4: Price Discrimination

1. _____ is charging different customers different _____ for the same product.

2. Dumping is setting a _____ on goods sold domestically than on goods sold in foreign markets.

3. Predatory dumping is dumping to drive competitors out of the _____.

Section 5: Comparison of Perfect Competition and Monopoly

1. Compared with a perfectly competitive industry with the same costs, a monopoly firm will charge a _____ (higher, lower) price and produce a _____ (smaller, larger) quantity.

2. Compared with a perfectly competitive industry, a monopoly firm gets _____ (larger, smaller) profits and generates a _____ (larger, smaller) consumer surplus.

3. The deadweight loss from a monopoly is the difference between the reduction in _____ surplus and the increase in the firm's gain that is produced when a perfectly competitive industry is monopolized.

4. Monopolists can be forced to behave as if competition actually existed by the threat of _____ .

5. _____ is the tendency of a firm not faced with competition to become inefficient.

6. _____ is the use of resources simply to transfer wealth from one group to another without increasing production or total wealth.

THINKING ABOUT AND APPLYING MONOPOLY

I. Monopoly and Innovation: The Two Faces of Patents

The "Economically Speaking" piece in this chapter concerns the monopoly that patents provide to makers of new drugs, as well as some of the costs and benefits of that monopoly. Economists in general are not at all enthusiastic about monopolies, but patents can be an exception. As we'll see in more detail in later chapters, there are risks involved in innovation: you may work for years developing a new product that nobody wants. Patents, a temporary monopoly granted for seventeen years, can provide an incentive for innovation.

1. Explain why.

_____

_____

_____

_____

2. What negative effects of patents are illustrated in the "Economically Speaking" article?

_____

_____

_____

_____

3. One general cure for the problem associated with monopoly is providing competition for the monopolist. How does this seem to be working in the case of AZT?

_____

_____

_____

_____

4. One facet of patents not mentioned in the article is that, to get a patent, you must provide the U.S. Patent Office with detailed information on your innovation; this information is available to the public. Although no one can exactly copy your innovation, how does the public nature of patent information help reduce the monopoly effects of patents?

_____

_____

_____

_____

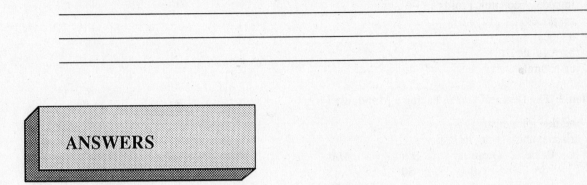

ANSWERS

Quick Check Quiz

Section 1: The Market Structure of Monopoly

1. e; 2. c; 3. b
   If you missed any of these questions, you should go back and review pages 280–283 in Chapter 11 (pages 652–655 in *Economics*, Chapter 25).

Section 2: The Demand Curve Facing a Monopoly Firm

1. e; 2. d; 3. a
   If you missed any of these questions, you should go back and review pages 283–287 in Chapter 11 (pages 655–659 in *Economics*, Chapter 25).

Section 3: Profit Maximization

1. a; 2. c; 3. b
   If you missed any of these questions, you should go back and review pages 287–289 in Chapter 11 (pages 659–661 in *Economics*, Chapter 25).

Section 4: Price Discrimination

1. e; 2. a; 3. a
   If you missed any of these questions, you should go back and review pages 289–294 in Chapter 11 (pages 661–666 in *Economics*, Chapter 25).

Section 5: Comparison of Perfect Competition and Monopoly

1. c; 2. c; 3. a
   If you missed any of these questions, you should go back and review pages 294–299 in Chapter 11 (pages 666–671 in *Economics*, Chapter 25).

Practice Questions and Problems

Section 1: The Market Structure of Monopoly

1. only; no close
2. barriers to entry
3. impedes; economic profits
4. set prices
5. a. local
   b. regulated
   c. natural

Section 2: The Demand Curve Facing a Monopoly Firm

1. market (or industry)
2. elastic; unit-elastic; inelastic
3. a.

Price	Quantity	TR	MR
$6	0	$0	
5	1	5	$5
4	2	8	3
3	3	9	1
2	4	8	−1
1	5	5	−3
0	6	0	−5

(a) Total Revenue

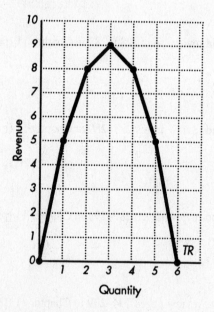

(b) Demand and Marginal Revenue

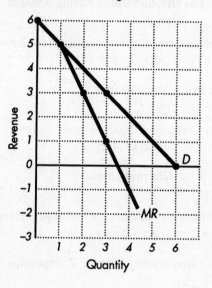

   b. from $6 down to $3
      In this range, cutting price increases total revenue.
   c. from $0 up to $3
      In this range, cutting price increases total revenue.

d. $3

  Demand is unit-elastic in the middle of a demand curve.

  If these didn't seem familiar, refer back to the chapter on elasticity.

4. more than; equal to

Section 3: Profit Maximization

1. *MR; MC;* demand curve
2.

Burgers	TC	Price	TR	MR	AFC	AVC	ATC	MC
1	$ 9.00	$6.00	$6.00	$6.00	$5.50	$3.50	$9.00	$3.50
2	10.00	5.50	11.00	5.00	2.75	2.25	5.00	1.00
3	10.50	5.00	15.00	4.00	1.83	1.67	3.50	.50
4	11.50	4.50	18.00	3.00	1.38	1.50	2.88	1.00
5	13.00	4.00	20.00	2.00	1.10	1.50	2.60	1.50
6	15.00	3.50	21.00	1.00	.92	1.58	2.50	2.00
7	17.50	3.00	21.00	0.00	.79	1.71	2.50	2.50
8	20.50	2.50	20.00	−1.00	.69	1.88	2.56	3.00
9	24.00	2.00	18.00	−2.00	.61	2.06	2.67	3.50
10	28.00	1.50	15.00	−3.00	.55	2.25	2.80	4.00

Quantity: 5 burgers
Price: $4.00
Profit: $7.00

  The quantity that maximizes Joe's profit is 5 burgers. The fifth burger is the last one where *MR* is greater than or equal to *MC*. The price comes from the demand curve at 5 units; profit is just *TR – TC* again.

Section 4: Price Discrimination

1. Price discrimination; prices
2. higher price
3. market

Section 5: Comparison of Perfect Competition and Monopoly

1. higher; smaller
2. larger; smaller
3. consumer
4. potential competition
5. X-inefficiency
6. Rent seeking

Thinking About and Applying Monopoly

I. Monopoly and Innovation: The Two Faces of Patents

1. If successful, the innovation will generate monopoly profits, at least for a while. The possibility of monopoly profits, over and above a normal rate of return, makes risk taking worthwhile.
2. Like most monopolies, patent monopolies lead to higher prices. When the demand for a patented product is very inelastic, like the demand for AZT, the price can be driven very high.

3. The high profits made by Burroughs-Wellcome on AZT attract new competitors into the market. No one can directly copy AZT, but other drug companies can try to find different drugs that have similar effects, as Bristol-Myers seems to have done.

4. Looking at other people's patents can help a company develop similar but not identical products, providing competition for the patented product. Many innovators prefer not to patent new innovations, reasoning that it is better not to give their competitors that much information.

CHAPTER 12*
Monopolistic Competition, Oligopoly, and the Economics of Information

1. What is monopolistic competition?

   As its name suggests, monopolistic competition is a market structure with some of the characteristics of monopoly and some of the characteristics of perfect competition. Like perfect competition, there are a large number of firms, and entry into the market is easy. Because entry into the market is easy, monopolistically competitive firms earn a normal rate of return in the long run.

   The difference between monopolistic competition and perfect competition is in the type of product sold: a standardized product in perfect competition and a differentiated product in monopolistic competition. Each firm in monopolistic competition has a monopoly on its own versions or brands of the product: as in a monopoly, the firm's demand curve is downward sloping. Unlike in a real monopoly, however, in monopolistic competition many competitors make almost identical products.

   Monopolistically competitive firms are not economically efficient: they do not produce where $P = MC$, or at the minimum ATC. This inefficiency is the price consumers have to pay to get differentiated products instead of the standardized, identical product of perfect competition.

2. Why are there so many different brands of beer, detergent, fast food, cereal, and other products?

   In monopolistic competition, successful products create economic profits, which attract new competitors. New firms enter the market by introducing their own, slightly different brands of the product. McDonald's success and profits encouraged the owners of Burger King, Wendy's, Hardee's, and many others to start their own hamburger stands.

   Introducing new, different brands of a product is also one of the ways existing firms compete with each other and with new entrants. Many of the new brands of beer put on the market in the 1980s came from existing breweries expanding their brand lists to compete in new market niches.

3. What is oligopoly?

   Oligopoly is a market structure in which there are a few large firms and entry is difficult but not impossible. Oligopolies can produce either identical products, like steel or cement, or differentiated products, like automobiles or colas. Oligopoly is different from other market structures because firms are interdependent: any action taken by one firm usually provokes a reaction by other firms. If General Motors cuts the prices of its cars, Ford and Chrysler (plus Toyota, Volkswagen, Honda, and the rest) will find some way to react.

*Economics Chapter 26.

4. In what form does rivalry occur in an oligopoly?

In oligopolies, **strategic behavior** is the rule. When making their decisions, firms have to keep in mind how their rivals will respond. Although strategic behavior can take many forms, several are fairly common. In the *kinked demand curve*, competitors match price decreases but ignore price increases. In *price leadership*, a dominant firm decides on prices and price changes and other firms follow along. In a **cartel,** or shared monopoly, independent firms organize themselves and agree on prices and production limits.

Secret cooperation agreements (collusion) are used to help reduce competition. Several other **facilitating practices** can be used to increase cooperation among firms, including **cost-plus pricing** to ensure that firms with the same costs charge the same price, and **most-favored-customer** policies, which discourage selective price cutting.

5. How do market structure models explain image advertising and brand names?

Obtaining information frequently has costs, and rational consumers try to economize on those costs. Rather than do intensive market research on the characteristics of every brand, consumers frequently buy brands they are familiar with, either from past experience or from advertising. Many firms invest large amounts of resources in building and maintaining their images. Before McDonald's opened their store in Moscow, they imported American potatoes and beef cattle into the Soviet Union so that a Big Mac and fries would taste the same in Moscow as it does in New York or Los Angeles, or in London, Paris, or Tokyo.

When information is costly or unobtainable, problems can arise in the way markets operate. **Adverse selection** occurs when buyers misvalue product qualities that they cannot easily observe. **Moral hazard** is another information problem that occurs when it is difficult or expensive to determine whether people have changed their behavior after an agreement or contract has been defined.

KEY TERMS

vertical merger	concentration ratios	cost-plus pricing
horizontal merger	Herfindahl index	most-favored customer
conglomerate mergers	strategic behavior	adverse selection
hostile takeover	cartel	moral hazard
economies of scope	facilitating practices	

QUICK CHECK QUIZ

Section 1: Monopolistic Competition

1. Monopolistic competition is a market structure in which firms produce a
   a. differentiated product, and entry is difficult but not impossible.
   b. standardized product, and entry is difficult but not impossible.
   c. standardized product, and entry is impossible.
   d. differentiated product, and entry is easy.
   e. standardized product, and entry is easy.

2. In the short run, a monopolistically competitive firm can receive
   a. only a normal rate of return.
   b. only a positive economic profit.
   c. only a negative economic profit.
   d. only either a normal rate of return or a negative economic profit.
   e. a positive or negative economic profit, or a normal rate of return.

3. Compared with a perfectly competitive market structure, firms in a monopolistically competitive market structure in the long run produce at
   a. higher costs and lower output.
   b. higher costs and higher output.
   c. lower costs and lower output.
   d. lower costs and higher output.
   e. higher costs, and either a higher or lower output.

4. In both perfect competition and monopolistic competition, firms
   a. produce differentiated products.
   b. produce standardized products.
   c. receive only a normal rate of return in the long run.
   d. engage in nonprice competition.
   e. always receive only a normal rate of return in the short run.

Section 2: Oligopoly and Interdependence

1. Which of the following is NOT a characteristic of oligopoly?
   a. Entry is difficult but not impossible.
   b. There are a few firms.
   c. Either differentiated or standardized products are produced.
   d. Firms make strategic decisions without considering their competitors.
   e. All of the above are characteristics of oligopoly.

2. Which of the following does NOT belong on a list of factors that can result in oligopoly?
   a. innovations
   b. cost conditions
   c. control of an essential resource
   d. legal restrictions
   e. successful differentiation
   f. large fixed costs
   g. mergers
   h. All of the above can result in oligopoly.

3. Which of the following occurs only in an oligopoly?
   a. a downward-sloping market demand curve
   b. a downward-sloping demand curve for the individual firm
   c. interdependence and strategic behavior
   d. a differentiated product
   e. a standardized product

4. The shape of the demand curve for an oligopolist depends on
   a. the market marginal-revenue curve.
   b. how rival firms react to price changes.
   c. the amount of monopolistic competition in the market.
   d. whether price is more or less than marginal revenue.
   e. the prevalence of adverse selection.

5. A merger between two grocery stores in the same small town would be an example of a
   a. horizontal merger.
   b. vertical merger.
   c. specialized merger.
   d. conglomerate merger.
   e. deglomerate merger.

6. A merger between an oil refinery and a chain of gas stations would be an example of a
   a. horizontal merger.
   b. vertical merger.
   c. specialized merger.
   d. conglomerate merger.
   e. deglomerate merger.

7. A merger between a gas station and a barbershop would be an example of a
   a. horizontal merger.
   b. vertical merger.
   c. specialized merger.
   d. conglomerate merger.
   e. deglomerate merger.

8. A kinked demand curve occurs when
   a. other firms follow price cuts but not price increases.
   b. other firms follow price increases but not price cuts.
   c. price leadership is operating.
   d. economic profits exist for all firms in an oligopoly.
   e. economic profits exist for some but not all firms in an oligopoly.

9. An oligopoly using explicit cooperation achieved through formal agreement is called
   a. a hostile takeover.
   b. a cartel.
   c. a shared monopoly.
   d. Both a and b above.
   e. Both b and c above.

Section 3: Summary of Market Structures

1. In which market structure or structures do firms produce the output level where $P = MC$?
   a. perfect competition
   b. monopolistic competition
   c. oligopoly
   d. monopoly
   e. Firms produce the output level where $P = MC$ in all of the above market structures.

2. In which market structure or structures do firms receive no economic profits in the long run?
   a. only in perfect competition
   b. only in monopoly
   c. only in monopolistic competition
   d. in both perfect competition and monopolistic competition
   e. in both monopoly and monopolistic competition

Section 4: The Economics of Information

1. Which of the following statements is correct?
   a. Market structure models usually assume that information is costly to obtain, but in reality it is sometimes free.
   b. Market structure models usually assume that information is costly to obtain, but in reality it is always free.
   c. Market structure models usually assume that information is free; in reality it always is.
   d. Market structure models usually assume that information is free, but in reality it is sometimes costly to obtain.
   e. None of the above statements is correct.

2. Adverse selection occurs when
   a. fully informed consumers make mistaken choices.
   b. low-quality consumers or producers force higher-quality consumers or producers out of the market.
   c. people alter their behavior in an unanticipated way after an agreement or contract has been defined.
   d. consumers rely on brand names in making decisions.
   e. collusion forces some producers from the market.

3. Moral hazard occurs when
   a. fully informed consumers make mistaken choices.
   b. low-quality consumers or producers force higher-quality consumers or producers out of the market.
   c. people alter their behavior in an unanticipated way after an agreement or contract has been defined.
   d. consumers rely on brand names in making decisions.
   e. collusion forces some producers from the market.

PRACTICE QUESTIONS AND PROBLEMS

Section 1: Monopolistic Competition

1. Monopolistic competition is a market structure in which _____ firms are producing a _____ product and entry is _____ .

2. Firms in monopolistic competition compete primarily through _____ (product differentiation, price).

3. Monopolistically competitive firms maximize their profits by producing the output level where

   _____ = _____ .

4. Compared with firms in perfectly competitive markets, monopolistically competitive firms charge

_____ (higher, lower) prices and produce a _____ (larger,

smaller) amount of output.

5. The diagram below shows the demand, marginal-revenue, and cost curves for Paul's Pizza, a monopolistically competitive firm.

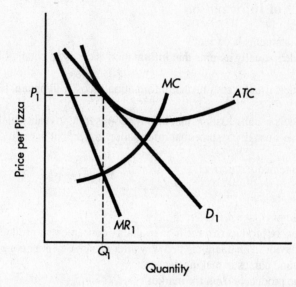

At the price and quantity marked, is Paul's Pizza maximizing its profits? _____

How do you know? _____ At the price and quantity marked, is Paul's Pizza receiving a positive economic profit, negative economic profit, or a normal rate of return?

_____ How do you know? _____

6. Suppose Paul develops a new, "Super Spicy" pizza that many people start buying. Assuming that "Super Spicy" does not cost any more to make than Paul's other pizzas, sketch in new demand and marginal-revenue curves for Paul's Pizza that reflect the increased demand for his pizza, and shade in the rectangle that measures Paul's economic profits.

7. Why will Paul's economic profits probably last for only a little while?

_____

_____

_____

_____

Section 2: Oligopoly and Interdependence

1. Oligopoly is a market structure in which _____ firms are producing a

_____ product and entry is _____ .

2. Strategic behavior occurs in oligopolies because firms are _____ .

3. The shape of the demand curve and marginal-revenue curve for an oligopolist depends on

_____ .

4. Match these terms with the definitions below.

      concentration ratio   horizontal merger

      conglomerate merger   hostile takeover

      economies of scope   vertical merger

      Herfindahl index

  a. _____ : combination of two firms that were buyers from or sellers to each other

  b. _____ : acquisition of a firm over the opposition of the firm's management

  c. _____ : measure of the percentage of the total industry that is accounted for by

    the largest firms

  d. _____ : measure of concentration calculated as the sum of the squares of the

    market share of each firm in an industry

  e. _____ : combination of two firms that were direct rivals

  f. _____ : lower cost per unit of producing goods that results when a firm offers

    several unrelated products

  g. _____ : combination of two firms in different lines of business

5. Let's look at two different industries, each with four firms. In industry *A*, each of the four firms has 25 percent of the market. In industry *B*, one firm has 80 percent of the market, one firm has 10 percent, and the other two have 5 percent each. Calculate the four-firm concentration ratio and Herfindahl index for each industry.

	Four-Firm Concentration Ratio	**Herfindahl Index**
Industry *A:*	_____	_____
Industry *B:*	_____	_____

6. Does the concentration ratio or the Herfindahl index give more information about how concentrated these

industries are? _____

7. Briefly describe how a price-leadership oligopoly operates.

_____

_____

_____

_____

8. Briefly explain how cost-plus pricing and most-favored-customer agreements facilitate cooperation among oligopolists.

_____

_____

_____

_____

Section 3: Summary of Market Structures

1. Summarize the characteristics of the four market structures you've been studying by filling in the table below.

Characteristic	Perfect Competition	Monopoly	Monopolistic Competition	Oligopoly
Number of firms	_____	_____	_____	_____
Type of product	_____	_____	_____	_____
Entry conditions	_____	_____	_____	_____
Demand curve for firm	_____	_____	_____	_____
Price and marginal cost	_____	_____	_____	_____
Long-run profit	_____	_____	_____	_____

Section 4: The Economics of Information

1. The models of market structure usually assume that information is _____ (free, costly), but in the real world it is frequently _____ (free, costly).

2. _____ occurs when low-quality producers force higher-quality producers out of the market.

3. _____ exists when people can alter their behavior after a contract has been defined.

4. Professors know that most college students are honest and will not cheat on exams. They also know that some students will cheat if they have an opportunity. Since professors cannot tell which students are likely to cheat, all students are inconvenienced when professors try to prevent cheating. This is an example of

_____.

5. Suppose you are sick the day of a sociology exam and have to take a make-up exam later. After you solemnly promise not to cheat, your professor leaves you alone to take the test in a room full of sociology textbooks. The possibility that you might cheat despite your promise is an example of

_____.

6. Why do you think the sociology professor left you alone when you might cheat? (Hint: Think about the situation in terms of information costs.)

_____

_____

_____

_____

THINKING ABOUT AND APPLYING MONOPOLISTIC COMPETITION, OLIGOPOLY, AND THE ECONOMICS OF INFORMATION

I. Is Advertising Profitable in Monopolistic Competition?

Paul's Pizza is thinking about using advertising to differentiate its pizza from all the other pizzas in town. An advertising agency has developed two possible campaigns: a smaller-scale campaign that will add $5.00 per hour to Paul's costs, and a larger campaign that will add $10.00 per hour to Paul's costs. The agency also estimated the increases in demand it expects Paul's Pizza to get from each campaign. Using the cost and demand information in the tables, find the profit-maximizing price and output for each case, and calculate Paul's economic profits.

Paul's Pizza: Current Demand and Costs

Quantity Sold/Hour	ATC	MC	P	MR
1	$26.50	$12.50	$12.00	$12.00
2	16.25	6.00	11.00	10.00
3	11.50	2.00	10.00	8.00
4	9.25	2.50	9.00	6.00
5	8.00	3.00	8.00	4.00
6	7.25	3.50	7.00	2.00
7	6.79	4.00	6.00	.00
8	6.50	4.50	5.00	−2.00

Profit-maximizing quantity: _____

Profit-maximizing price: _____

Economic profit: _____

Paul's Pizza: With Smaller Advertising Campaign

Quantity Sold/Hour	ATC	MC	P	MR
1	$31.50	$12.50	$15.00	$15.00
2	18.75	6.00	13.75	12.50
3	13.17	2.00	12.50	10.00
4	10.50	2.50	11.25	7.50
5	9.00	3.00	10.00	5.00
6	8.08	3.50	8.75	2.50
7	7.50	4.00	7.50	.00
8	7.13	4.50	6.25	-2.50

Profit-maximizing quantity: _____

Profit-maximizing price: _____

Economic profit: _____

Paul's Pizza: With Larger Advertising Campaign

Quantity Sold/Hour	ATC	MC	P	MR
1	$36.50	$12.50	$15.60	$15.60
2	21.25	6.00	14.30	13.00
3	14.83	2.00	13.00	10.40
4	11.75	2.50	11.70	7.80
5	10.00	3.00	10.40	5.20
6	8.92	3.50	9.10	2.60
7	8.21	4.00	7.80	.00
8	7.75	4.50	6.50	-2.60

Profit-maximizing quantity: _____

Profit-maximizing price: _____

Economic profit: _____

If you were Paul, which campaign (smaller, or larger) would you choose? _____

Explain. _____

_____

II. Cartel Cheating

The key difference between oligopoly and other market structures is that oligopolists are interdependent: the decisions of one affect others. In many situations, interdependence creates conflicting incentives both to cooperate with others and to "cheat" in one's cooperation. The "Economically Speaking" section in this chapter describes an experiment that illustrates this conflict. Read through that section and use the table to answer the questions below.

1. If there are 30 students in the class and they all agree to cooperate and pick "1," how much money will

   each get? _____ How much money will all 30 students get in total?

   _____

2. If one student "cheats" and picks "0," how much money will the cheater get? _____

   How much money will the other 29 students each receive? _____

   What will be the total received by all 30 students in this case? _____

   You can see that although everyone taken together is better off if all cooperate (the group takes in more money), any one individual is better off if he or she cheats (that one person takes in more money).

3. We can see how the same thing happens in oligopolies by looking at the choices faced by a member of a cartel such as OPEC. Let's make you the Oil Minister of Scheherazade, a hypothetical small member of OPEC. You are responsible for managing your country's oil output and price, and your objective is to maximize your country's total revenues from oil (your marginal cost of producing more oil is so low that you don't have to pay any attention to costs).

   Last week, the OPEC countries met and agreed to charge $25 per barrel for oil. Scheherazade was given an output quota of 300,000 barrels per day. The diagram below shows your current position and possible options; D_1 is the demand curve for your oil if the rest of OPEC ignores any price changes you make, and D_2 is your demand curve if the rest of OPEC matches any price changes. Like the kinked demand curve model, the rest of OPEC will ignore any price increases you make but will match any price cuts that they know about. Use this information to answer the questions below.

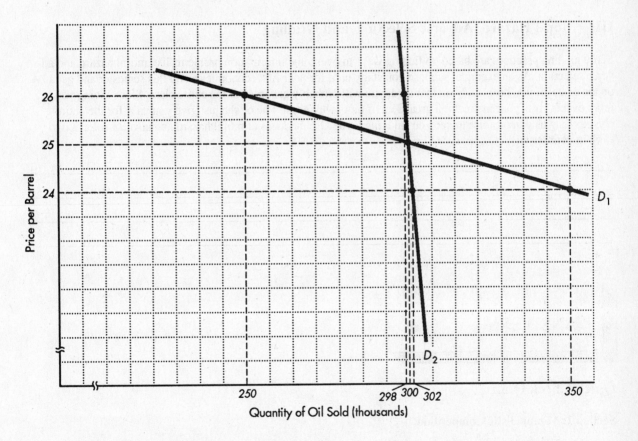

Quantity of Oil Sold (thousands)

   a. How much money is Scheherazade taking in from selling 300,000 barrels at $25 per barrel?

   _____

   b. If you could get the rest of OPEC to go along with raising its price to $26 per barrel, how much would Scheherazade take in? _____

c. Unfortunately, the rest of OPEC thinks that $25 is the best price and will not go along with a higher price. If only Scheherazade raises its price to $26, how much will you take in?

_____

d. Since raising your price will not increase revenues, you can try cutting the price to $24. How much will Scheherazade take in if the rest of OPEC matches your price cut? _____

That doesn't seem to leave you any better off.

e. Late one night, the buyer for Euro-Oil, a large oil refiner, knocks quietly on your door. She offers to buy 350,000 barrels of oil a day from Scheherazade if you cut the price to $24 and keep the price cut a secret. Will this deal be profitable for Scheherazade, and why?

_____

_____

_____

_____

III. Moral Hazard, Adverse Selection, and Grading

Many grading practices are based on finding ways to overcome information problems like moral hazard and adverse selection. As an example, suppose you study hard for your first economics exam this semester and get an *A* on the exam. If you keep studying that hard, you will probably get an *A* for the entire class. Since giving you more exams costs your instructor a great deal of time, why doesn't he or she just give you an *A* for the entire class as long as you promise to keep on studying hard? Use the ideas of moral hazard and adverse selection to explain your answer.

_____

_____

_____

_____

ANSWERS

Quick Check Quiz

Section 1: Monopolistic Competition

1. d.; 2. e; 3. a; 4.c

If you missed any of these questions, you should go back and review pages 306–315 in Chapter 12 (pages 678–687 in *Economics*, Chapter 26).

Section 2: Oligopoly and Interdependence

1. d; 2. h; 3. c; 4. b; 5. a; 6. b; 7. d; 8. a; 9. e
    If you missed any of these questions, you should go back and review pages 315–329 in Chapter 12 (pages 687–701 in *Economics*, Chapter 26).

Section 3: Summary of Market Structures

1. a; 2. d
    If you missed any of these questions, you should go back and review pages 329–330 in Chapter 12 (pages 701–702 in *Economics*, Chapter 26).

Section 4: The Economics of Information

1. d; 2. b; 3. c
    If you missed any of these questions, you should go back and review pages 330–334 in Chapter 12 (pages 702–706 in *Economics*, Chapter 26).

Practice Questions and Problems

Section 1: Monopolistic Competition

1. many; differentiated; easy
2. product differentiation
3. *MR; MC*
4. higher; smaller
5. yes; $MR = MC$ at quantity marked; normal rate of return; $P = ATC$
6.

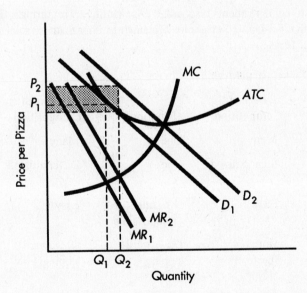

7. Other pizza makers will emulate Paul's innovation, shifting the demand for Paul's pizzas downward.

206 / Chapter 12

Section 2: Oligopoly and Interdependence

1. few; differentiated or standardized; difficult but not impossible
2. interdependent
3. how rivals react to changes in price and product
4. a. vertical merger
   b. hostile takeover
   c. concentration ratio
   d. Herfindahl index
   e. horizontal merger
   f. economies of scope
   g. conglomerate merger

5.

	Four-Firm Concentration Ratio	Herfindahl Index
Industry *A:*	100 (25+25+25+25)	2,500 ($25^2+25^2+25^2+25^2$)
Industry *B:*	100 (80+10+5+5)	6,500 ($80^2+10^2+5^2+5^2$)

6. Herfindahl index
   The four-firm concentration ratio came out the same in both cases, whereas the Herfindahl index shows that industry *A*, with four equal-sized firms, is less concentrated than industry *B*, where one firm has a large majority of the market.
7. One firm determines the price, and all other firms follow along and match any price changes.
8. If firms with the same production costs figure their prices by adding the same profit margin to their costs, their prices will all come out the same without any need for collusion.

   Most-favored-customer agreements discourage price cutting by requiring a firm to cut its price to the price of all firms with most-favored-customer agreements rather than use selective price cuts to attract new customers from other firms.

Section 3: Summary of Market Structures

1.

Characteristic	Perfect Competition	Monopoly	Monopolistic Competition	Oligopoly
Number of firms	Many	One	Many	Few
Type of product	Standardized	One	Differentiated	Differentiated or standardized
Entry conditions	Easy	Difficult or impossible	Easy	Difficult
Demand curve for firm	Horizontal (perfectly elastic)	Downward sloping	Downward sloping	Downward sloping
Price and marginal cost	$MC = P$	$MC < P$	$MC < P$	$MC < P$
Long-run profit	Zero	Yes	Zero	Depends on whether entry occurs

Section 4: The Economics of Information

1. free; costly
2. Adverse selection
3. Moral hazard
4. adverse selection
5. moral hazard
6. Monitoring your behavior to be sure you didn't cheat has some costs: it requires finding a different room, watching you take the test, or finding some other way to gain information about whether or not you cheated.

Thinking About and Applying Monopolistic Competition, Oligopoly, and the Economics of Information

I. Is Advertising Profitable in Monopolistic Competition?

Paul's Pizza: Current Demand and Costs

Profit-maximizing quantity: 5
> The first 5 pizzas have $MR > MC$. The sixth pizza's MR is $2.00, less than its MC of $3.50, so it is not worth making and selling.

Profit-maximizing price: $8.00
> $8.00 is the price at which consumers will buy 5 pizzas.

Economic profit: $.00
> Price = ATC

Paul's Pizza: With Smaller Advertising Campaign

Profit-maximizing quantity: 5
> The first 5 pizzas have $MR > MC$. The sixth pizza's MR is $2.50, less than its MC of $3.50, so it is not worth making and selling.

Profit-maximizing price: $10.00
> $10.00 is the price at which consumers will buy 5 pizzas.

Economic profit: $5.00
> Profit per pizza = $10.00 (price) – $9.00 ($ATC$) = $1; $1 profit per pizza × 5 pizzas = $5.00

Paul's Pizza: With Larger Advertising Campaign

Profit-maximizing quantity: 5
> The first 5 pizzas have $MR > MC$. The sixth pizza's MR is $2.60, less than its MC of $3.50, so it is not worth making and selling.

Profit-maximizing price: $10.40
> $10.40 is the price at which consumers will buy 5 pizzas.

Economic profit: $2.00
> Profit per pizza = $10.40 (price) – $10.00 ($ATC$) = $.40; $.40 profit per pizza × 5 pizzas = $2.00

The smaller advertising campaign gives Paul $5.00 economic profits, compared with the normal rate of return he is currently receiving. The larger advertising campaign gives Paul only $2.00 economic profits; compared with the smaller campaign, it adds more to Paul's costs than it generates in increased demand and revenue, so it is not worth the money. The law of diminishing returns applies to advertising campaigns, too: the first few dollars spent on advertising frequently have more impact on demand than additional dollars have.

II. Cartel Cheating

1. $1.20; $1.20 × 30 = $36.00
2. $1.70; $1.16; $1.16 × 29 + $1.70 = $35.34
3. a. $7,500,000 ($25 × 300,000)
    b. $7,748,000 ($26 × 298,000)
    c. $6,500,000 ($26 × 250,000)
    d. $7,248,000 ($24 × 302,000)
    e. Scheherazade will take in $8,400,000 ($24 × 350,000), so it will be quite profitable. What makes it profitable is keeping it secret so that the rest of OPEC does not match your price. Secret cheating on cartel agreements is usually profitable for any member of the cartel as long as the rest of the cartel does not find out about the cheating and match the price cut immediately.

III. Moral Hazard, Adverse Selection, and Grading

Without more exams, your instructor has no way to monitor whether or not you are keeping your promise to study hard; this is an example of moral hazard. Even though many students will keep their promises to study hard, we all know that some will not. Since your instructor can't tell who the honest, "high-quality" students are, all students end up being treated as though they might not keep their promises. This is an example of adverse selection.

CHAPTER 13*
Antitrust Policy and the Regulation of Monopoly

FUNDAMENTAL QUESTIONS

1. How do policymakers attempt to minimize the allocative inefficiency of monopoly?

   As we've seen in previous chapters, monopoly is a market structure that is allocatively inefficient and frequently wastes resources through X-inefficiency and rent seeking. Policymakers in the United States have used two tools to try to reduce the negative effects of monopoly: **antitrust policy** and regulation. In other countries, nationalization has also been used to reduce the effects of monopoly.

   Antitrust laws attempt to enhance competition in markets by restricting business activities that can be anticompetitive, such as price fixing and other conspiracies, restraints on trade, deceptive and unfair practices, and monopolization of a market. Antitrust policy in the United States has gone through three phases. Beginning with the **Sherman Antitrust Act** in 1890, antitrust law was very loosely applied, although some large monopolies, such as Standard Oil, were broken up into several smaller firms. After the passage of the **Clayton Antitrust Act** and the **Federal Trade Commission Act** in 1914, enforcement became stricter, with courts relying on the **per se rule** rather than the **rule of reason.** In the 1980s, antitrust policy was loosened considerably as courts and the Department of Justice returned more to the rule of reason approach.

   Regulation is used to control natural monopolies, where competition is not practical. Under regulation, firms remain privately owned and the firm's owners and managers make most decisions. Some decisions, particularly about the price to be charged, are made by a regulatory commission rather than by the firm. In most parts of the United States, the rates charged by local telephone companies, electric companies, and natural gas suppliers are regulated.

2. Is big necessarily bad?

   Antitrust policy's answer to this question has varied over the years. Currently, being big is considered bad only if the firm behaves unreasonably and if its actions have measurable negative effects on other firms or on the firm's customers. Although this viewpoint has been adopted by the legal system, many economists disagree and believe that dominant firms often act in uncompetitive ways.

3. How are the antitrust statutes interpreted and enforced?

   An antitrust case begins when the Department of Justice or private plaintiffs file a lawsuit, or when the Federal Trade Commission files an administrative complaint. Except for cases of price fixing, which is always illegal, processing the case requires defining the market and the defendants' market power, identifying their anticompetitive activity and intent, and measuring damages. If the defendants are found guilty, remedies can include a variety of penalties, including payment of fines and damages by

*Economics Chapter 27.

the firm (tripled when private plaintiffs win), breaking up of the firm, and fines and jail terms for guilty individuals.

4. How are natural monopolies regulated?

In the United States, regulation of natural monopolies has usually been based on **rate-of-return regulation,** whereby a regulatory commission specifies the rate of return the monopoly is allowed to earn, the prices charged, and the level of output produced. In other countries, nationalization has been a more common way to regulate natural monopolies.

5. Why have governments deregulated and privatized certain lines of business in recent years?

In the United States, regulation of transportation—railroads, trucks, and airlines—resulted in very inefficient operations in the airline and trucking industries, as well as the bankruptcy of several major railroads. Deregulation of long-distance telephone service followed the 1982 breakup of AT&T. Relying on competition instead of regulation is intended to promote more efficient use of resources in these industries.

In some developed countries, particularly France and the United Kingdom, governments have been privatizing previously nationalized industries, again with the intent of improving efficiency.

KEY TERMS

antitrust policy	per se rule	tying
Sherman Antitrust Act	vertical relationships	rate-of-return regulation
Clayton Antitrust Act	resale price maintenance	privatization
Federal Trade Commission Act	exclusive dealing	contracting out
rule of reason		

QUICK CHECK QUIZ

Section 1: Antitrust Policy

1. Which of the following is NOT one of the U.S. antitrust laws?
   a. Clayton Act
   b. Sherman Act
   c. Wagner Act
   d. Federal Trade Commission Act
   e. All of the above are U.S. antitrust laws.

2. Which of the following best describes the sequence of the three phases of antitrust policy in the United States?
   a. (1) strict enforcement based on the Clayton Act and the Federal Trade Commission Act; (2) loose enforcement of the Sherman Act; (3) strict enforcement currently based on the per se rule
   b. (1) loose enforcement of the Sherman Act; (2) strict enforcement based on the Clayton Act and the Federal Trade Commission Act; (3) strict enforcement currently based on the per se rule
   c. (1) loose enforcement of the Sherman Act; (2) strict enforcement based on the Clayton Act and the Federal Trade Commission Act; (3) loose enforcement currently based on the view that most business practices are part of the competitive process
   d. (1) loose enforcement based on the Clayton Act and the Federal Trade Commission Act; (2) strict enforcement of the Sherman Act; (3) loose enforcement currently based on the rule of reason
   e. (1) strict enforcement of the Sherman Act; (2) loose enforcement based on the Clayton Act and the Federal Trade Commission Act; (3) strict enforcement currently based on the per se rule

3. Internationally, antitrust laws
   a. are very similar, but not identical.
   b. are all the same, since they've been developed by an international agency.
   c. are all the same, since all other countries have adopted U.S. laws.
   d. vary from country to country, with U.S. laws being the least strict.
   e. vary from country to country, with U.S. laws being the most strict.

Section 2: The Regulation of Monopoly

1. Natural monopolies are regulated to
   a. provide profits for the government.
   b. protect the monopoly from improper competition.
   c. protect the public from the abuse of monopoly power.
   d. increase the profits received by the monopoly.
   e. protect international competition.

2. When regulating a natural monopoly, the government may regulate
   a. price.
   b. profit.
   c. output.
   d. all of the above, as part of rate-of-return regulation.
   e. none of the above.

3. Regulation
   a. is a perfect substitute for the pressures of competition.
   b. distorts the regulated firm's incentives.

4. Price regulation of railroads, trucking, and airlines began
   a. because these industries are all natural monopolies.
   b. because large fixed costs limited entry, requiring price regulation to prevent monopolistic actions.
   c. as part of the penalty for antitrust violations.
   d. because of the international nature of these industries.
   e. because antitrust laws were not in effect yet.

5. During the period from 1887 to 1940, regulatory agencies in the United States
   a. arose to regulate the communications and transportation industries.
   b. were eliminated in the transportation industry.
   c. were eliminated in the communications industry.
   d. nationalized the transportation and communications industries.
   e. privatized the transportation and communications industries.

6. In recent years,
   a. deregulation and privatization have become the trend within developed nations.
   b. regulation by international agencies is increasing.
   c. regulation by international agencies has disappeared.
   d. both a and b have happened.
   e. both a and c have happened.

212 / Chapter 13

PRACTICE QUESTIONS AND PROBLEMS

Section 1: Antitrust Policy

1. Antitrust policies are designed to control the growth of _____ and to enhance
    _____.

2. List the three main U.S. antitrust laws, and circle the agencies or groups that are primarily responsible for
    enforcing each law.

Act	Enforcement Agencies or Groups		
a. _____	Justice Department	Federal Trade Commission	Private parties
b. _____	Justice Department	Federal Trade Commission	Private parties
c. _____	Justice Department	Federal Trade Commission	Private parties

3. Number the blanks to show the time sequence of antitrust enforcement policies.

    a. _____ Passage of the Clayton Act and Federal Trade Commission Act leads to strict enforcement
        against both horizontal and vertical restrictions.

    b. _____ Reconsideration of antitrust policy by the Justice Department and courts leads to much looser
        enforcement.

    c. _____ Passage of the Sherman Act leads to loose enforcement of antitrust law.

4. In what years were the following antitrust laws passed?

    a. _____ Sherman Antitrust Act

    b. _____ Clayton Antitrust Act

    c. _____ Federal Trade Commission Act

5. For each of the following provisions, write the appropriate antitrust law.

    a. _____: prohibits certain practices that might keep other firms from entering an
        industry or competing with an existing firm

    b. _____: forbids monopolization and attempts to monopolize

    c. _____: prohibits unfair methods of competition and unfair or deceptive acts

    d. _____: bans price discrimination that substantially lessens competition or
        injures competitors

    e. _____: outlaws contracts and conspiracies in restraint of trade

    f. _____: outlaws mergers that substantially lessen competition

6. Which of the following best describes the *rule of reason* approach to antitrust enforcement?
   a. Some actions that could be anticompetitive are illegal when they yield large profits.
   b. Some actions that could be anticompetitive are illegal, regardless of their effects.
   c. To be illegal, an action must be unreasonable in a competitive sense and the anticompetitive effects must be demonstrated.
   d. To be illegal, an action must be reasonable in a competitive sense and have no anticompetitive effects.
   e. Some actions that are normally illegal become legal when other competitors are helped.

7. Which of the following best describes the *per se rule* approach to antitrust enforcement?
   a. Some actions that could be anticompetitive are illegal when they yield large profits.
   b. Some actions that could be anticompetitive are illegal, regardless of their effects.
   c. To be illegal, an action must be unreasonable in a competitive sense and the anticompetitive effects must be demonstrated.
   d. To be illegal, an action must be reasonable in a competitive sense and have no anticompetitive effects.
   e. Some actions that are normally illegal become legal when other competitors are helped.

8. Under present antitrust enforcement standards, what is the only action that is per se illegal?
   _____

9. The relationships between suppliers and distributors are known as _____ relationships.

10. Which of the following best describes the change that has recently taken place in the way antitrust policy-makers view vertical relationships?
    a. Until the 1980s, concerns about vertical relationships were a large part of the antitrust agenda. In recent years, vertical relationships have caused little concern.
    b. Until the 1980s, vertical relationships caused little concern. In recent years, concerns about vertical relationships have become a large part of the antitrust agenda.

11. Define the following terms:
    a. resale price maintenance: _____
       _____

    b. exclusive dealing: _____
       _____

    c. tying: _____
       _____

12. Some makers of personal computers have put tight controls on their dealers: the dealers must maintain minimum prices, stock a variety of supplies and repair parts, and sell only certain brands of computers. Do you think these actions restrain or promote competition? _____ Explain why.
    _____
    _____
    _____
    _____

Section 2: The Regulation of Monopoly

1. A natural monopoly is characterized by _____ fixed costs and

    _____ economies of scale.

2. In the United States, regulatory commissions normally determine a natural monopoly's price and profit

    rate. This process is known as _____ .

3. The objective of regulating natural monopolies is to make them behave less like monopolies and more like
    perfectly competitive firms. The diagram below shows the demand, marginal-revenue, and cost curves for
    Hometown Electric, your local electric utility.

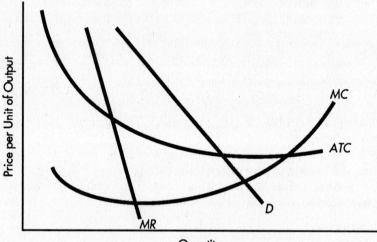

a. Find the price and quantity that Hometown Electric would choose if it were not regulated. Mark these
    P_M and Q_M.
b. Find the price and quantity that Hometown's regulatory commission will set if it wants to achieve allo-
    cative efficiency, as perfectly competitive markets do. Mark these P_0 and Q_0. What problem do you
    see for Hometown if this price and quantity are chosen?

    _____

    _____

c. Find the price and quantity that Hometown's regulatory commission will set if it wants to give Home-
    town just a normal rate of return, like firms in perfectly competitive markets get. Mark these P_A and
    Q_A.

d. Suppose the president of Hometown Electric decides to buy 20 Rolls-Royce limousines (for $250,000 each) for the company's executives. What will happen to Hometown's *ATC* curve? Under rate-of-return regulation, what will happen to the price Hometown is allowed to charge for electricity? What would happen to a firm in a perfectly competitive market if it bought 20 limousines?

_____

_____

_____

_____

4. In addition to natural monopolies, several other industries in the United States have been regulated for various reasons. Several reasons for regulation are given below; match the industries listed with the reason why they were regulated.

Reasons

a. Industry was a natural monopoly when it was initially regulated.
b. Marginal costs are low relative to fixed costs, so free entry and competition could lead to the failure of the entire industry.
c. Without regulation, a key resource would be available to all without cost, and overuse of the resource would destroy the industry.
d. A competing industry was already regulated.

Industries

_____ railroads

_____ trucks

_____ airlines

_____ radio and television broadcasting

_____ telephone telecommunications

5. During the 1970s and early 1980s, many of the industries listed above were _____ ;

in other industrialized countries, previously nationalized industries have been

_____ .

6. Privatization means transferring a _____ owned enterprise to

_____ ownership.

7. As an alternative to completely privatizing a government enterprise, sometimes an outside firm is hired by government to provide a product or service that the government used to provide. This is known as

_____ .

THINKING ABOUT AND APPLYING ANTITRUST POLICY AND THE REGULATION OF MONOPOLY

I. College Cartels

1. The "Economically Speaking" section of the chapter discusses an "Ivy League Cartel" involving colleges exchanging information on financial-aid packages to be offered to potential students. After reviewing the material, identify the section of the U.S. antitrust laws that these colleges may be violating.

   _____

2. Can some students benefit from the information exchange? (Hint: Think about the money the schools have available for giving financial aid as a limited resource, and look at the effects of the colleges' information exchange on the way the money is allocated.)

   _____
   _____
   _____
   _____

3. If you are a student who thinks you have been overcharged by one of the colleges, do you have any way to recover the money you lost?

   _____
   _____
   _____
   _____

II. Garbage Economics

This chapter has looked at several ways to handle natural monopoly, including regulation, nationalization, and contracting out. The different ways that U.S. cities and towns organize garbage and trash collection illustrate the costs and benefits of these different methods.

1. The garbage collection industry has two stages: collection of garbage and trash by garbage trucks, and disposal of garbage and trash in a dump or landfill. Both stages are natural monopolies in some ways. For all but the largest cities, one landfill is cheaper to operate than several landfills because of very large economies of scale. Why is collecting garbage and trash in garbage trucks a natural monopoly? (Hint: Think about the patterns that several competing garbage trucks would have to follow to serve a neighborhood.)

   _____
   _____
   _____

2. Many U.S. cities and towns have effectively nationalized the garbage industry, running garbage trucks and landfills as a government enterprise, with expenses paid by taxes or by fees designed to cover costs; others have organized it as a regulated industry under rate-of-return regulation. Based on what you have read in the chapter, why do you think that these ways of organizing the garbage industry might be inefficient?

_____

_____

_____

_____

3. As part of the movement toward deregulation and privatization, some cities have considered changing the way they organize garbage and trash collection. For a city looking at privatizing the garbage industry, which stage (collection trucks or landfill operation) is more suitable for complete privatization, and which stage is more suitable for contracting out? (Hint: For each stage, think about the size of the economies of scale and the possibilities for having several competitive firms.)

_____

_____

_____

_____

ANSWERS

Quick Check Quiz

Section 1: Antitrust Policy

1. c; 2. c; 3. e
   If you missed any of these questions, you should go back and review pages 343–352 in Chapter 13 (pages 715–724 in *Economics*, Chapter 27).

Section 2: The Regulation of Monopoly

1. c; 2. d; 3. b; 4. b; 5. a; 6. d
   If you missed any of these questions, you should go back and review pages 353–362 in Chapter 13 (pages 725–734 in *Economics*, Chapter 27).

Practice Questions and Problems

Section 1: Antitrust Policy

1. monopoly; competition
2. a. Sherman Act: Justice Department, private parties
   b. Clayton Act: Federal Trade Commission, private parties
   c. Federal Trade Commission Act: Federal Trade Commission

3. a. 2; b. 3; c. 1
4. a. 1890; b. 1914; c. 1914
5. a. Clayton Act; b. Sherman Act; c. Federal Trade Commission Act; d. Clayton Act; e. Sherman Act; f. Clayton Act
6. c
7. b
8. price fixing
9. vertical
10. a
11. a. definition by the product's manufacturer of the price a distributor can set on the product
    b. definition by a manufacturer of a distributor's product, customers, or business location
    c. the ability to purchase one product only if another product is also purchased
12. In different ways, these actions both restrain and promote competition. You could argue that these controls limit *competition among that maker's dealers*. On the other hand, these controls help build a strong network of dealers, which promotes *competition with other makers' dealers*. Although economists disagree about which effect is more important to consumers, antitrust policymakers and the courts have adopted the position that vertical restrictions are not important.

Section 2: The Regulation of Monopoly

1. high; large
2. rate-of-return regulation

3.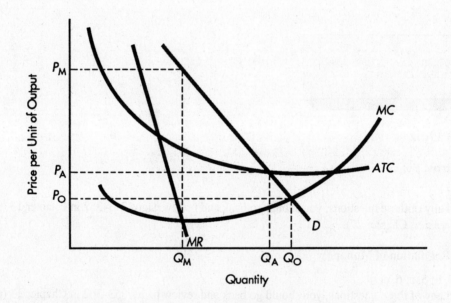

a. Q_M is where $MR = MC$. P_M comes from the demand curve at that quantity.
b. Allocative efficiency occurs when $P = MC$, where the demand curve crosses the MC curve. This price is below ATC, so Hometown will end up bankrupt and out of business.
c. A normal rate of return occurs when $P = ATC$, where the demand curve crosses the ATC curve.
d. The extra cost will raise ATC, requiring that Hometown raise its price to keep receiving a normal rate of return. Since perfectly competitive firms receive only a normal profit, extra expenses usually force a firm out of the market.

4. b railroads
    d trucks
    b airlines
    c radio and television broadcasting
    a telephone telecommunications
5. deregulated; privatized
6. publicly; private
7. contracting out

Thinking About and Applying Antitrust Policy and the Regulation of Monopoly

I. College Cartels

1. Sherman Act, Section 1: Conspiracies in restraint of trade are illegal.
2. By avoiding "bidding wars" for the best students, the colleges will spend less money on those students and have more money available for other uses. If the colleges do set aside a specific amount of money for financial aid, some of the money they save can go to provide financial aid to more students.
3. You can file an antitrust suit against the colleges as a private party. If you win, you will collect triple damages—that is, you will get back three times the amount you were overcharged.

II. Garbage Economics

1. If there were several competing garbage and trash collection companies serving a neighborhood, all the trucks would have to drive up and down each street to serve all customers. One truck could serve all homes on a street for less money. For example, if there were 5 miles of streets in a neighborhood and 4 companies were competing, their trucks would have to drive 20 miles total to serve all customers. One truck could serve all customers and only have to drive 5 miles, incurring lower costs for gasoline, maintenance, and so on. The cost savings would not be very large, but they would exist.
2. There are no real incentives to hold down costs in either case. Governments, as well as regulated monopolies, pass on their costs to their customers.
3. Landfills do have large economies of scale, so completely privatizing the landfill operation stage will create a private monopoly that could abuse its position; contracting out landfill operations usually works out better. Competition among garbage and trash collectors, although a little more expensive in theory, may be less expensive in practice if the firms are under pressure from competitors. Complete privatization will work better in this stage of the garbage and trash industry.

CHAPTER 14*
An Overview of Resource Markets

FUNDAMENTAL
QUESTIONS

1. Who are the buyers and sellers of resources?

   In any large shopping mall, almost anything you would ever want seems to be there for sale—candy, clothing, camping equipment, computer disks, maybe even cars. And if the mall does not have what you want, the grocery store does. But there is a vast constellation of products you never see for sale at the mall: things like railroad locomotives, factory buildings, aluminum ore, and farmland. You can't go to the mall and hire a business manager, a baseball player, or a ballerina either.

   Resources like these are not bought because they create utility for consumers. Nobody buys a ton of iron ore to enjoy looking at it; instead, the demand for resources like iron ore is derived from the value of the resources to businesses, in terms of producing other products that satisfy consumer wants. Economists classify resources into four groups: land, labor, capital, and entrepreneurial ability. These resources are sold by households to obtain income to buy the goods and services the households want.

2. How are resource prices determined?

   Resource prices are set by the same kind of equilibrium process that we've studied for consumer markets: through the interactions of buyers and sellers. This equilibrium process determines the rate of pay of each resource and the quantity of that resource used. The payment received by a resource consists of two parts: the rate of pay needed to keep the resource in its current use, called **transfer earnings,** and any pay in excess of transfer earnings, called **economic rent.**

   The rate of pay needed to keep a resource in its current use depends on opportunity costs: how much some *other* buyer is willing to pay for a particular resource. For example, a very talented basketball player is worth millions to a professional basketball team, but he will not quit playing basketball if his salary is cut. Most of his salary is economic rent (there's nobody else that can play basketball as he does).

3. Why will a firm selling its output in a perfectly competitive market use more resources than an identical firm selling its output in a market structure other than perfect competition?

   Buying a resource adds to the firm's costs; selling the output produced by the resource adds to the firm's revenues. Economists use the term **marginal factor cost (MFC)** to refer to the added costs a firm pays to get a resource unit, and the term **marginal revenue product (MRP)** to refer to the added revenues. Firms find it profitable to use resources up to the amount where $MRP = MFC$. The MRP of a resource depends on the amount of added output produced by the resource (the marginal physical product, or MPP) and on the value of that output to the firm (the marginal revenue, or MR).

   For firms selling their output in a perfectly competitive market, the marginal revenue is the same as the market price. For firms selling in other market structures, the marginal revenue is less than the price. We end up with these equations:

*Economics Chapter 28.

222 / Chapter 14

$$MRP = MPP \times P \text{ for perfectly competitive markets}$$

$$MRP = MPP \times MR \text{ for other market structures}$$

Since P is more than MR, resources are more valuable to firms selling in perfectly competitive markets; for the same resource cost, firms in perfectly competitive markets will find it profitable to use more resources than would identical firms selling in other market structures.

4. How does a firm allocate its expenditures among the various resources?

A firm allocates its expenditures among resources in the same way that consumers allocate their incomes: so that the value per dollar is equal at the margin. Consumers get the most value from their incomes when the last dollar spent on all goods bought gives the same marginal utility. Firms are using resources efficiently when the last dollar spent gives the same marginal revenue product for all resources.

KEY TERMS

derived demand
residual claimants
transfer earnings
economic rent

marginal revenue product (MRP)
value of the marginal product (VMP)
marginal factor cost (MFC)
monopsonist

QUICK CHECK QUIZ

Section 1: Buyers and Sellers of Resources

1. The demand for resources is called a "derived demand" because the demand for resources comes from
   a. the supply of resources.
   b. the marginal utility of owning a resource.
   c. what a resource can produce.
   d. consumers' needs for resources to use.
   e. how much a resource consumes.

2. What do economists call the price paid for the use of land?
   a. interest
   b. proceeds
   c. profits
   d. rent
   e. wages

3. What do economists call the price paid for the use of labor?
   a. interest
   b. proceeds
   c. profits
   d. rent
   e. wages

4. What do economists call the price paid for the use of capital?
   a. interest
   b. proceeds
   c. profits
   d. rent
   e. wages

5. Who are the residual claimants?
   a. entrepreneurs
   b. bankers
   c. workers
   d. government employees
   e. the unemployed

6. Which of the following correctly identifies the buyers and sellers of resources?
   a. Firms buy resources; households sell resources.
   b. Firms and households buy resources; governments sell resources.
   c. Governments and households buy resources; firms sell resources.
   d. Households buy resources; firms sell resources.
   e. Governments buy resources; firms and households sell resources.

Section 2: The Market Demand for and Supply of Resources

1. Transfer earnings are
   a. labor earnings used to support nonworking family members.
   b. the part of total earnings needed to keep a resource in its current use.
   c. earnings shifted from one resource category to another.
   d. the same as economic rent.
   e. excess residual incomes received by entrepreneurs.

2. The payment needed to keep a resource in its current use depends mostly on
   a. the resource's opportunity cost.
   b. the taxes paid by the resource's owner.
   c. the taxes paid by the resource's user.
   d. the resource's economic rent.
   e. the derived demands for other resources.

3. Economic rent is
   a. the total price paid for renting an apartment.
   b. the price paid for renting an apartment minus taxes and utilities.
   c. the portion of earnings above transfer earnings.
   d. the difference between transfer earnings and opportunity costs.
   e. the payment to residual claimants.

4. Firms buy resources with the goal of
   a. maximizing output quantity.
   b. using all resources equally.
   c. maximizing profits.
   d. providing maximum utility to consumers.
   e. minimizing costs.

Section 3: The Demand for a Resource by a Single Firm

1. The marginal revenue product (MRP) is the
   a. value of the additional output that an extra unit of a resource can produce.
   b. additional cost of an additional unit of a resource.
   c. additional cost of an additional unit of output.
   d. value of the additional revenue that an extra unit of output can produce.
   e. cost of the additional output that an extra unit of a resource can produce.

2. The marginal factor cost (MFC) is the
   a. value of the additional output that an extra unit of a resource can produce.
   b. additional cost of an additional unit of a resource.
   c. additional cost of an additional unit of output.
   d. value of the additional revenue that an extra unit of output can produce.
   e. value of the additional input used to make an extra unit of a resource.

3. The value of the marginal product (VMP) is
   a. the marginal revenue product in a perfectly competitive output market, $P \times MPP$.
   b. the marginal revenue product in a monopolistic output market, $MR \times MPP$.
   c. equal to the difference between the MRP and the MFC.
   d. zero when MRP is at its maximum.
   e. zero when MFC is at its minimum.

4. A monopsonist is
   a. the only seller of a resource.
   b. the only seller of a product.
   c. the only buyer of a resource.
   d. a firm that maximizes MRP.
   e. a firm that minimizes VMP.

5. A firm's demand curve for a resource is the
   a. upward-sloping portion of the firm's MC curve.
   b. downward-sloping portion of the firm's MFC curve.
   c. downward-sloping portion of the resource's MRP curve.
   d. upward-sloping portion of the resource's MFC curve.
   e. downward-sloping portion of the resource's MC curve.

6. To maximize profits, a firm should hire resources up to the point where
   a. $MR = MC$.
   b. $P = MC$.
   c. $MRP = MFC$.
   d. $MRP = MC$.
   e. $MR = MFC$.

PRACTICE QUESTIONS AND PROBLEMS

Section 1: Buyers and Sellers of Resources

1. List the four types of resources and what each type's price is called.

Type	Price
_____	_____
_____	_____
_____	_____
_____	_____

2. The buyers of resources are _____ ; the sellers of resources are

    _____ .

3. Who are the residual claimants? _____

Section 2: The Market Demand for and Supply of Resources

1. On a graph, the market demand curve for a resource looks _____ (the same as,

    different from) the demand curve for a consumer product.

2. What equation do you use to calculate the price elasticity of resource demand?

    _____

3. List the four factors that determine the elasticity of resource demand.

    _____

    _____

    _____

    _____

4. List the five factors that can shift the demand curve for a resource.

    _____

    _____

    _____

    _____

    _____

5. List the three factors that can shift the supply curve for a resource.

    _____

    _____

    _____

Section 3: The Demand for a Resource by a Single Firm

1. The firm's demand curve for a resource is the _____ -sloping portion of the re-

    source's _____ curve.

2. To maximize profits, a firm should hire a resource up to the amount where _____ =

    _____ .

3. In perfectly competitive resource markets, resources are paid an amount _____

    (equal to, more than, less than) their marginal revenue product.

4. In monopsonistic resource markets, resources are paid an amount _____ (equal to,

    more than, less than) their marginal revenue product.

5. A firm will allocate its budget on resources so that the last dollar spent yields

    _____ no matter which resource the dollar is spent on.

6. You have decided to make some extra money and gain some real-world experience by starting your own
    business. You have observed that there is a good market for handwoven doormats made of recycled rope.
    You can get old rope for free and can use your apartment as work space. Your only costs will be for hiring
    other students to work on making the mats. The table below shows how many mats you can make with
    different numbers of workers, how much you can sell the mats for, and how much you have to pay to at-
    tract workers. Fill in all the blanks in the table, plot the *MRP* and *MFC* curves on the graph, and figure out
    how many workers you want to hire.

Number of Workers	Mats per Hour	MPP	Price per Mat	Total Revenue	MR	MRP	Wage per Hour	Total Labor Cost	MFC
1	8	___	$2.00	$___	$___	$___	$4.00	$___	$___
2	19	___	2.00	___	___	___	4.00	___	___
3	26	___	2.00	___	___	___	4.00	___	___
4	30	___	2.00	___	___	___	4.00	___	___
5	32	___	2.00	___	___	___	4.00	___	___
6	33	___	2.00	___			4.00	___	___

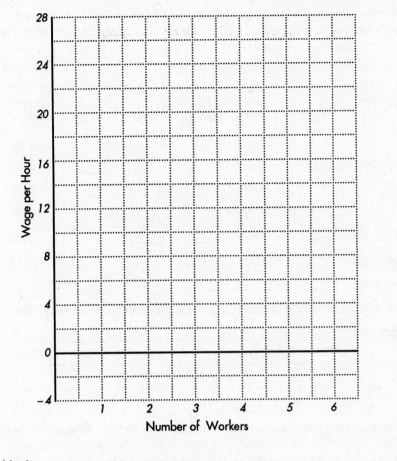

a. Workers hired: _____

b. In what kind of market structure are your doormats selling? _____ How can you tell? _____

c. In what kind of market structure are you hiring workers? _____ How can you tell? _____

7. You have become so successful making doormats that all other sellers of doormats have quit the market; you are now a monopolist, and the demand for your mats has changed. Recalculate your total revenue, *MR,* and *MRP* figures; graph your new *MRP* on the graph *above;* and find how many workers you want to hire now.

Number of Workers	Mats per Hour	MPP	Price per Mat	Total Revenue	MR	MRP	Wage per Hour	Total Labor Cost	MFC
1	8	8	$2.00	$____	$____	$____	$4.00	$ 4.00	$4.00
2	19	11	1.90	____	____	____	4.00	8.00	4.00
3	26	7	1.80	____	____	____	4.00	12.00	4.00
4	30	4	1.70	____	____	____	4.00	16.00	4.00
5	32	2	1.60	____	____	____	4.00	20.00	4.00
6	33	1	1.50	____	____	____	4.00	24.00	4.00

a. Workers hired: _____

b. How can you tell from the table that you aren't selling your doormats in a perfectly competitive market anymore? _____

_____

_____

_____

8. When you started, many other students were willing to work for you. Most of those who tried weaving doormats hated the job, though, and now there are only six students in town who are willing to work for you. A few of them like the job enough to be willing to work for low wages, but you have to keep increasing your pay rate to attract more workers. Refigure your labor costs and *MFC,* plot the *MRP* and *MFC* curves and the supply curve for your workers on the graph *below,* and decide how many workers you want to hire now.

Number of Workers	Mats per Hour	MPP	Price per Mat	Total Revenue	MR	MRP	Wage per Hour	Total Labor Cost	MFC
1	8	8	$2.00	$16.00	$2.00	$16.00	$2.00	$____	$____
2	19	11	1.90	36.10	1.83	20.10	3.00	____	____
3	26	7	1.80	46.80	1.53	10.70	4.00	____	____
4	30	4	1.70	51.00	1.05	4.20	5.00	____	____
5	32	2	1.60	51.20	.10	.20	6.00	____	____
6	33	1	1.50	49.50	−1.70	−1.70	7.00	____	____

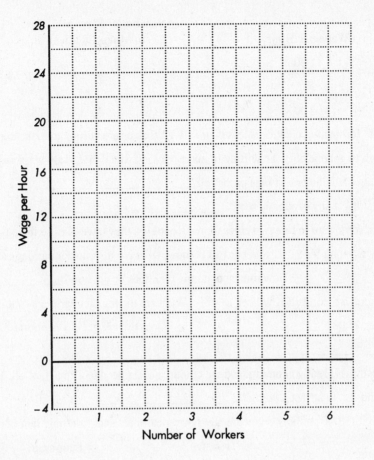

a. Workers hired: _____

b. How can you tell from the table that you aren't hiring workers in a perfectly competitive market anymore? _____

_____

_____

_____

THINKING ABOUT AND APPLYING AN OVERVIEW OF RESOURCE MARKETS

I. Cookies, Elves, and Economic Rent

If you've watched much television in the past few years, you've seen ads for a cookie company in which cute little cartoon elves make all the cookies. Let's take a look at elf economics.

In many ways, the elves in these commercials act like people; for example, they respond to incentives. Some elves really enjoy making cookies, so they will work for the cookie company for a low rate of pay. Other elves enjoy other things and will only work for the cookie company at higher rates of pay. The table below shows the supply curve for cookie-making elves.

Wage per Hour	Number of Elves Willing to Make Cookies
$1.00	1
2.00	2
3.00	3
4.00	4

1. If the wage rate for making cookies is less than $1.00, no elves are willing to make cookies, but a wage of $1.00 is enough to get one elf to be willing to make cookies. Since that $1.00 wage is just enough to attract that elf, what are the transfer earnings of that elf? _____ At a wage of $1.00 per hour, does this elf get any economic rent? _____

2. If the cookie makers want to hire two elves to make cookies, they have to raise the pay to $2.00. If the elf who is already working for $1.00 gets paid $2.00 now, what are his transfer earnings after the raise? _____ How much economic rent does he get now? _____

3. At $2.00 per hour, a second elf is willing to work. What are the transfer earnings of this second elf when the wage rate is $2.00? _____ Does this elf get any economic rent? _____

4. The cookie business is really booming, and the cookie makers need to hire a third elf. How high do they have to raise the rate to attract a third elf? _____

5. If the wage rate is $3.00 per hour, what are the transfer earnings and economic rent of each of the elves?

	Transfer Earnings	Economic Rent
First elf	_____	_____
Second elf	_____	_____
Third elf	_____	_____

6. Why don't all of the elves have the same transfer earnings? _____

II. Demand and Supply for Aerospace Engineers

The "Economically Speaking" section for this chapter describes the effects of a change in trademark law on the demand, supply, and equilibrium pay rate for lawyers in that specialty, and illustrates the way resource markets react to economic changes. Let's expand on those ideas, looking at the market for aerospace engineers.

Aerospace engineers design airplanes and spaceships. As in most engineering areas, becoming a specialist in aerospace engineering takes several years of study even if you already are an engineer, and even longer if you are just starting out in engineering. The time it takes to train new engineers makes the market for engineers behave differently than the market for lawyers, since changing legal specialties is much easier and quicker.

Let's say that the market for aerospace engineers is shown by MRP_1 and S_1 on the graph below; salaries average $60,000 per year, and there are 40,000 aerospace engineers working. If the United States decides next year to start working on sending people to visit Mars and starts paying aerospace engineering firms to design spaceships for the trip, the MRP of aerospace engineers will increase to MRP_2.

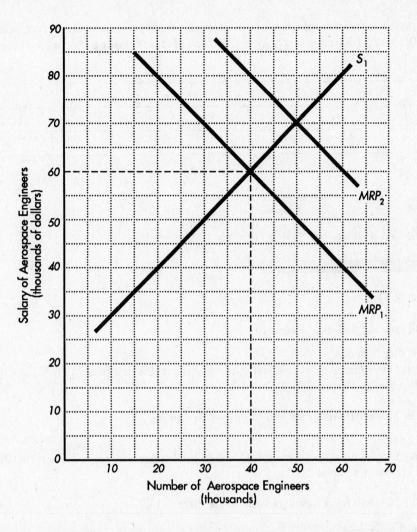

1. The supply curve on the diagram shows the long-run supply of aerospace engineers, after people have had time to become aerospace engineers. On the graph, sketch in a supply curve for aerospace engineers that shows how the number of available aerospace engineers will respond to an overnight increase in salaries. (Hint: Can you change the number of engineers overnight, when it takes several years of study to become an aerospace engineer?)

2. Use this "overnight" supply curve to find the salaries that current aerospace engineers will get shortly after MRP shifts to MRP_2. _____

3. How much of the increase in salary is transfer earnings, and how much of it is economic rent?

    _____
    _____
    _____
    _____

4. After there has been enough time for new aerospace engineers to enter the market, salaries will end up at $70,000, with 50,000 engineers working. Will any of these engineers still be receiving economic rent? Explain why or why not.

_____

_____

_____

_____

ANSWERS

Quick Check Quiz

Section 1: Buyers and Sellers of Resources

1. c; 2. d; 3. e; 4. a; 5. a; 6. a

If you missed any of these questions, you should go back and review pages 370–372 in Chapter 14 (pages 742–744 in *Economics*, Chapter 28).

Section 2: The Market Demand for and Supply of Resources

1. b; 2. a; 3. c; 4. c

If you missed any of these questions, you should go back and review pages 372–380 in Chapter 14 (pages 744–752 in *Economics*, Chapter 28).

Section 3: The Demand for a Resource by a Single Firm

1. a; 2. b; 3. a; 4. c; 5. c; 6. c

If you missed any of these questions, you should go back and review pages 380–392 in Chapter 14 (pages 752–764 in *Economics*, Chapter 28).

Practice Questions and Problems

Section 1: Buyers and Sellers of Resources

1. land; rent
   labor; wages
   capital; interest
   entrepreneurship; profit
2. firms; households
3. entrepreneurs

Section 2: The Market Demand for and Supply of Resources

1. the same as

2. $e_r = \dfrac{\text{percentage change in quantity demanded of resource}}{\text{percentage change in price of resource}}$

3. price elasticity of the product
   proportion of total costs
   number of substitutes
   time period

4. prices of the product the resource is used to produce
   productivity of the resource
   number of buyers of the resource
   prices of related resources
   quantities of other resources

5. tastes
   number of suppliers
   prices of other uses of the resource

Section 3: The Demand for a Resource by a Single Firm

1. downward; *MRP*
2. *MRP; MFC*
3. equal to
4. less than
5. the same marginal revenue product

6.

Number of Workers	Mats per Hour	*MPP*	Price per Mat	Total Revenue	*MR*	*MRP*	Wage per Hour	Total Labor Cost	*MFC*
1	8	8	$2.00	$16.00	$2.00	$16.00	$4.00	$ 4.00	$4.00
2	19	11	2.00	38.00	2.00	22.00	4.00	8.00	4.00
3	26	7	2.00	52.00	2.00	14.00	4.00	12.00	4.00
4	30	4	2.00	60.00	2.00	8.00	4.00	16.00	4.00
5	32	2	2.00	64.00	2.00	4.00	4.00	20.00	4.00
6	33	1	2.00	66.00	2.00	2.00	4.00	24.00	4.00

MPP = the change in output (mats per hour) from using another worker
Total revenue = mats per hour × price per mat
MR = change in total revenue divided by change in output, or *TR/MPP*
MRP = change in total revenue from using another worker
Total labor cost = number of workers × wage per hour
MFC = change in total labor cost from hiring one more worker

If you need help on these calculations, refer to Figures 4, 5, and 7 in the text.

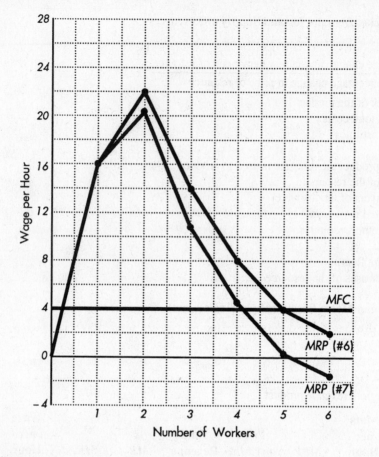

a. Workers hired: 5

   MRP = MFC for the fifth worker

b. perfect competition; because output price (price per mat) is constant

c. perfectly competitive market; because resource price (wage per hour) is constant

7.

Number of Workers	Mats per Hour	MPP	Price per Mat	Total Revenue	MR	MRP	Wage per Hour	Total Labor Cost	MFC
1	8	8	$2.00	$16.00	$2.00	$16.00	$4.00	$ 4.00	$4.00
2	19	11	1.90	36.10	1.83	20.10	4.00	8.00	4.00
3	26	7	1.80	46.80	1.53	10.70	4.00	12.00	4.00
4	30	4	1.70	51.00	1.05	4.20	4.00	16.00	4.00
5	32	2	1.60	51.20	.10	.20	4.00	20.00	4.00
6	33	1	1.50	49.50	−1.70	−1.70	4.00	24.00	4.00

a. Workers hired: 4

   With the decrease in output price, the fifth worker's MRP has dropped below his MFC, so profit is higher now with only 4 workers.

b. The output price decreases as quantity increases—you're not facing a perfectly elastic demand curve anymore.

8.

Number of Workers	Mats per Hour	MPP	Price per Mat	Total Revenue	MR	MRP	Wage per Hour	Total Labor Cost	MFC
1	8	8	$2.00	$16.00	$2.00	$16.00	$2.00	$ 2.00	$ 2.00
2	19	11	1.90	36.10	1.83	20.10	3.00	6.00	4.00
3	26	7	1.80	46.80	1.53	10.70	4.00	12.00	6.00
4	30	4	1.70	51.00	1.05	4.20	5.00	20.00	8.00
5	32	2	1.60	51.20	.10	.20	6.00	30.00	10.00
6	33	1	1.50	49.50	−1.70	−1.70	7.00	42.00	12.00

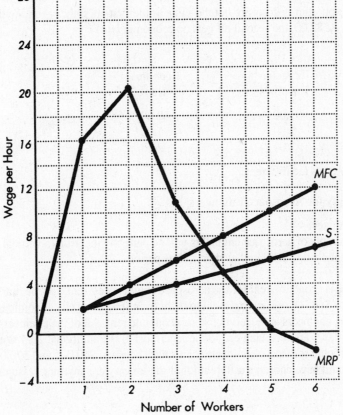

a. Workers hired: 3
With the increasing *MFC*, only the first 3 workers now have an *MRP* that is more than their *MFC*.

b. You have to increase wages to attract more workers, so you aren't facing a perfectly elastic supply curve for workers anymore.

Thinking About and Applying an Overview of Resource Markets

I. Cookies, Elves, and Economic Rent

1. $1.00; no

   Transfer earnings are the amount needed to keep a resource in its current employment. Since the $1.00 wage is barely enough to make working worthwhile, all of the elf's wage is transfer earnings: there is no economic rent.

2. $1.00; $1.00

   Transfer earnings are determined by opportunity costs. Since the first elf was willing to work for $1.00, any payment over $1.00 is economic rent to that elf.

3. $2.00; no

   The second elf's opportunity costs are not the same as the first elf's: the second will work only if the wage is $2.00 or more. At $2.00, the second elf gets no economic rent.

4. $3.00

5.

	Transfer Earnings	Economic Rent
First elf	$1.00	$2.00
Second elf	2.00	1.00
Third elf	3.00	zero

6. Their opportunity costs are different.

II. Demand and Supply for Aerospace Engineers

1. See graph on next page.

   The "overnight" supply of aerospace engineers will be perfectly inelastic (a vertical line), since the number of engineers cannot change at all in that short a time period.

2. $80,000

3. All of the increase is economic rent for the aerospace engineers currently in the market. They were all willing to work for $60,000, so any payment to them over $60,000 is all economic rent.

4. Almost all of these engineers are receiving some economic rent. All of the engineers who were willing to work before at $60,000 are receiving economic rent; most of the additional 10,000 engineers would have been willing to become aerospace engineers for a salary between $60,000 and $70,000. Only those few engineers who would have chosen a different job if the salary were anything less than $70,000 receive no economic rent.

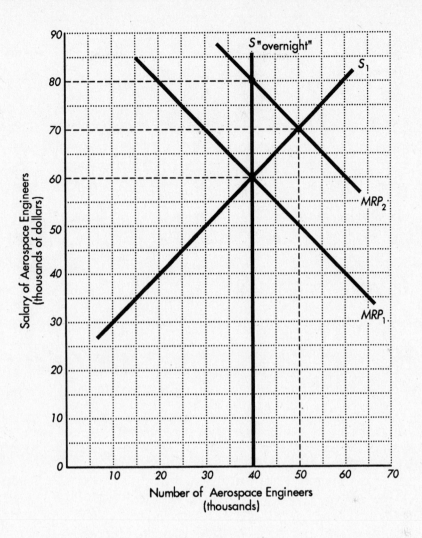

CHAPTER 15*
The Labor Market

1. Are people willing to work more for higher wages?

   Most people work to earn money to spend when they're not working. Even for people who really enjoy their jobs, the size of the paycheck affects how much they are willing to work. For individual workers, a higher wage rate has two effects: it encourages them to work more hours, but it also lets them enjoy more leisure time without lowering their standard of living. When wage rates get high enough, most people will cut back on hours worked and take more leisure time, producing a **backward-bending labor supply curve.**

2. What are compensating wage differentials?

   The supply of and demand for different labor markets determine the wage and the number of people employed in those markets. If people and jobs were like wheat, there would be only one wage rate. But people and jobs differ, so wages are not all the same. **Compensating wage differentials** exist when differences in job characteristics result in wage differences. Economists are paid more than fast-food workers partly because much more education is required before one can become an economist.

3. Why might wages be higher for people with more human capital than for those with less human capital?

   Human capital is the training, education, and physical health people accumulate during their lives. Human capital increases productivity, making workers more valuable to employers. Acquiring human capital has opportunity costs (time and money); therefore, it reduces the supply of labor for those jobs relative to the supply for jobs not requiring as much human capital.

4. Why do older workers tend to earn more than younger workers?

   Older workers usually have more human capital, especially in the form of on-the-job training. Many employers base wages on seniority (number of years with the firm) to encourage experienced workers to stay with the firm, since keeping experienced workers reduces the firm's training costs.

5. What accounts for earnings disparities between males and females and between whites and nonwhites?

   A wide variety of factors affects the earnings of different groups of people. On average, people in some groups have more human capital than people in other groups; differences in human capital usually lead to differences in earnings. Other factors that account for some of the differences among groups are **occupational segregation,** age differences, immigration, differences in educational opportunities, and **discrimination.**

*Economics Chapter 29.

6. Are discrimination and freely functioning markets compatible?

Labor market discrimination occurs when wages are affected by something other than workers' marginal products. Discrimination can occur because of personal prejudice: an individual's dislike of people with particular characteristics. Hiring people on the basis of personal prejudice adds to employers' costs and is not compatible with free markets. **Statistical discrimination** occurs when employers wrongly perceive that all members of a group have characteristics that make them less productive. This kind of discrimination can persist as long as employers' perceptions remain incorrect.

7. What is the role of comparable worth and affirmative action?

Comparable worth and **affirmative action** are ways to modify labor markets to help resolve wage differentials associated with occupational segregation and discrimination. Comparable worth is based on the idea that pay should be based on job characteristics rather than supply and demand: thus jobs with similar characteristics should be given similar pay rates. Affirmative action plans are commitments by employers to eliminate any unequal opportunities for women and minorities, usually by actively trying to recruit and retain minority and women employees.

KEY TERMS

backward-bending labor supply
   curve
labor force participation
compensating wage differentials
human capital

discrimination
statistical discrimination
crowding
occupational segregation

comparable worth
disparate treatment
disparate impact
affirmative action plans

QUICK CHECK QUIZ

Section 1: The Supply of Labor

1. Which of these graphs shows a backward-bending supply curve for labor?

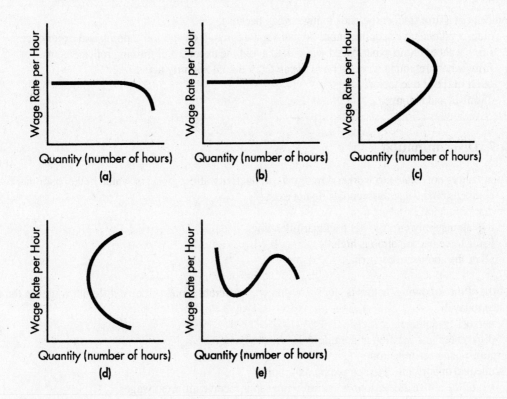

2. As wage rates increase in the economy, labor force participation
   a. is unaffected.
   b. increases.
   c. decreases at a steady rate.
   d. decreases at first, then increases.
   e. decreases slowly at first, then decreases more rapidly.

Section 2: Wage Differentials

1. Wage differences that make up for higher risk or poorer working conditions among different jobs are called
   a. human capital.
   b. disparate treatment.
   c. labor force participation differentials.
   d. compensating wage differentials.
   e. affirmative action plans.

2. Skills, training, and personal health acquired through education and on-the-job training are called
   a. disparate treatment.
   b. labor force participation differentials.
   c. human capital.
   d. compensating wage differentials.
   e. affirmative action plans.

3. Seniority at a firm frequently leads to higher pay because
   a. older workers have acquired more human capital through on-the-job training and experience.
   b. firms want to retain experienced workers to avoid the expenses of training replacements.
   c. firms who hire young workers have to pay extra Social Security taxes.
   d. of all of the above factors.
   e. of only a and b above.

Section 3: Discrimination

1. When factors not related to workers' marginal productivity affect workers' value in the labor market,
   a. compensating wage differentials do not exist.
   b. discrimination is occurring.
   c. the labor supply curve is not backward-bending.
   d. labor force participation is high.
   e. all of the above are occurring.

2. Which of the following factors is NOT a reason why different groups receive different wages in the United States today?
   a. personal prejudice
   b. differences in education and training
   c. statistical discrimination
   d. unequal opportunities to acquire human capital
   e. All of the above are reasons why different groups receive different wages.

3. Statistical discrimination can occur when
   a. wages are based on individual workers' actual marginal productivity.
   b. employers base wage decisions on personal prejudice.
   c. employers with imperfect information on people's productivity rely on incorrect assumptions to set wages.
   d. occupational segregation causes labor market crowding.
   e. immigration of unskilled people lowers the wages for all unskilled workers.

Section 4: Comparable Worth and Affirmative Action

1. Comparable worth is the idea that pay should be based on
   a. the supply and demand for different types of labor.
   b. only the supply side of the labor market.
   c. the characteristics of the job.
   d. the degree of occupational segregation in a labor market.
   e. the percentage of jobs filled by minorities.

2. In legal terms, the disparate impact standard judges employers on
   a. whether they are personally prejudiced against certain groups.
   b. whether their employment policies are intended to discriminate against certain groups.
   c. whether their employment policies affect different groups differently, regardless of whether or not the employer intended to discriminate.
   d. the degree of occupational segregation within their firms.
   e. whether their affirmative action plans are properly written.

PRACTICE QUESTIONS AND PROBLEMS

Section 1: The Supply of Labor

1. Sketch a backward-bending labor supply curve on the graph below.

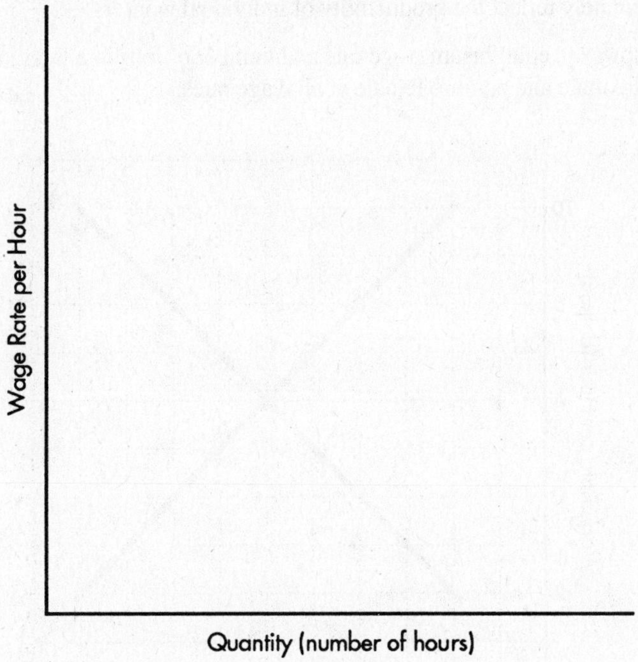

2. In the overall labor market, as wages increase, labor force _____ also increases.

3. In any labor market, the wage rate and number of jobs depend on the _____ and _____ curves for labor.

Section 2: Wage Differentials

1. Employers must pay _____ to get people to do unpleasant or dangerous jobs.

2. _____ is the skills, training, and personal health acquired through education and on-the-job training.

3. Higher opportunity costs for acquiring the human capital needed for a job result in

_____ (larger, smaller) numbers of people in that occupation, leading to wages that
are _____ (higher, lower) than for other jobs.

Section 3: Discrimination

1. Job market discrimination occurs when wages are based on anything besides workers'

_____ .

2. Discrimination based on personal prejudice is usually _____ (costly, profitable) for
a firm.

3. _____ discrimination can occur when employers use indicators of group perform-
ance that do not accurately reflect the productivity of individual workers.

4. The graph below shows the equilibrium wage rate and number of jobs in a labor market where half the
supply of workers are male and half are female at all wage rates.

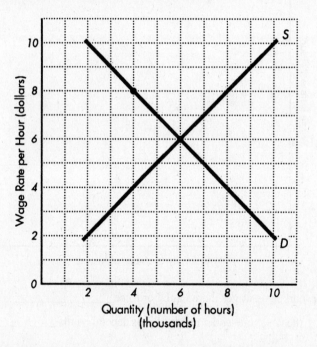

a. If employers' prejudices lead them to refuse to hire any women, what wage rate will the employers
end up paying? (Hint: If women will not be hired, they are not part of the supply as far as the employers are concerned, so draw in the supply curve for men to find the wage.)

_____

b. If you are a profit-maximizing employer, how can you take advantage of the other employers' prejudice?

_____

_____

_____

_____

c. When women are excluded from some labor markets, they are forced into some other labor markets; this is called _____. What effect will this have on women's wages in these other labor markets? _____

_____

Section 4: Comparable Worth and Affirmative Action

1. Comparable worth uses _____ rather than demand and supply to determine wage rates.

2. _____ commit firms to a schedule for eliminating any unequal opportunities for women and minorities.

3. Enforcement of civil rights laws regarding employment discrimination has led to two standards or tests of discrimination. Give the name of the standard that matches each description below.

   a. _____: Individuals are treated differently by the company because of their race, sex, color, religion, or national origin.

   b. _____: Company policies have effects that differ according to an employee's race, sex, color, religion, or national origin, regardless of any intent to discriminate.

THINKING ABOUT AND APPLYING THE LABOR MARKET

I. Human Capital and Skilled Workers

The "Economically Speaking" section of the chapter looks at the growing shortage of workers with technical skills in the United States. You can use what you have learned in the last two chapters about resource markets in general and labor markets in particular to analyze this problem further. (You should refer back to Section 2.b on market supply in the previous chapter.)

1. The graph on the left below shows the current market demand and supply for these skilled workers. Sketch in a new supply curve that shows what will happen to the market if people with technical skills keep retiring from the labor force faster than new workers are being trained in these skills.

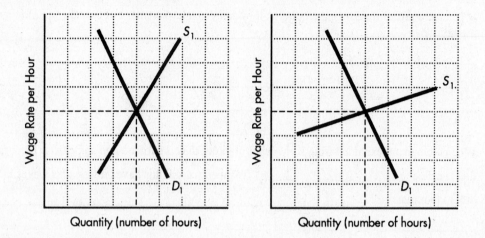

2. The current supply curve is very inelastic. What factors discussed in the last two chapters explain this, and what does it imply about future changes in the costs of hiring technically skilled workers? What effects will these costs have on U.S. firms' ability to compete internationally with countries that have larger supplies of technically skilled workers?

_____

_____

_____

_____

3. The graph on the right above shows a much more elastic supply curve for labor. If U.S. firms want to expand their use of technically skilled labor, will their production costs increase substantially? What implications does this have for U.S. firms' ability to compete?

_____

_____

_____

_____

4. Explain why the policies followed by the firms described in the "Economically Speaking" section will help change the supply curve for technically skilled labor.

_____

_____

_____

_____

II.   Comparable Worth and High School Teachers

Labor markets in the United States have frequently resulted in wage patterns that seem discriminatory: minorities and women are on average paid substantially less than white males. One approach (known as comparable worth) to making wage patterns more equal is to disregard the market forces of demand and supply and to set wages for jobs based on the jobs' characteristics. Using this approach, jobs that take place in the same sort of environment, that require the same levels of responsibility, and that require the same amounts of education should receive the same rate of pay.

The job market for high school teachers in most of the United States has worked this way for many years. In most high schools, teachers with the same education and years of experience are paid the same salary, regardless of the subject area they teach. This fits the comparable worth idea: the working conditions and demands on English teachers are the same as for math teachers. But ignoring the effects of demand and supply has some economic effects worth looking at.

1. Let's look at what will happen if U.S. high schools decide to improve the training of skilled workers by requiring students to take more math classes. The graphs on the following page show the demand and supply (D_1 and S_1) for math teachers and English teachers before adding math classes, with both math and English teachers earning \$30,000, and a new demand curve (D_2) for math teachers after adding more math classes. Mark on the graph the old and new equilibrium salary and number of math teachers.

What is the market equilibrium salary for math teachers now? _____

Using the ideas in Sections 1 and 2 of the chapter, explain why the salary has to go up to attract new math teachers.

_____

_____

_____

_____

2. If the schools maintain equal salaries for all teachers, English teachers will also be given a salary of \$35,000. Mark on the graph the quantity demanded and quantity supplied of English teachers when the salary is \$35,000. Explain what will happen in the market for English teachers if their salaries are raised to \$35,000.

_____

_____

_____

_____

3. One of the most useful characteristics of a market economy is that price changes signal changes in the relative scarcity of different products and resources, and encourage people to respond to those changes. Can you think of any ways that labor markets, by setting salaries through comparable worth, can do the same thing, without the math teachers receiving higher salaries than the English teachers?

_____

_____

_____

_____

(a) Market for Math Teachers

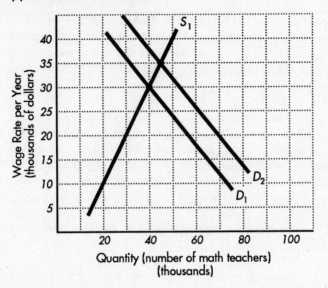

Quantity (number of math teachers)
(thousands)

(b) Market for English Teachers

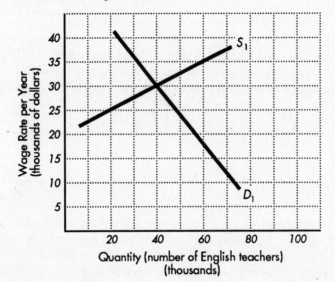

Quantity (number of English teachers)
(thousands)

ANSWERS

Quick Check Quiz

Section 1: The Supply of Labor

1. c; 2. b

If you missed either of these questions, you should go back and review pages 398–401 in Chapter 15 (pages 770–773 in *Economics*, Chapter 29).

Section 2: Wage Differentials

1. d; 2. c; 3. e

If you missed any of these questions, you should go back and review pages 402–407 in Chapter 15 (pages 774–779 in *Economics*, Chapter 29).

Section 3: Discrimination

1. b; 2. e; 3. c

If you missed any of these questions, you should go back and review pages 408–417 in Chapter 15 (pages 780–789 in *Economics*, Chapter 29).

Section 4: Comparable Worth and Affirmative Action

1. c; 2. c

If you missed either of these questions, you should go back and review pages 417–421 in Chapter 15 (pages 789–793 in *Economics*, Chapter 29).

Practice Questions and Problems

Section 1: The Supply of Labor

1.

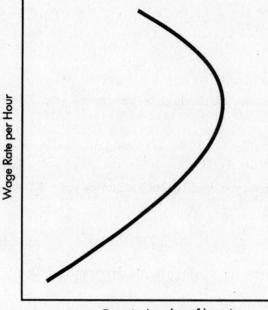

The bend backward comes at higher wage levels, where the income effect of wage increases becomes larger than the substitution effect. At lower wages, the labor supply curve looks like a regular supply curve, sloping upward to the right.
2. participation
3. demand; supply

Section 2: Wage Differentials

1. compensating wage differentials
2. Human capital
3. smaller; higher

Section 3: Discrimination

1. marginal productivity (or marginal physical product)
2. costly
3. Statistical
4. a. Equilibrium wage: $8.00

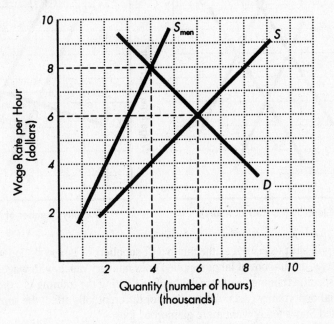

b. If other employers insist on hiring men at high wages, you can hire women at a lower wage, sell your product at a lower price, and receive substantial profits.
c. crowding; Wages in "crowded" labor markets will be lower than otherwise because of the larger supply.

Section 4: Comparable Worth and Affirmative Action

1. job characteristics
2. Affirmative action plans
3. a. disparate treatment
   b. disparate impact

Thinking About and Applying the Labor Market

I. Human Capital and Skilled Workers

1.

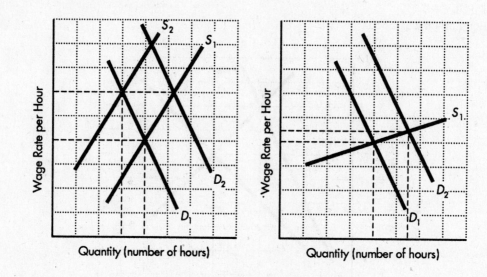

The supply curve will shift to the left as the number of suppliers of labor (skilled workers) gets smaller.

2. For this supply curve, the amount of labor supplied does not vary much with wages (it is inelastic) because only people with specific training can enter the market. Getting the training is expensive for individuals: there are substantial opportunity costs. Also, tastes for different jobs affect the supply curve; many young people in the United States today want more glamorous jobs.

    When an inelastic supply curve shifts to the left, the equilibrium wage will rise sharply, as shown above. Skilled workers become much more expensive, increasing production costs and making it more difficult for U. S. firms to compete with firms in other countries whose wages are not increasing as fast.

3. With a more elastic supply, wages will not increase much when demand increases; therefore production costs will not rise very much. This in turn will make it easier to compete than if wages were much higher.

4. The policies address the "tastes" problem by providing more information to young people who might be interested in technical jobs. They lower the opportunity costs to young people by paying them while they learn, and in one case by using public education for part of the training.

II. Comparable Worth and High School Teachers

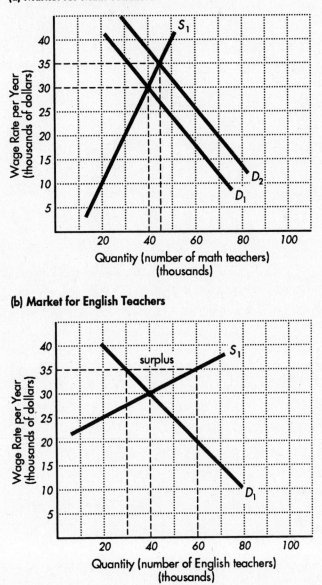

(a) Market for Math Teachers

(b) Market for English Teachers

1. $35,000

   The salary has to increase to pay the costs of acquiring the human capital needed to be a math teacher and to compete with other occupations for people with mathematical training and ability.
2. There will be a surplus in the market for English teachers as the salary increase attracts more people into that occupation; at the same time, schools may hire fewer English teachers at the higher salary.
3. There does not seem to be any way to do it: you can either you keep salaries equal, or you can respond to changes, but not both.

CHAPTER 16*
Unions

1. What is a bilateral monopoly?

   A **bilateral monopoly** is the market structure that results when a monopolistic seller faces a monopsonistic buyer: there is a monopoly on both sides of the market. Many labor bargaining situations, where a single union representing all the workers bargains with a committee representing employers, can be analyzed as bilateral monopolies.

2. What is the purpose of a union?

   Unions are formed to allow workers to speak with one voice when bargaining with an employer. By bargaining as a monopolist, the union can gain higher wages for its members.

3. Are unions and business always on opposite sides of an issue?

   On issues such as pay rates and employee benefits, unions and employers are on opposite sides. They engage in **collective bargaining** to try to reach an agreement; if they cannot agree by themselves, negotiated settlements may be reached through the use of a **mediator,** who will try to get both sides to compromise on an agreement, or through **compulsory arbitration,** during which a neutral individual or group resolves the conflicts. Failures to agree can result in strikes or lockouts.

   On other issues, unions and businesses work together. Unions can help employers find and screen new employees, improve morale and communication, and provide benefits for employees. Negotiating with one union rather than many individuals can also reduce costs.

4. How are craft unions and industrial unions different?

   Craft unions and industrial unions define their markets in different ways. Craft unions organize workers who have the same skills and practice the same trade, even though they work for many employers in different industries. The Carpenters' Union is made up of carpenters, regardless of where they work. Industrial unions organize workers in the same industry, even if they have many different skills or jobs. The United Auto Workers union represents people who work in the automobile industry, regardless of their specific jobs.

5. What is the government's attitude toward unions?

   In the United States, government's attitude toward unions has changed over the years. Until the 1930s, government attitudes were negative, slowing union growth. Beginning with the New Deal in the 1930s, unions became legal, and the federal government encouraged their growth. In 1947, attitudes changed again with the passage of the Taft-Hartley Act. Taft-Hartley limited union tactics and allowed states to pass **right-to-work laws** that make it illegal to require union membership.

*Economics Chapter 30.

6. Have unions been able to increase the wages of union members relative to the wages of non-unionized workers?

On average, union wages are higher than wages in nonunionized sectors of the economy. Among the reasons for higher union wages are differences in skills and experience, unions' ability to decrease supply and increase demand for union labor, and the impact of unions on monopsonistic markets.

7. What effects do minimum wages and job security rules have on employment?

The effects are uneven. Some employees, particularly those with jobs now, receive benefits from these laws. New entrants, and low-skill workers in general, are harmed.

KEY TERMS

bilateral monopoly
collective bargaining
mediator

compulsory arbitration
closed shop
right-to-work laws

union shop
featherbedding

QUICK CHECK QUIZ

Section 1: Monopsony and Bilateral Monopoly

1. Bilateral monopoly occurs when
   a. two monopolists sell different products in the same market.
   b. two monopolists sell the same product in different markets.
   c. a monopsonist sells to a monopolist.
   d. a monopolist sells to a monopsonist.
   e. a firm is both a monopolist and a monopsonist.

2. The outcome of negotiations in a bilateral monopoly depends primarily on
   a. the relative bargaining strengths of the buyer and seller.
   b. the shape of the *MRP* curve.
   c. the shape of the *MFC* curve.
   d. the difference between the *MRP* and *MFC* curves.
   e. the sum of the *MRP* and *MFC* curves.

3. A mediator is
   a. given the power to decide how to resolve issues between employer and union.
   b. an essential part of collective bargaining.
   c. the chief negotiator for the management side.
   d. an impartial observer who attempts to resolve conflicts between union and management.
   e. the chief negotiator for the union.

4. In compulsory arbitration, an arbitrator is
   a. given the power to decide how to resolve issues between employer and union.
   b. an essential part of collective bargaining.
   c. the chief negotiator for the management side.
   d. an impartial observer who attempts to resolve conflicts between union and management.
   e. the chief negotiator for the union.

Section 2: The History and Status of Unions

1. The three basic types of unions are called
    a. open, restricted, and exclusive.
    b. craft, industrial, and public employee.
    c. closed shop, right-to-work, and public.
    d. local, regional, and national.
    e. collective, independent, and neutral.

2. Which of the following statements is false?
    a. The Knights of Labor was the first national political union in the United States.
    b. The American Federation of Labor (AFL) was a federation of craft unions.
    c. The Congress of Industrial Organizations (CIO) was a federation of industrial unions.
    d. The AFL and CIO merged in the 1950s.
    e. Since the 1970s, craft and industrial unions have grown, while public employee unions have lost a large fraction of their members.

3. Which of the following descriptions is NOT historically accurate?
    a. Until the 1930s, the attitude of the U.S. government was basically anti-union.
    b. The Wagner Act of 1935 gave employees the right to organize.
    c. The National Labor Relations Board runs union elections and investigates unfair labor practices.
    d. The Taft-Hartley Act gave unions new powers that made strikes easier to win.
    e. Right-to-work laws allow individual states to make union shops illegal.

Section 3: The Economic Effects of Unions

1. Union wages
    a. are always higher than nonunion wages.
    b. are always lower than nonunion wages.
    c. are higher than nonunion wages in most but not all industries.
    d. are lower than nonunion wages in most but not all industries.
    e. are generally the same as nonunion wages.

2. Which of the following are ways that unions can increase wages?
    a. They can increase the demand for union labor by improving productivity.
    b. They can decrease the supply of labor to unionized sectors through barriers to entry.
    c. They can decrease the supply of labor by pushing for immigration restrictions.
    d. All of the above are ways that unions can increase wages.
    e. Only b and c above are ways that unions can increase wages.

3. Which of the following statements about minimum wage laws is false?
    a. Minimum wage laws require that certain jobs pay no less than the prescribed minimum wage.
    b. In competitive labor markets, minimum wage laws can cause unemployment.
    c. In monopsonistic labor markets, minimum wage laws can increase employment.
    d. Minimum wage increases tend to reduce teenage employment.
    e. All of the above are true statements about minimum wage laws.

PRACTICE QUESTIONS AND PROBLEMS

Section 1: Monopsony and Bilateral Monopoly

1. Most monopsonies arise because buyers _____.

2. When one buyer confronts one seller, the market structure is called a _____. In this market structure, the price will depend on _____.

3. The process of negotiating contracts between business firms and labor unions is

    _____. When labor and management cannot agree, they may decide to call in a

    _____ to help them reach an agreement, or they may use

    _____, whereby a neutral third party resolves the conflict.

Section 2: The History and Status of Unions

1. What type of union matches these descriptions?

    a. _____ union: Membership is made up of people who work in the same industry, regardless of what job they do.

    b. _____ union: Membership is made up of people who have the same skills and do the same job, regardless of what industry they work in.

    c. _____ union: Membership is made up of government employees.

2. In the United States, government's attitude toward unions has gone through several phases. Give the dates that match the three periods described, and name the laws that marked the turning points.

    a. _____ : Government attitude was anti-union.

    b. _____ : Government attitude became much more favorable toward unions, and unions were given the right to bargain collectively.

    Laws: _____

    c. _____ : Government imposed restrictions on union tactics.

    Law: _____

3. In a _____ shop agreement, employers are allowed to hire only people who are already members of the union. The _____ Act made this type of agreement _____ (always illegal, sometimes illegal) everywhere in the United States.

4. In a _____ shop agreement, employers may hire people who are not members of the union, but these new employees must join the union to keep their jobs. Individual states can pass _____ laws to make this type of agreement illegal.

5. In recent years, the fastest-growing unions have been _____ unions.

Section 3: The Economic Effects of Unions

1. On average, union wages are _____ (higher than, lower than, about the same as) nonunion wages in the United States.

2. Unions can increase wages by _____ the demand for union labor or by _____ the supply of labor available.

3. Union contracts in the railroad industry required railroads to have at least five people on each train, even after changes in technology cut the number needed to two. This is an example of

   _____ .

4. The diagrams below show the competitive labor market for stone carvers and the *MRP* and *MFC* curves for Hal's Headstones, an employer of stone carvers. Sketch in what would happen to this market and to Hal's Headstones, if the stone carvers' union developed a training program that increased the *MPP* of union stone carvers by 25 percent.

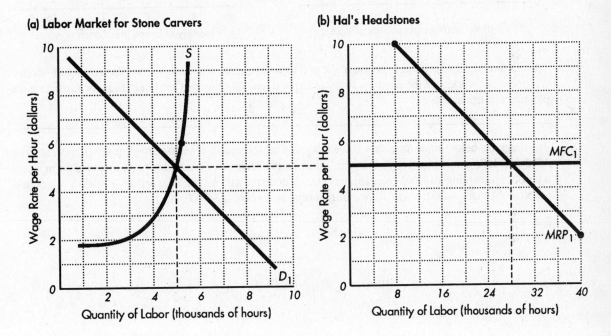

(a) **Labor Market for Stone Carvers**

(b) **Hal's Headstones**

5. The diagrams below show the competitive labor market for carpenters and the *MRP* and *MFC* curves for A-1 Homes, a home builder that employs carpenters. Suppose that you have to get a license to be a carpenter and that the only way to get a license is to pass the carpenters' union's two-year training program. Sketch in what will happen if the carpenters' union decides to lengthen the training program to three years.

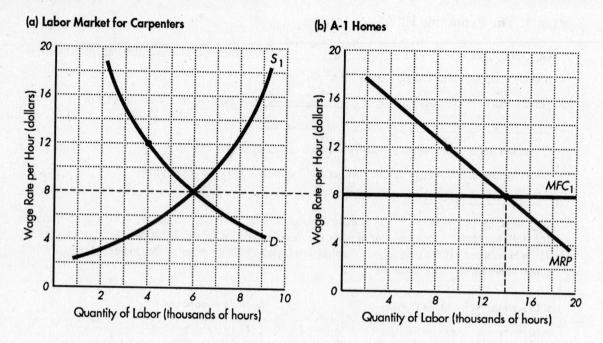

(a) Labor Market for Carpenters

(b) A-1 Homes

6. The "Economically Speaking" section in the text looks at the movement to restrict the number of hours teenagers can work. Use the diagram above to explain why labor unions are likely to favor restricting employment of teenagers.

7. The diagrams below show the competitive labor market for unskilled teenage hamburger flippers and the *MRP* and *MFC* curves for Tony's Burgers. Show on the diagrams what will happen in this labor market if a union representing all hamburger flippers signs a contract with all hamburger stands raising wages to $6.00. How many workers will Tony's Burgers choose to hire at $6.00?

(a) Labor Market for Unskilled Teenage Hamburger Flippers

(b) Tony's Burgers

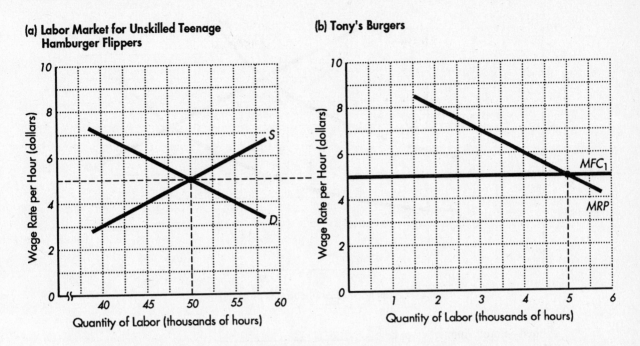

Quantity of Labor (thousands of hours)

8. Referring to the diagram above, explain the effects on the market for unskilled teenage workers of a minimum wage law that raises the minimum wage to $6.00 per hour.

_____

_____

_____

_____

9. In question 8, you assumed that the market for unskilled teenage labor was competitive. Suppose that it is monopsonistic instead. Use the diagram on the following page to find the effects on employment of a $6.00 minimum wage.

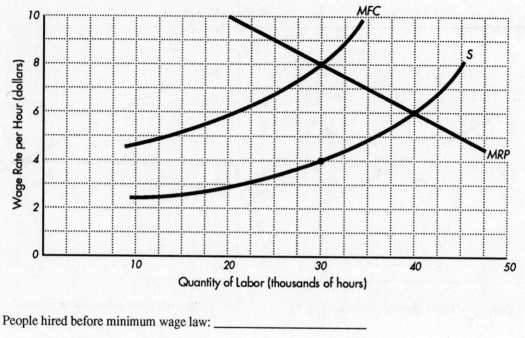

People hired before minimum wage law: _____

People hired after minimum wage law: _____

THINKING ABOUT AND APPLYING UNIONS

I. Study Time for Barbers

Arizona's barbers are required to spend at least 1,250 hours studying barbering, according to the quote from Arizona's governor in the "Preview" section of the text. Use the ideas you have been learning in the last three chapters about resource supply, labor markets, and unions to explain why the barbers' union in Arizona wanted this requirement put into the law.

II. Discrimination and Minimum Wage Laws

Your text quotes Walter Williams, an economist and columnist, as saying, "The brunt of the minimum wage law is borne by low-skilled workers . . . particularly black teenagers." A few questions ago, we looked at the effects of minimum wage laws on labor markets and found that in competitive labor markets minimum wage laws create a surplus. Combine this information with what you learned about discrimination in the last chapter to explain the logic behind Walter Williams's statement. (Hint: Think about the effects of a surplus on the costs of discriminating.)

_____

_____

_____

_____

Quick Check Quiz

Section 1: Monopsony and Bilateral Monopoly

1. d; 2. a; 3. d; 4. a
   If you missed any of these questions, you should go back and review pages 428–433 in Chapter 16 (pages 800–805 in *Economics*, Chapter 30).

Section 2: The History and Status of Unions

1. b; 2. e; 3. d
   If you missed any of these questions, you should go back and review pages 433–438 in Chapter 16 (pages 805–810 in *Economics*, Chapter 30).

Section 3: The Economic Effects of Unions

1. c; 2. d; 3. e
   If you missed any of these questions, you should go back and review pages 439–445 in Chapter 16 (pages 811–817 in *Economics*, Chapter 30).

Practice Questions and Problems

Section 1: Monopsony and Bilateral Monopoly

1. form cartels
2. bilateral monopoly; the negotiating strengths of the two sides
3. collective bargaining; mediator; compulsory arbitration

Section 2: The History and Status of Unions

1. a. industrial
   b. craft
   c. public-employee
2. a. before 1930s
   b. 1930s–1947
      Laws: Norris-LaGuardia Act
         Wagner Act
   c. after 1947
      Law: Taft-Hartley Act
3. closed; Taft-Hartley; always illegal
4. union; right-to-work
5. public-employee

Section 3: The Economic Effects of Unions

1. higher than
2. increasing; decreasing
3. featherbedding
4. Increasing the *MPP* by 25 percent will raise the *MRP* of each of Hal's workers by 25 percent, shifting Hal's MRP_1 to MRP_2. Since the market demand curve comes from the sum of individual firms' *MRP* curves, the market demand curve will shift to D_2. Wages will be higher, and there will be more jobs.

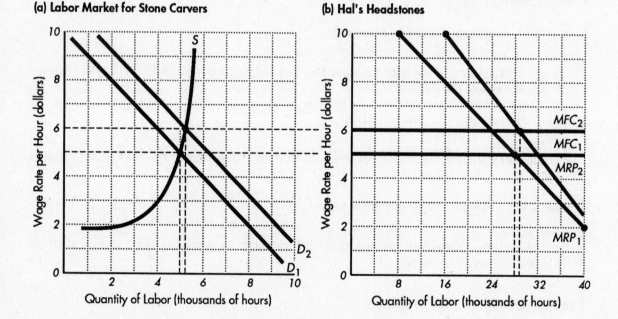

(a) Labor Market for Stone Carvers

(b) Hal's Headstones

5. The supply curve for carpenters will shift to the left, since the opportunity cost of becoming a carpenter went up because of the increased training required. Wages will go up, and the number of jobs will go down.

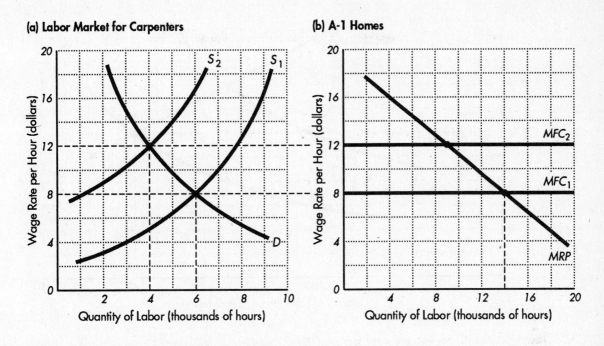

(a) Labor Market for Carpenters

(b) A-1 Homes

6. Restricting the supply of labor increases wage rates.
7. 4 workers
   In the labor market, a surplus of 10,000 workers will now exist.

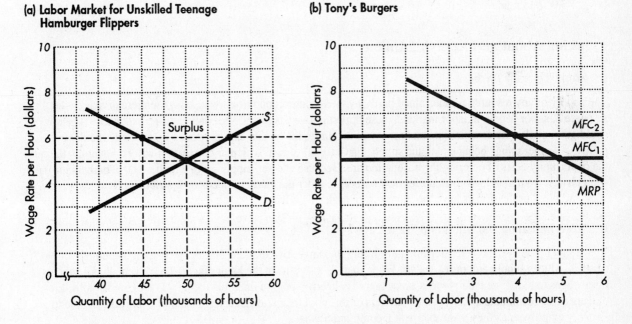

(a) Labor Market for Unskilled Teenage Hamburger Flippers

(b) Tony's Burgers

8. The effects of a $6.00 minimum wage are the same as above: employers will hire fewer workers, and a surplus will exist in the market.

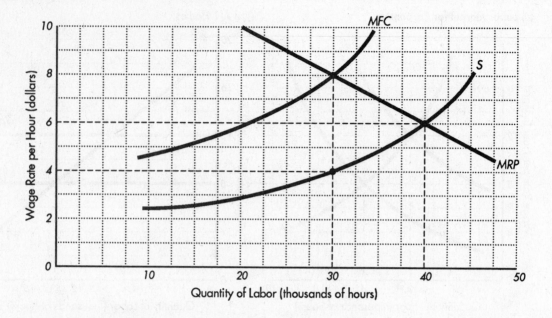

People hired before minimum wage law: 30,000

People hired after minimum wage law: 40,000

In the monopsonistic market, workers are hired up to the point where *MRP = MFC,* with their wage rate determined from the supply curve at that quantity. The minimum wage law changes the *MFC* curve: since employers cannot pay less than $6.00, they can hire up to 40,000 people at an additional cost *(MFC)* of $6.00 per hour.

Thinking About and Applying Unions

I. Study Time for Barbers

The supply of any resource is determined partly by the resource's opportunity costs: what alternative uses the resource has. For people in labor markets, these opportunity costs include not only the alternative jobs a person could get, but also the costs in time and money of acquiring the human capital needed to enter a particular occupation. All other things being equal, the supply curve for labor in a particular occupation will be lower the higher the opportunity costs of entering the occupation are. Because a lower supply gives a higher wage, barbers in Arizona benefit from making it difficult for new barbers to enter the market. Licensing restrictions for doctors, lawyers, and other professionals have the same sort of logic and effects.

II. Discrimination and Minimum Wage Laws

As we saw in the last chapter, discriminatory hiring in competitive markets is usually costly to the employer because it reduces supply and raises wages. When there is a surplus in the labor market, employers do not have to raise wages to attract new employees, since there is already a pool of unemployed people looking for jobs. Employers can discriminate against some members of this pool (black teenagers, for example) and still be able to get as many employees as they want to hire at the minimum wage.

CHAPTER 17*
Land, Capital, and Entrepreneurial Ability

FUNDAMENTAL QUESTIONS

1. **Does economic rent serve the allocative role that other resource prices serve?**

   One of the functions of prices in a market economy is to allocate resources: workers are employed by those who will pay them the most, diamonds are sold to the highest bidder, and so on. Remember from the chapter on resource markets that economic rent is the payment to resources beyond that needed to keep the resource in its current use. The huge salaries of movie stars, for example, are mostly economic rent, since they would still work as movie actors for much less money. Their huge salaries do serve to allocate their services among movie studios. Only those studios that can make the most profitable use of their talents will be willing to pay for them.

2. **What role does saving play in the economy?**

   In effect, **saving** is the way an economy can trade some current consumption for more future consumption. Saving permits accumulation of capital, which in turn increases production. The more capital—machines, factory buildings, trucks, computers, information libraries, and so on—a society's workers have to use, the more output the society can produce. The only way a society can accumulate more capital is to give up some current consumption: to save some of its output rather than consume all of it. The process of sacrificing current consumption to accumulate capital with which more output can be produced in the future is known as **roundabout production.**

3. **What is present value?**

   Present value is the value to you today of an amount of money you will receive in the future. Let's say that a lawyer just stopped by to tell you that your rich Aunt Iris passed away and left you $10,000; the only catch is that the check is dated 1999, so you cannot cash it until then. You have plenty of things you'd like to buy now, so you try to find someone who will pay you something for the check now. Unless you come across someone who does not understand present value, however, you will not be able to sell that $10,000 check for $10,000. Anyone with $10,000 now could put the money in the bank (instead of buying your check), get paid interest, and have more than $10,000 by 1999. The present value of future income is always less than the amount of the income; how much less depends on the interest rate.

   These same sorts of considerations come into play when businesses are deciding whether to buy new machinery or other forms of capital: they have to pay for the capital now, but the income from the new machinery does not all come in right away.

*Economics Chapter 31.

4. Why does the entrepreneur receive profit?

An **entrepreneur** is someone who sees an opportunity to earn a profit and acts to take advantage of that opportunity. The profit successful entrepreneurs receive can come from several sources. Profit can be compensation for entrepreneurial ability, or the ability to recognize opportunities to turn resources into something worth more than the cost of the resources used. Entrepreneurs take risks in starting new activities: profits come when they are successful, and losses when they are not. Innovations created by entrepreneurs can create at least a temporary monopoly and can generate some monopoly profits.

5. How are the resource markets tied together?

Resource markets are tied together through households, which own the resources and offer them for sale to firms. As part of a household, you usually have some choices about what resources to own. You can use your savings to buy land or stock in a corporation (capital), and you can use whatever entrepreneurial abilities you have to start your own business—you can even decide to own different labor resources by entering or leaving the labor force, or increasing your human capital through education and training, as you are doing now by studying economics.

When making decisions about resource ownership, you and everyone else will pay attention to the expected rate of return on different resources. Your presence in a college economics class says that you (or maybe your parents) believe that the expected return on your time is higher if it is spent in college increasing your human capital than if you spent the time working or running your own business. Your decisions about what resources to own affect the supplies of different resources, in turn affecting the prices and rates of return of the different resources. In the long run, rates of return on different resources should be equal as households allocate their savings to those resources offering the highest rate of return.

KEY TERMS

pure economic rent	present value	entrepreneurial ability
roundabout production	future value	intrapreneurial ability
saving	entrepreneur	

QUICK CHECK QUIZ

Section 1: Land

1. When a resource has a fixed supply, payments to the resource are
   a. pure interest.
   b. increased to their future value, depending on the interest rate.
   c. pure economic rent.
   d. pure transfer earnings.
   e. partial transfer earnings.

2. Because land is fixed in supply, all land receives
   a. the same pure economic rent.
   b. the same pure transfer earnings.
   c. differing amounts of economic rent, depending on the supply of land.
   d. differing amounts of economic rent, depending on the demand for different pieces of land.
   e. the same economic rent but different transfer earnings.

3. Pure economic rent
   a. performs the allocative function of a price but not the incentive function of a price.
   b. performs the incentive function of a price but not the allocative function of a price.
   c. performs both the allocative function and the incentive function of a price.
   d. performs neither the allocative function nor the incentive function of a price.
   e. always performs the incentive function of a price but only performs the allocative function when land is scarce.

Section 2: Capital

1. The process of saving and accumulating capital in order to increase production and consumption in the future is called
   a. roundabout production.
   b. piecemeal production.
   c. delayed gratification of savings.
   d. the present value/future value metaphor.
   e. current consumptionism.

2. To an economist, delaying consumption is called
   a. minimizing future value.
   b. maximizing present value.
   c. saving.
   d. capital.
   e. rounding production.

3. Present value is
   a. the value of savings forgone to acquire capital.
   b. the value of capital forgone to acquire savings.
   c. the difference between the rate of return and the rate of interest.
   d. the equivalent value in the future of some amount received today.
   e. the equivalent value today of some amount to be received in the future.

4. Future value is
   a. the value of savings forgone to acquire capital.
   b. the value of capital forgone to acquire savings.
   c. the difference between the rate of return and the rate of interest.
   d. the equivalent value in the future of some amount received today.
   e. the equivalent value today of some amount to be received in the future.

5. Which of the following statements about the demand and supply of capital is false?
   a. The demand for capital is represented by a downward-sloping curve.
   b. The supply of capital is represented by an upward-sloping curve.
   c. The demand for and supply of capital determine the price of capital.
   d. An increase in the price of capital lowers the rate of return on capital.
   e. The demand for capital shifts outward when interest rates rise.

6. When the rate of interest rises above the rate of return on capital, the
   a. demand for capital declines, the price of capital declines, and the rate of return on capital increases.
   b. demand for capital declines, the price of capital increases, and the rate of return on capital increases.
   c. demand for capital declines, the price of capital increases, and the rate of return on capital declines.
   d. demand for capital declines, the price of capital declines, and the rate of return on capital declines.
   e. demand for capital increases, the price of capital declines, and the rate of return on capital increases.

Section 3: Entrepreneurial Ability

1. An entrepreneur is someone who
   a. does the routine management work for an existing firm.
   b. sees an opportunity and acts to take advantage of it.
   c. is an employee of an existing firm who has the freedom and support to create new goods and services for the firm.
   d. is an employee of an existing firm who has the freedom and support to create new goods and services for his or her own benefit.
   e. exploits other members of society for private gain.

2. An intrapreneur is someone who
   a. does the routine management work for an existing firm.
   b. sees an opportunity and acts to take advantage of it.
   c. is an employee of an existing firm who has the freedom and support to create new goods and services for the firm.
   d. is an employee of an existing firm who has the freedom and support to create new goods and services for his or her own benefit.
   e. exploits other members of society for private gain.

3. Successful entrepreneurs receive profits because
   a. they recognize opportunities to turn resources into something more valuable.
   b. they take risks.
   c. their innovations can create monopoly profits.
   d. of all three reasons above.
   e. of only reasons a and b above.

Section 4: Tying Resource Markets Together

1. Prices in resource markets are tied together by
   a. government regulations on the sale of resources.
   b. the actions of households that own resources.
   c. business preferences for resource sellers.
   d. monopolistic resource buyers who are also monopsonistic resource sellers.
   e. the monopolistic ownership of capital.

2. In the long run, the rates of return on different resources
   a. are determined by government controls.
   b. should be unequal, reflecting differences in resource supply.
   c. should be unequal, reflecting differences in resource demand.
   d. should be equal.
   e. may or may not be equal, because resource markets are independent of each other.

PRACTICE QUESTIONS AND PROBLEMS

Section 1: Land

1. When a resource has a fixed supply, the payment it receives is _____ .

2. Rent serves to _____ the fixed supply of a resource among competing uses.

3. The graph below shows the demand for farmland in Finney County, Kansas. All the land in Finney County is used to grow wheat.

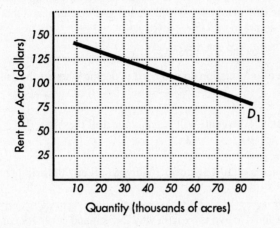

Quantity (thousands of acres)

a. Like all resource demand curves, the demand for land is based on its _____

    and on the price of _____ .

b. Last year, land in Finney County rented for $100 per acre. Draw in the supply curve for land that matches that price and the demand curve shown.

c. Because of unexpected increases in world production of wheat, the price of wheat dropped this year

    from $5.00 per bushel to $2.50 per bushel, and it is expected to stay at $2.50 in the future. On the

    graph, draw in a new demand curve for Finney County land. What is the rent for Finney County land

    now? _____

Section 2: Capital

1. The process of saving and accumulating capital in order to increase production and consumption in the

    future is called _____ .

2. To an economist, saving is _____ .

3. Consumers and producers match their future plans with their current actions through

    _____ .

4. As the price of capital rises, the quantity of capital demanded will _____ (rise, fall,

    stay the same) and the quantity of capital supplied will _____ (rise, fall, stay the

    same).

5. When the interest rate rises, the present value of the marginal revenue product of capital

   _____ (rises, falls, stays the same), so the demand curve for capital will shift

   _____ (inward, outward).

6. When the interest rate falls, the present value of the marginal revenue product of capital

   _____ (rises, falls, stays the same), so the demand curve for capital will shift

   _____ (inward, outward).

7. You're the owner of the Best Machine Shop. You've just seen a new computerized drill press that you're thinking about buying. The drill press costs $10,000, and you've calculated that buying it will add $1,000 per year (in present value terms) to the shop's revenues.

   a. What is the rate of return on the drill press? _____

   b. What additional piece of information do you need to decide whether the drill press is worth buying?

      _____

   c. The current interest rate is 9 percent. Will you buy the drill press? _____
      Why? _____

   d. The interest rate just increased to 11 percent. Will you still buy the drill press? _____
      Why? _____

   e. Use your answers to c and d above to explain why the demand curve for capital shifts inward when the

      interest rate rises. _____

      _____

      _____

      _____

   f. Because the interest rate increased to 11 percent, machine shops have not bought as many computer-

      ized drill presses as the manufacturer had expected. As a result, the price of the drill presses just

      dropped to $9,000. What is the rate of return on the drill press now? _____

      Is it worthwhile for you to buy the drill press now? _____

Section 3: Entrepreneurial Ability

1. Individuals who recognize opportunities for profit and then organize resources and take risks to gain those

   profits are known as _____.

2. People who perform entrepreneurial functions within existing firms are known as

   _____.

3. Successful entrepreneurs are paid _____.

4. List three reasons why successful entrepreneurs receive profits.

   _____

   _____

   _____

5. You are the proud owner of City Slickers, Inc., manufacturers of plastic raincoats. Starting with nothing but your entrepreneurial ability, you have built this business into an operation that yields a profit of $100,000 per year. You are sure your profits will continue at this level for 5 years into the future. Use Table 1 in the text chapter to find the present value of City Slickers, Inc., if the interest rate is 10 percent.

   Present value: _____

Section 4: Tying Resource Markets Together

1. As owners of resources, decisions by _____ connect resource markets and resource

   prices together. Their decisions make the long-run rates of return on different resources

   _____.

2. Let's say you have saved $50,000. You are trying to decide whether to use your savings to buy stock in General Motors or to pay for going back to school for 2 years to get an MBA. You expect the GM stock to pay $8,000 per year in dividends and increases in the value of the stock; you expect the MBA to increase your salary and pension by $10,000 per year.

   Which use of your resources gives you a better financial return? _____

3. Let's change the situation in problem 2 a little bit. You currently own 1,000 shares of General Motors stock that generates $8.00 per year income ($8,000 total); you expect that income to continue in the future. You can sell the stock for $50 per share ($50,000 total) and get your MBA, increasing your future income by $10,000.

   a. In financial terms, should you sell the stock and get your MBA? _____

   b. Let's look at what is going to happen in the markets for GM stock and MBAs, if there are a lot of other people making the same decision you are making. The left graph shows the market for GM stock, and the right graph shows the market for MBAs, in terms of the extra income people get with an MBA. Sketch on the graphs below the effects of your decision (and the decisions of many others) to sell GM stock and get an MBA.

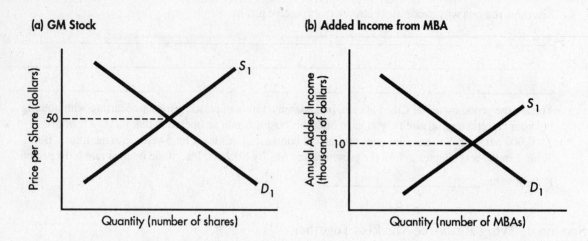

(a) GM Stock

(b) Added Income from MBA

c. Why do these changes bring about equal rates of return on investments in GM stock and MBAs?

_____

_____

_____

_____

THINKING ABOUT AND APPLYING LAND, CAPITAL, AND ENTREPRENEURIAL ABILITY

I. Rent Control and Capital Markets

The "Economically Speaking" section discusses New York City's controls on apartment rents. Almost all economists agree that rent control is a bad idea. As the reading shows, it creates shortages of housing and inequities in the distribution of what housing is available.

Let's use rent controls and the market for rental housing to explore how capital markets work and how rent control interferes with markets. From the viewpoint of the owner or potential buyer of an apartment building, the building is capital that has a rate of return derived from the rent paid on the apartments in the building. If the rate of return on apartment buildings is as high as or higher than the interest rate (the opportunity cost of capital), then it is worthwhile to invest in apartment buildings; if the rate of return is lower, it is not worthwhile.

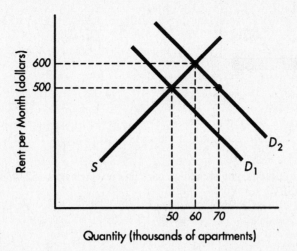

1. The graph above shows the market for rental housing. For demand curve D_1, the equilibrium rent is $500 per month, or $6,000 per year (in present value terms). If the cost of building an apartment is $60,000, what is the rate of return? _____ For the housing market to be in equilibrium, what must the rate of interest be? _____

2. If the city's population is growing and the demand for apartments shifts to D_2, the equilibrium rent is $600 per month, or $7,200 per year. What is the rate of return on apartments now? _____ Is it worthwhile to build more apartments than before? _____

3. If the city freezes rents at $500 per month, what is the rate of return on apartments? _____ Is there any incentive to build more apartments? _____

4. Although some of the 20,000 "surplus" families who want apartments but can't find them may end up homeless, most will find alternative housing: apartments without rent control, houses in the suburbs, and so on. The demand for housing in these uncontrolled markets will then expand. What will happen to the rate of return to building houses in the suburbs? If you were an intelligent, profit-maximizing builder, would you build rent-controlled apartments, or uncontrolled houses in the suburbs?

_____

_____

_____

_____

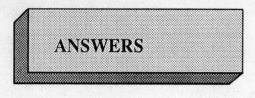

ANSWERS

Quick Check Quiz

Section 1: Land

1. c; 2. d; 3. a

If you missed any of these questions, you should go back and review pages 452–456 in Chapter 17 (pages 824–828 in *Economics*, Chapter 31).

Section 2: Capital

1. a; 2. c; 3. e; 4. d; 5. e; 6. a

If you missed any of these questions, you should go back and review pages 456–463 in Chapter 17 (pages 828–835 in *Economics*, Chapter 31).

Section 3: Entrepreneurial Ability

1. b; 2. c; 3. d

If you missed any of these questions, you should go back and review pages 463–466 in Chapter 17 (pages 835–838 in *Economics*, Chapter 31).

Section 4: Tying Resource Markets Together

1. b; 2. d

If you missed either of these questions, you should go back and review pages 466–467 in Chapter 17 (pages 838–839 in *Economics*, Chapter 31).

Practice Questions and Problems

Section 1: Land

1. economic rent
2. allocate

3. a. marginal physical product; output

    b.

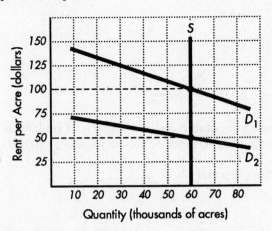

     The supply of land in Finney County is perfectly inelastic: a vertical line. For the rent to be $100 per acre, the supply of land must be 60,000 acres.

    c. $50

     The price of wheat is part of what determines the marginal revenue product of farmland, and thus the demand for farmland. If the price of wheat drops 50 percent, the *MRP* of farmland drops 50 percent, and so the demand for farmland will also drop 50 percent, as shown by D_1 on the graph. The new rent will be 50 percent of the old rent, or $50.

Section 2: Capital

1. roundabout production
2. delaying consumption
3. capital markets
4. fall; rise

    The demand and supply curves for capital work like other demand and supply curves.

5. falls; inward

    When interest rates rise, present value always falls, making capital less valuable to firms. When capital is less valuable, firms will not demand as much.

6. rises; outward

    When interest rates fall, present value always rises, making capital more valuable to firms. When capital is more valuable, firms will demand more than before.

7. a. 10 percent

     The rate of return is the income ($1,000) divided by the price of the asset ($10,000), in percentage terms.

    b. interest rate

     Capital is worth buying if its rate of return is at least equal to the interest rate, the opportunity cost of capital.

    c. yes; The rate of return is more than the interest rate.

    d. no; Now the rate of return is less than the interest rate. You'd get a better return from just putting the money in the bank and collecting interest.

    e. When the interest rate went up, capital that used to be worth buying became unprofitable. Since less capital would be bought at the same price of capital, the demand curve must have shifted inward.

    f. 11.1 percent; ($1,000/$9,000); yes

     Now it is worthwhile to buy the drill press again, because the rate of return at least equals the interest rate. These changes—the rate of interest rising, and the price of capital falling because the demand for capital dropped—are the way capital markets reach equilibrium.

Section 3: Entrepreneurial Ability

1. entrepreneurs
2. intrapreneurs
3. profits
4. They are successful traders.
   They bear risks.
   They create temporary monopolies by innovating.
5. Present value: $379,080
   Table 1 shows that the present value of receiving $1 per year for 5 years when the interest rate is 10 percent is 3.7908. Multiply this by 100,000 to get the present value of a $100,000 income.

Section 4: Tying Resource Markets Together

1. households; equal
2. MBA
   The rate of return on the MBA is 20 percent ($10,000 income per year/$50,000 investment), while the rate of return on the General Motors stock is only 16 percent ($8,000/$50,000).
3. a. The GM stock still has a rate of return of 16 percent, while the MBA again has a rate of return of 20 percent. You can increase your income by $2,000 per year by selling the stock and getting the MBA.

   b.

(a) GM Stock

(b) Added Income from MBA

People selling GM stock decreases the demand for GM stock and decreases the price of GM stock. More people getting MBAs increases the supply of MBAs, decreasing the added income people with MBAs receive. While you should be able to figure out the directions of the shifts, the specific shifts and prices shown above are just for illustration.

c. The decreased price of GM stock increases the rate of return. When the price of GM stock was $50 per share, the rate of return was 16 percent ($8/$50). If the price of GM stock fell to $44.44 per share as shown, the rate of return would rise to 18 percent ($8/$44.44). The increased supply of MBAs lowers the rate of return on MBAs by reducing the added income from having the degree. If the added income from an MBA drops to $9,000 as shown, the rate of return will decrease to 18 percent ($9,000/$50,000). At this point, both the stock and the MBA has the same expected rate of return, and people have no incentive to change from owning one resource (GM stock, which means ownership of GM capital) to another (more human capital from the MBA).

Thinking About and Applying Land, Capital, and Entrepreneurial Ability

I.   Rent Controls and Capital Markets

1.   10 percent; 10 percent ($6,000/$60,000)
     The rate of interest must also be 10 percent for the market to be in equilibrium with the rest of the economy.

2.   12 percent; ($7,200/$60,000); yes
     Since the rate of return on apartments is higher than the interest rate, building more apartments will be profitable.

3.   still 10 percent; no
     There is no incentive to build more apartments; apartment building is no more profitable than putting your money in the bank.

4.   The rate of return to building houses in the suburbs will rise because of increased demand and higher prices. Since building houses in the suburbs is more profitable, you would be working in the suburbs.

CHAPTER 18*
The Economics of Aging and Health Care

1. Why is the U.S. population aging?

    In the United States, as well as in most other industrialized countries, the average age of the population is increasing: there are relatively fewer young people and relatively more older people than before. One reason is that fewer babies are being born because of changes in the market for children. A second reason is that people are living longer than they used to live.

2. What does it mean to say that there is a market for children?

    When economists talk about the market for children, they're not talking about buying and selling children. Instead, they're talking about using the tools of demand and supply to analyze people's decisions about having children.

    Parents demand children because children provide utility to the parents, although, like other things, the marginal utility decreases as the number of children in a family increases: the demand curve for children slopes downward. The marginal costs of supplying and maintaining children increase as the number of children increases, giving an upward-sloping supply curve. The number of children in a family is determined by the intersection of demand and supply. Factors that change the costs and benefits of having children will cause changes in the number of children.

3. What was the purpose of mandatory retirement?

    The economic reason for mandatory retirement derives from the difference between the average worker's **age-earnings profile** and that worker's **age-productivity profile.** Workers' productivity usually rises with age until about age 45 and then declines, whereas workers' earnings usually rise throughout their working years. In their early years, workers are underpaid relative to productivity, whereas in later years workers are overpaid relative to productivity. This pattern encourages workers to stay in a firm's labor force during their younger years but also encourages them to remain in the labor force longer than employers want. By forcing retirement at a specific age, **mandatory retirement** policies prevent employees from staying in the work force too long.

4. Why do pension plans exist, and what is the role of Social Security?

    Pension plans serve several functions in the economy. They provide income for people after they retire and stop working, and they also provide an incentive for older workers to retire and leave their jobs. Social Security is a mandatory, government-run pension program, and benefits are paid for through taxes on employers and employees. It has the same economic functions as other pensions.

*Economics Chapter 32.

5. What accounts for the increasing percentage of expenditures allocated to health care?

    People in the United States already spend more than 14 percent of their income—one dollar out of every seven—on health care, and the percentage is steadily increasing. Several factors are responsible: expensive improvements in the quality of medical care, an aging population, and the way the U.S. health-care system is set up.

    For most people in the United States, medical bills are primarily paid by private or public insurance programs. Since we pay little of our medical bills directly out of our own pockets, we don't pay much attention to prices—our demand is inelastic. Other countries using different payment systems have developed health-care systems that cost considerably less but that provide equal quality in terms of infant mortality and life expectancy.

KEY TERMS

age-earnings profile
age-productivity profile
mandatory retirement
incidence of a tax
Medicare

Medicaid
prospective payment system (PPS)
health maintenance organization (HMO)
preferred provider organization (PPO)

QUICK CHECK QUIZ

Section 1: The Household

1. To economists, the number of children a family has depends on
    a. random events.
    b. the costs and benefits of children.
    c. the value of additional children to society.
    d. the size of the army wanted by society.
    e. fashion.

2. Which of the following will decrease the number of children?
    a. decreasing the value of children to parents
    b. increasing the opportunity costs of having children
    c. postponing having children until a large amount of human capital has been acquired
    d. All of the above will decrease the number of children.
    e. Only b and c above will decrease the number of children.

Section 2: Aging and Retirement

1. Which of the following can affect the timing of retirement?
    a. the size and timing of pension benefits
    b. Social Security benefits
    c. the relationship between the age-earnings profile and the age-productivity profile
    d. All of the above can affect the timing of retirement.
    e. Only a and b above can affect the timing of retirement.

2. If the age-earnings profile is steeper than the age-productivity profile, then workers are paid
   a. less than their marginal revenue product when they are younger, and more than their marginal revenue product when they are older.
   b. more than their marginal revenue product when they are younger, and less than their marginal revenue product when they are older.
   c. more than their marginal revenue product throughout their lives.
   d. less than their marginal revenue product throughout their lives.
   e. the same as their marginal revenue product throughout their lives.

3. Mandatory retirement policies
   a. require workers to retire from their jobs when their productivity has declined to a specified level.
   b. require workers to retire from their jobs when they reach a specific age.
   c. are now illegal in the United States.
   d. are characterized by all of the above.
   e. are characterized by only b and c above.

4. The incidence of a tax
   a. is determined by who is required to send money to the government to pay the tax.
   b. depends on whether it is a state or federal tax.
   c. depends on whether the tax is a percentage or a fixed amount.
   d. can only be determined for income taxes.
   e. is determined by who bears the burden of the tax.

5. The portion of Social Security taxes paid by an employer
   a. is completely paid from the profits of the business.
   b. is completely offset by other tax credits.
   c. increases the value of workers to the firm.
   d. is paid partly by workers in the form of lower wages.
   e. is accurately described by both c and d above.

Section 3: Health Economics

1. In the United States, the fastest-growing segment of national expenditures is for
   a. military spending.
   b. housing.
   c. health care.
   d. transportation.
   e. welfare payments.

2. Health-care costs are rising because
   a. hospital and nursing-home costs are increasing.
   b. physicians' fees are increasing.
   c. the population is aging.
   d. of all of the above factors.
   e. of only b and c above.

284 / Chapter 18

3. Demand for health care is relatively inelastic because
   a. individual consumers don't directly pay the cost of medical care, so they don't respond much to price increases.
   b. people spend only a small portion of their incomes on health care.
   c. health care is considered by most people to be a luxury rather than a necessity.
   d. most health-care spending is for the rapidly growing number of babies in the United States.
   e. growing numbers of people in the United States lack health insurance.

4. Medicare is
   a. a federal program providing health care for the elderly and disabled.
   b. a private charity that gives medical care to the poor.
   c. provided by doctors and nurses who are employees of the federal government.
   d. provided by doctors and nurses who are employees of state governments.
   e. a joint federal-state program providing health care for those who otherwise can't afford it.

5. Medicaid is
   a. a federal program providing health care for the elderly and disabled.
   b. a private charity that gives medical care to the poor.
   c. provided by doctors and nurses who are employees of the federal government.
   d. provided by doctors and nurses who are employees of state governments.
   e. a joint federal-state program providing health care for those who otherwise can't afford it.

6. The prospective payment system (PPS) is
   a. the use of a preassigned reimbursement rate by Medicare to reimburse hospitals and physicians.
   b. an organization that provides comprehensive medical care to a voluntarily enrolled consumer population in return for a fixed, prepaid amount of money.
   c. a group of physicians who contract to provide services at a price discount.
   d. a payment plan whereby workers pay for medical care after retirement while they are still working.
   e. a system for deciding which individuals will not be given any more medical care.

7. A health maintenance organization (HMO) is
   a. the use of a preassigned reimbursement rate by Medicare to reimburse hospitals and physicians.
   b. an organization that provides comprehensive medical care to a voluntarily enrolled consumer population in return for a fixed, prepaid amount of money.
   c. a group of physicians who contract to provide services at a price discount.
   d. a payment plan whereby workers pay for medical care after retirement while they are still working.
   e. a system for deciding which individuals will not be given any more medical care.

8. A preferred provider organization (PPO) is
   a. the use of a preassigned reimbursement rate by Medicare to reimburse hospitals and physicians.
   b. an organization that provides comprehensive medical care to a voluntarily enrolled consumer population in return for a fixed, prepaid amount of money.
   c. a group of physicians who contract to provide services at a price discount.
   d. a payment plan whereby workers pay for medical care after retirement while they are still working.
   e. a system for deciding which individuals will not be given any more medical care.

PRACTICE QUESTIONS AND PROBLEMS

Section 1: The Household

1. The number of children a family chooses depends on the _____ a child produces and on the _____ of a child.

2. The benefits of children include consumption benefits, such as _____ , and production benefits, such as _____ .

3. List some of the costs involved in raising children.

   _____

   _____

   _____

4. As more women have entered the labor force and have acquired larger amounts of human capital, the cost of having children has _____ (increased, decreased), leading to a/an _____ (increase, decrease) in the supply of children and a _____ (higher, lower) birthrate.

Section 2: Aging and Retirement

1. List three factors that affect the timing of retirement.

   _____

   _____

   _____

2. Social Security taxes in the United States are imposed on both _____ and _____ , and both groups are charged _____ (the same, different) amounts.

3. If the supply of labor is upward sloping, _____ (none, part, all) of the Social Security tax imposed on employers is actually paid by workers.

4. If the supply of labor is perfectly inelastic, _____ (none, part, all) of the Social Security tax imposed on employers is actually paid by workers.

Section 3: Health Economics

1. Compared with other industrialized countries, the United States spends a _____ (smaller, about equal, larger) percentage of its output on health care.

2. Compared with other expenditures in the U.S. economy, spending on health care is growing _____ (slowly, at about the same rate, rapidly).

3. In the United States today, the demand for health care is usually _____ (elastic, inelastic, unit-elastic) because the individual consumer _____ (does, does not) pay much, if any, of the cost of health care.

4. Assume that you are covered by health insurance that pays all of your medical-care costs.
    a. Your doctor charges $30 for an office visit. If you start feeling a little bit ill and are trying to decide whether to see your doctor, how will the $30 cost of seeing your doctor affect your decision?

    _____

    _____

    b. If you decide to see your doctor and the doctor wants to do blood tests that cost $500, do you have any reason to tell her to skip the tests, since you're not very sick anyway?

    _____

    _____

    c. Does the doctor have any reason not to do the tests?

    _____

    _____

    d. Suppose that instead of having regular health insurance, you and your doctor are part of an HMO. In an HMO, why does the doctor have a reason not to do the tests?

    _____

    _____

5. The "Economically Speaking" section in this chapter discusses a group of large businesses that are pushing for government to provide "national health insurance."
    a. Summarize the two themes, or objectives, of this group of businesses.

    _____

    _____

    _____

    _____

    b. Why can't we provide unlimited amounts of health care to everyone who wants it?

    _____

    _____

    _____

    _____

THINKING ABOUT AND APPLYING THE ECONOMICS OF AGING AND HEALTH CARE

I. Who Pays for Social Security?

According to current law, both workers and employers pay equal amounts in Social Security taxes; in 1990, both paid 7.65 percent of the worker's wages in Social Security taxes. But who really pays these taxes? Let's look at the effects of Social Security taxes on labor markets and on an employer's decisions about employment.

Remember the company making handwoven doormats from recycled rope that you started back in the chapter on resource markets? Let's use those figures to analyze the effects of Social Security taxes. From the employer's point of view, the tax reduces the *MRP* of labor, since the employer doesn't get to keep all the income the workers produce—some of that income goes to the government.

1. In the following table, calculate the amount of the Social Security tax (7.65 percent of *MFC*), and the *MRP* after the tax. Draw the *MRP* before tax and after tax on the right-hand graph, and find the number of workers hired before and after the tax.

Number of Workers	Mats per Hour	MPP	Price per Mat	Total Revenue	MR	MRP	Wage per Hour	Total Labor Cost	MFC (before tax)	Tax (7.65% of MFC)	MRP (after tax)
1	8	8	$2.00	$16	$2	$16	$4.00	$ 4.00	$4.00	_____	_____
2	19	11	2.00	38	2	22	4.00	8.00	4.00	_____	_____
3	26	7	2.00	52	2	14	4.00	12.00	4.00	_____	_____
4	30	4	2.00	60	2	8	4.00	16.00	4.00	_____	_____
5	32	2	2.00	64	2	4	4.00	20.00	4.00	_____	_____
6	33	1	2.00	66	2	2	4.00	24.00	4.00	_____	_____

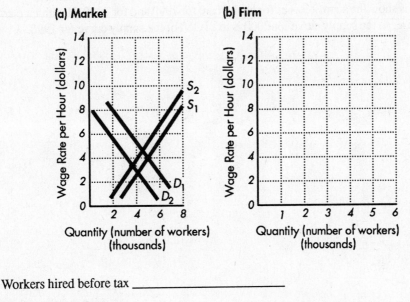

(a) Market   (b) Firm

Workers hired before tax _____

Workers hired after tax _____

2. The tax reduced the demand for labor, didn't it? Social Security taxes are also levied on individual workers (7.65 percent of your pay), so the tax reduces the wages you get to spend, and this reduction in wages will reduce the supply of labor. Curves D_2 and S_2 on the left graph show the effects of the decrease in the supply and demand for labor and the drop in equilibrium price to $3.80 per hour. In the following table, recalculate the tax and the *MRP* after tax, and find the number of workers hired.

Number of Workers	Mats per Hour	*MPP*	Price per Mat	Total Revenue	*MR*	*MRP*	Wage per Hour	Total Labor Cost	*MFC* (before tax)	Tax (7.65% of *MFC*)	*MRP* (after tax)
1	8	8	$2.00	$16	$2	$16	$4.00	$ 4.00	$3.80	____	____
2	19	11	2.00	38	2	22	4.00	8.00	3.80	____	____
3	26	7	2.00	52	2	14	4.00	12.00	3.80	____	____
4	30	4	2.00	60	2	8	4.00	16.00	3.80	____	____
5	32	2	2.00	64	2	4	4.00	20.00	3.80	____	____
6	33	1	2.00	66	2	2	4.00	24.00	3.80	____	____

Workers hired after tax _____

3. Before the tax, what was the wage rate? _____ After the tax, what is the wage rate a worker actually gets to take home and spend? _____

II. The Inelastic Demand for Health Care

As medical technology has developed and as doctors have raised their fees, the cost of providing health care has risen sharply. Part of the reason why cost increases have resulted in large price increases is that the demand for health care is inelastic: since private or government health insurance pays for most health care, individual consumers don't respond much to price increases by reducing the amount of health care demanded.

The following graphs show the supply curves for health care for 1990 and for 2000. Health-care costs are expected to continue to rise, so the supply curve for 2000 is to the left of the supply curve for 1990.

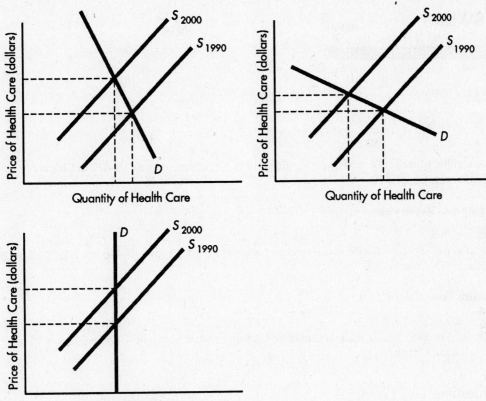

1. The graph on the left has an inelastic demand curve for health care, like the current situation in the United States today. When the supply curve shifts from 1990 to 2000, does this have a large or small effect on the price paid for health care? _____ A large or small effect on the quantity of health care bought? _____

2. The graph on the right shows a more elastic demand curve for health care, which would result if individual consumers had to pay directly for any health-care services they chose to buy. Compared with the graph on the left, does the supply shift cause a larger or smaller change in the price of health care?

   _____ In the quantity of health care bought? _____

3. The graph on the bottom shows a perfectly inelastic demand curve for health care. This demand curve might result from developing a national health insurance plan like that discussed in the "Economically Speaking" section of the text. Explain why the demand curve for health care would be perfectly inelastic if government paid for all health-care costs, and describe how government could limit health care expenses under this proposal. You'll need to refer back to the "Economically Speaking" section before you answer.

_____

_____

_____

_____

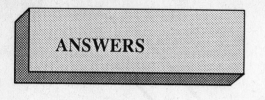

ANSWERS

Quick Check Quiz

Section 1: The Household

1. b; 2. e

If you missed either of these questions, you should go back and review pages 476–479 in Chapter 18 (pages 848–851 in *Economics*, Chapter 32).

Section 2: Aging and Retirement

1. d; 2. a; 3. e; 4. e; 5. d

If you missed any of these questions, you should go back and review pages 479–486 in Chapter 18 (pages 851–858 in *Economics*, Chapter 32).

Section 3: Health Economics

1. c; 2. d; 3. a; 4. a; 5. e; 6. a; 7. b; 8. c

If you missed any of these questions, you should go back and review pages 487–498 in Chapter 18 (pages 859–870 in *Economics*, Chapter 32).

Practice Questions and Problems

Section 1: The Household

1. benefits; costs
2. utility; labor
3. costs of caring for children
   costs of feeding children
   time involved in raising children
4. increased; decrease; lower

Section 2: Aging and Retirement

1. relationship between age, earnings, and productivity
   pension benefits
   Social Security benefits
2. workers; employers; the same
3. part
4. all

Section 3: Health Economics

1. larger
2. rapidly
3. inelastic; does not

4. a. It won't. With health insurance, the office visit is free to you. Of course, it's not free to the insurance company.
    b. No. Again, the tests don't cost you anything directly.
    c. No. If the doctor owns the testing lab or is worried about malpractice suits, she has an incentive to order as many tests as possible.
    d. In an HMO, the doctor is paid a set amount to take care of you for the year. Spending money on tests costs the doctor money, so she has an incentive to avoid unnecessary tests or other expenses.
5. a. (1) Government should pay the costs for some groups, such as retirees. (2) Government should set standards for medical practice in order to ration the amount of care available.
    b. Like other goods and services, health care takes resources. Providing unlimited amounts of health care to everyone would not leave enough resources for other things like food and shelter.

Thinking About and Applying the Economics of Aging and Health Care

I. Who Pays for Social Security?

1.

Number of Workers	Mats per Hour	MPP	Price per Mat	Total Revenue	MR	MRP	Wage per Hour	Total Labor Cost	MFC (before tax)	Tax (7.65% of MFC)	MRP (after tax)
1	8	8	$2.00	$16	$2	$16	$4.00	$ 4.00	$4.00	$.31	$15.69
2	19	11	2.00	38	2	22	4.00	8.00	4.00	.31	21.69
3	26	7	2.00	52	2	14	4.00	12.00	4.00	.31	13.69
4	30	4	2.00	60	2	8	4.00	16.00	4.00	.31	7.69
5	32	2	2.00	64	2	4	4.00	20.00	4.00	.31	3.69
6	33	1	2.00	66	2	2	4.00	24.00	4.00	.31	1.69

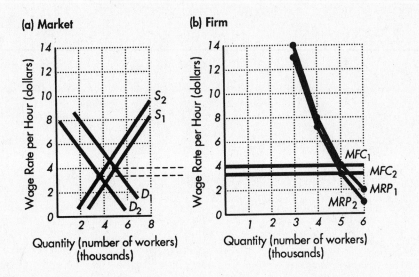

Workers hired before tax: 5
Workers hired after tax: 4
Refer back to the chapter on resource markets if you don't remember how to find the number of workers hired.

2.

Number of Workers	Mats per Hour	MPP	Price per Mat	Total Revenue	MR	MRP	Wage per Hour	Total Labor Cost	MFC (before tax)	Tax (7.65% of MFC)	MRP (after tax)
1	8	8	$2.00	$16	$2	$16	$4.00	$ 4.00	$3.80	$.29	$15.71
2	19	11	2.00	38	2	22	4.00	8.00	3.80	.29	21.71
3	26	7	2.00	52	2	14	4.00	12.00	3.80	.29	13.71
4	30	4	2.00	60	2	8	4.00	16.00	3.80	.29	7.71
5	32	2	2.00	64	2	4	4.00	20.00	3.80	.29	3.71
6	33	1	2.00	66	2	2	4.00	24.00	3.80	.29	1.71

Workers hired after tax: 4

3. Wage rate before tax: $4.00

Wage rate after tax: $3.51

The wage rate after tax is $3.80 minus 7.65 percent ($.29): $3.80 − .29 = $3.51.

II. The Inelastic Demand for Health Care

1. large; small
2. smaller; larger
3. Under a national health insurance plan, where all health-care costs are paid by the government, there is no incentive for an individual consumer to reduce the amount of health care consumed when the price rises. The demand for health care will be perfectly inelastic—completely insensitive to price.

   Restricting access to some kinds of health care (fewer coronary bypass operations, for example) or providing lower-quality care (requiring tonsil removals to be outpatient procedures, for example), are some of the possible ways to lower costs. Almost any way of lowering costs significantly would require providing less health care than people would want.

CHAPTER 19*
Income Distribution, Poverty, and Government Policy

FUNDAMENTAL QUESTIONS

1. Are incomes distributed equally in the United States?

   No. In a market system, income is derived from ownership of resources: people with more resources, or with more highly valued resources, receive higher incomes. Doctors are more highly paid than ditch diggers; people who have accumulated lots of capital receive more interest than people without any savings. In the United States, the top 5 percent of income earners receives 16 percent of the total national income, and the bottom 20 percent of the population gets only 5 percent of the national income.

   A **Lorenz curve** shows the degree of income inequality within a society. If all incomes are the same, the Lorenz curve is a straight line; the more unequally distributed incomes are, the more bowed the Lorenz curve becomes. Lorenz curves provide an easy way to compare income distributions across countries or within the same country at different times in history.

2. How is poverty measured, and does poverty exist in the United States?

   Poverty can be measured in two different ways. The statistics and Lorenz curve look at poverty in relative terms: by what share of the national income the poorest people get. Poverty can also be looked at in absolute terms: by what standard of living is necessary to meet basic human needs. The official U.S. poverty statistics gathered by the federal government use an absolute standard to set the minimum income level that avoids poverty, based on the cost of a nutritionally adequate diet. Officially, income includes earnings and **cash transfers,** but not **in-kind transfers** such as food stamps or Medicaid. Using this standard, about 13 percent of the U.S. population—about 30 million people—live in poverty.

3. Who are the poor?

   The incidence of poverty is distributed unevenly across groups within the United States. The percentage of families headed by a female that are below the poverty line is much higher than that of families headed by a male; black and Hispanic families have larger percentages below the poverty line than do white families. The poor are primarily those without jobs, those residing either in the centers of large cities or in rural areas, and those without much education.

   Many people who are poor stay that way for only a little while; they find new jobs, for example, and move back above the poverty line again. But there are a large number of people for whom poverty is a normal condition. Of those people in poverty at any specific time, about half of them will still be in poverty in ten years.

*Economics Chapter 33.

4. What are the determinants of income?

For individuals, the major determinants of income are things that affect the marginal productivity of a person's labor: endowments of skill and intelligence, human capital, work intensity, and age. Other factors include luck, compensating wage differentials, risk taking, inherited wealth, and discrimination. For nations, resource endowments and the political and social environment are important determinants of income.

5. How does the government try to reduce poverty?

Changing the income distribution in society has been the main target of government policy to reduce poverty; since 1929, income inequality in the United States has decreased. **Progressive income taxes,** whereby richer people pay proportionately more of their income in taxes, reduce income inequality and generate revenue that can be used for transfer payments to the poor. The main transfer programs are as follows:

social insurance (Social Security, unemployment compensation, Medicare)
cash welfare (Aid to Families with Dependent Children, Supplemental Security Income)
in-kind transfers (Medicaid, food stamps)
other programs (job training, Head Start)

These transfer programs may have reduced the incentives to work and may have increased the number of poor people. Several welfare reforms are under consideration, including tying benefits to work (**workfare**) and establishing parents' financial responsibility for their children's care. Economists have long proposed a **negative income tax** as a way to overcome the effects of welfare on incentives to work, but the idea has not been politically popular.

KEY TERMS

Lorenz curve	progressive income tax	workfare
cash transfers	proportional tax	negative income tax (NIT)
in-kind transfers	regressive tax	

QUICK CHECK QUIZ

Section 1: Income Distribution and Poverty

1. The graph showing the degree of income inequality within a society is called the
    a. Lorenz curve.
    b. in-kind curve.
    c. poverty line.
    d. poverty ratio plot.
    e. absolute income standard.

Use the graph below to answer question 2.

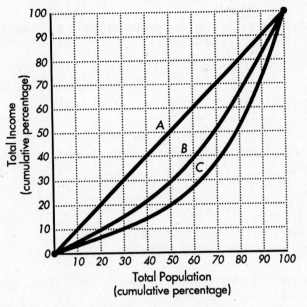

2. Which of the following statements about these Lorenz curves is/are correct?
   a. Line A shows the most unequally distributed income.
   b. Line C shows a more equal income distribution than line B does.
   c. Line A shows a perfectly equal distribution.
   d. All of the above are correct.
   e. Only a and b above are correct.

3. Relative to developed nations, less developed nations have
   a. the same income distribution.
   b. a more unequal income distribution.
   c. a more equal income distribution.
   d. an almost perfectly equal income distribution.
   e. an almost perfectly unequal income distribution.

4. The U.S. official statistics define poverty
   a. as a relative measure, based on the income level of the poorest 15 percent of the population.
   b. as an absolute measure, based on the cost of a nutritionally adequate diet.
   c. as an absolute measure, based on the cost of housing.
   d. as a relative measure, based on the income level of the poorest 5 percent of the population.
   e. as a relative measure, based on the accumulated wealth of the poorest 10 percent of the population.

5. In determining whether a family has a standard of living above or below the poverty line, the official U.S. statistics include as income
   a. only money earned by family members.
   b. money earned by family members, plus cash transfers.
   c. money earned by family members, plus in-kind transfers.
   d. money earned by family members, plus cash and in-kind transfers.
   e. money earned by the head of household, plus cash and in-kind transfers.

Section 2: The Poor

1. Of the people currently below the poverty line, what percentage are expected to still be below the poverty line in ten years?
   a. about 5 percent
   b. about 15 percent
   c. about 30 percent
   d. about 50 percent
   e. about 75 percent

2. Which of the groups below have a higher percentage of their members in poverty compared with the average for the United States?
   a. Hispanics
   b. blacks
   c. families headed by women
   d. All of the above have a higher poverty percentage.
   e. Only b and c above have a higher poverty percentage.

3. Which of the following is NOT a determinant of income?
   a. natural endowments of skill or intelligence
   b. luck
   c. work intensity
   d. human capital
   e. All of the above are determinants of income.

Section 3: Government Policies

1. A progressive tax has a rate that
   a. declines as income increases, leading to the more equal distribution of income.
   b. declines as income increases, leading to the less equal distribution of income.
   c. increases as income increases, leading to the more equal distribution of income.
   d. increases as income increases, leading to the less equal distribution of income.
   e. stays the same as income increases, having no effect on income distribution.

2. A regressive tax has a rate that
   a. declines as income increases, leading to the more equal distribution of income.
   b. declines as income increases, leading to the less equal distribution of income.
   c. increases as income increases, leading to the more equal distribution of income.
   d. increases as income increases, leading to the less equal distribution of income.
   e. stays the same as income increases, having no effect on income distribution.

3. A proportional tax has a rate that
   a. declines as income increases, leading to the more equal distribution of income.
   b. declines as income increases, leading to the less equal distribution of income.
   c. increases as income increases, leading to the more equal distribution of income.
   d. increases as income increases, leading to the less equal distribution of income.
   e. stays the same as income increases, having no effect on income distribution.

4. Workfare is a plan that
   a. requires welfare recipients to accept public-service jobs or participate in job training.
   b. encourages welfare recipients to join the military for training.
   c. limits the amount of time a person can receive welfare benefits.
   d. requires welfare recipients to spend a minimum of four hours per day looking for a job.
   e. bases welfare payments on a person's previous income.

5. When talking about income distribution, the term *equity* is used to mean
   a. equal distribution of income.
   b. equal opportunities to earn income.
   c. equal transfer payments for all.
   d. all of the above.
   e. only a and b above.

PRACTICE QUESTIONS AND PROBLEMS

Section 1: Income Distribution and Poverty

1. The _____ curve shows the amount of income inequality within a society.

2. The table below gives income distribution data for the United States and Mexico for the late 1980s. On the graph below, draw the Lorenz curves for the two countries. Which country has a more equal income distribution? _____

	Lowest 20%	Second 20%	Third 20%	Fourth 20%	Highest 20%
Mexico	3	7	12	20	58
U.S.	5	12	18	25	40

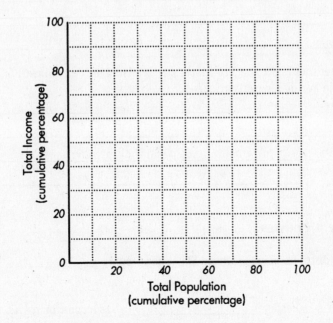

3. The poverty line for 1989 said that a family of four was in poverty if its income was less than
   a. $6,252.
   b. $8,752.
   c. $10,117.
   d. $12,675.
   e. $15,260.

4. The definition of income for calculating whether a family is below the poverty line includes

   _____ from resource markets and _____ transfers, but

   doesn't include _____ transfers.

5. Poverty _____ (increases, decreases) when the economy enters a recession, and

   _____ (increases, decreases) when the economy is growing strongly.

Section 2: The Poor

1. A nation may be poor because it lacks _____ endowments or because of the

   _____ and _____ environment created by its government.

2. The poor are primarily those without _____.

3. In terms of age, the highest incidence of poverty is for _____. Older people are

   _____ (more, less) likely to be poor than middle-aged people.

4. List several determinants of income.

   _____

   _____

   _____

   _____

   _____

5. Looking at all the statistics in Section 2 of the chapter, which of the determinants of income seems to be
   the most important in avoiding poverty? Explain.

   _____

   _____

   _____

   _____

Section 3: Government Policies

1. Since 1929, income distribution in the United States has become _____ (more

   equal, less equal).

2. A progressive tax has a rate that _____ as income increases.

3. A regressive tax has a rate that _____ as income increases.

4. A proportional tax has a rate that _____ as income increases.

5. The four main types of programs used to fight poverty in the United States are as follows:

   _____

   _____

   _____

   _____

6. List the three specific transfer programs that serve the most people. (Hint: Check Table 2 in the text.)

Program Name	Number of People Served
_____	_____
_____	_____
_____	_____

7. _____ is a plan that requires welfare recipients to accept public-service jobs or participate in job training.

THINKING ABOUT AND APPLYING INCOME DISTRIBUTION, POVERTY, AND GOVERNMENT POLICY

I. Welfare, Workfare, and Incentives to Work

The "Economically Speaking" section of the chapter looks at two examples of the effects of welfare programs on incentives to work. Let's look at this problem in some more detail.

1. Use what you have learned in this chapter and previous chapters about the supply of labor to explain why generous welfare programs in New York City might increase the number of people living in poverty in New York.

   _____

   _____

   _____

   _____

2. How would a workfare program change incentives? Do you think workfare is a good idea or a bad idea? Why?

   _____

   _____

   _____

   _____

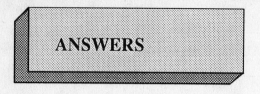

ANSWERS

Quick Check Quiz

Section 1: Income Distribution and Poverty

1. a; 2. c; 3. b; 4. b; 5. b

If you missed any of these questions, you should go back and review pages 504–512 in Chapter 19 (pages 876–884 in *Economics*, Chapter 33).

Section 2: The Poor

1. d; 2. d; 3. e

If you missed any of these questions, you should go back and review pages 513–516 in Chapter 19 (pages 885–888 in *Economics*, Chapter 33).

Section 3: Government Policies

1. c; 2. b; 3. e; 4. a; 5. e

If you missed any of these questions, you should go back and review pages 516–525 in Chapter 19 (pages 888–897 in *Economics*, Chapter 33).

Practice Questions and Problems

Section 1: Income Distribution and Poverty

1. Lorenz
2. U.S.

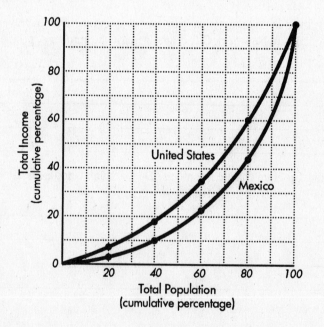

3. d
4. earnings; cash; in-kind

5. increases; decreases

Section 2: The Poor

1. resource; political; social
2. jobs
3. young people; more
4. endowments of skills and intelligence; work intensity; human capital; compensating wage differentials; luck; risk taking; age; inherited wealth; discrimination
5. Human capital, specifically education. Only 4 percent of those with one year or more of college fall below the poverty line, whereas 25 percent of the people with less than eight years of education are below the poverty line.

Section 3: Government Policies

1. more equal
2. increases
3. decreases
4. stays the same
5. social insurance
   cash welfare
   in-kind transfers
   employment programs
6. Social Security; 37.1 million people
   food stamps; 22.4 million people
   Medicaid; 21.9 million people
7. Workfare

Thinking About and Applying Income Distribution, Poverty, and Government Policy

I. Welfare, Workfare, and Incentives to Work

1. Welfare programs raise the opportunity cost of working. Not only do you have to give up leisure to work, but you also have to give up welfare benefits. The more generous the welfare benefits are, the more people will have opportunity costs of working that are too high to make working worthwhile: they're better off staying on welfare.
2. Workfare removes the choice of not working and staying on welfare. It reduces the opportunity cost of working by making nonworkers ineligible for welfare benefits. Whether it's a good idea or not depends partly on your values.

CHAPTER 20*
The Environment

1. How is the rate of use of exhaustible resources determined?

   Like other resources, the supply and demand for exhaustible resources determine the amount produced per year. Because exhaustible resources can be used only once, the markets for exhaustible resources take into account both present and future demand and supply. In general, exhaustible resources will be used at a rate that gives a rate of return on exhaustible resources that is comparable to rates of return on other assets. The higher the interest rate (the return on other assets) is, the faster an exhaustible resource will be used; the lower the interest rate, the slower the resource will be used.

   To illustrate this relationship, let's say you own an oil well. You can produce oil from the well this year or wait and produce the oil sometime in the future. If you're willing to wait until next year to spend your income from the oil well, you have two choices:

   a. You can produce the oil now, sell it, and put the money in the bank for a year.
   b. You can wait until next year to produce the oil, sell it then, and spend the money.

   Since you will earn interest on your money if you produce the oil now, the only reason why you would be willing to wait until next year to produce the oil is that you can get a higher price for it then. All other things equal, the rate of use of exhaustible natural resources will be just fast enough that the price rises at the rate of interest.

2. How do exhaustible natural resources differ from nonexhaustible natural resources?

   Exhaustible natural resources are those of which there is a fixed amount on and in the earth, with no practical way of making more. Examples are minerals such as coal, oil, gold, and so on. **Nonexhaustible natural resources** are those that can renew themselves: living organisms such as wheat, trees, or fish, and natural resources such as clean air and clean water that can, if not used too intensively, renew themselves naturally.

3. Why is an externality considered to be a source of market failure?

   Ideally, markets balance the marginal social costs and marginal social benefits of the product, and market failure occurs when **social costs** do not equal social benefits. **Externalities** exist whenever **private costs** or benefits are different from social costs or benefits. If market decision makers pay attention only to equating private costs and benefits, then social costs and benefits will not be the same.

Economics Chapter 34.

4. How can market failures be resolved?

Market failures can be resolved in several ways: by assigning private property rights instead of common ownership, or through regulation, taxes and subsidies, or public ownership.

5. How does agriculture contribute to U.S. environmental problems?

Agriculture is subsidized in several ways in the United States, many of which lead to environmental problems. When subsidy programs allow farmers to plant only a single crop year after year, damage to the soil is likely. Subsidies based on total production lead to increased use of fertilizer and pesticides, and subsidies based on the amount of land used tend to bring less-desirable pieces of land into cultivation, often leading to more erosion.

6. How do global environmental problems differ from domestic environmental problems?

The lack of property rights is a major problem in global environmental problems. Nobody owns the air that blows from the United States into Canada. If U.S. power plant emissions cause acid rain in Canada, there is no market or government mechanism that allows the Canadians to restrict the behavior of U.S. firms, unless the Canadian government can convince the U.S. government to intervene. Solving global pollution problems requires governments to cooperate, sometimes in ways that aren't beneficial to their own interests.

KEY TERMS

exhaustible natural resources	social costs	emission standard
nonexhaustible natural resources	principle of mutual exclusivity	Coase Theorem
	public good	bubble
private costs	free rider	emissions offset policy
externality		

QUICK CHECK QUIZ

Section 1: Natural Resources

1. Natural resources that cannot be replaced or renewed are known as
   a. scarce natural resources.
   b. nonexhaustible natural resources.
   c. unlimited natural resources.
   d. exhaustible natural resources.
   e. limited natural resources.

2. Natural resources that can be replaced or renewed are known as
   a. scarce natural resources.
   b. nonexhaustible natural resources.
   c. unlimited natural resources.
   d. exhaustible natural resources.
   e. limited natural resources.

3. The increase over time in the price of exhaustible natural resources generates a rate of return that is
    a. greater than the interest rate on comparable assets.
    b. equal to the interest rate on comparable assets.
    c. less than the interest rate on comparable assets.
    d. unrelated to the interest rate.
    e. the inverse of the interest rate.

4. The harvest rate of nonexhaustible natural resources is such that the rate of return on the resources is
    a. greater than the interest rate on comparable assets.
    b. equal to the interest rate on comparable assets.
    c. less than the interest rate on comparable assets.
    d. unrelated to the interest rate.
    e. the inverse of the interest rate.

5. From an economic point of view, conservation refers to
    a. saving all exhaustible natural resources for future use.
    b. saving all nonexhaustible natural resources for future use.
    c. using natural resources at the optimal rate.
    d. saving most but not all exhaustible natural resources for future use.
    e. saving most but not all nonexhaustible natural resources for future use.

Section 2: Market Failures

1. Externalities occur when
    a. someone outside a business makes decisions that affect the business.
    b. an activity creates costs or benefits that are borne by parties not directly involved in the activity.
    c. free riding does not exist.
    d. taxes affect the amount of a good produced.
    e. private benefits are equal to social benefits.

2. When private costs are less than social costs,
    a. an externality exists.
    b. a market failure exists.
    c. the market will produce too much of the good.
    d. All of the above are true.
    e. Only a and c above are true.

3. Public goods are goods
    a. for which the principle of mutual exclusivity does not apply.
    b. for which one person's consumption of the good doesn't reduce the amount of the good available for others to consume.
    c. concerning which free riding does not occur.
    d. for which all of the above are true.
    e. for which only a and b above are true.

4. Which of the following is *not* a public good?
   a. national defense
   b. police protection
   c. broadcast television
   d. pizza
   e. All of the above are public goods.

Section 3: Policies

1. Which of the following is NOT one of the policies followed by the U.S. government in attempting to improve the environment?
   a. public ownership
   b. regulations
   c. taxes and subsidies
   d. assignment of private property rights
   e. All of the above are policies of the U.S. government.

2. The Coase Theorem says that problems created by lack of property rights can be resolved by those affected as long as
   a. someone is assigned the property right—it doesn't matter who.
   b. the person causing an externality is assigned the property right.
   c. the person bearing the burden of an externality is assigned the property right.
   d. the government assigns the property right to a government agency.
   e. the parties to a problem assign the property right to the government.

3. In U.S. environmental policy, an emission standard is
   a. the minimum amount of clean air that may be emitted.
   b. a maximum allowable level of pollution from a specific source.
   c. a minimum allowable level of pollution from a wide area made up of many sources.
   d. a policy enabling a firm to trade off one type of emission for another as long as the total emissions remain below some standard.
   e. a policy wherein pollution permits are issued and a market in the permits then develops.

4. In U. S. environmental policy, a bubble is
   a. the minimum amount of clean air that may be emitted.
   b. a maximum allowable level of pollution from a specific source.
   c. a minimum allowable level of pollution from a wide area made up of many sources.
   d. a policy enabling a firm to trade off one type of emission for another as long as the total emissions remain below some standard.
   e. a policy wherein pollution permits are issued and a market in the permits then develops.

5. In U.S. environmental policy, an emissions offset policy is
   a. the minimum amount of clean air that may be emitted.
   b. a maximum allowable level of pollution from a specific source.
   c. a minimum allowable level of pollution from a wide area made up of many sources.
   d. a policy enabling a firm to trade off one type of emission for another as long as the total emissions remain below some standard.
   e. a policy wherein pollution permits are issued and a market in the permits then develops.

PRACTICE QUESTIONS AND PROBLEMS

Section 1: Natural Resources

1. Oil is a(n) _____ (exhaustible, nonexhaustible) natural resource because it _____ (can, cannot) be renewed.

2. Forests are a(n) _____ (exhaustible, nonexhaustible) natural resource because they _____ (can, cannot) be renewed.

3. The price of an exhaustible resource usually goes up at the same rate as the _____.

4. Higher interest rates lead to the _____ (faster, slower) use of natural resources.

5. Conservation refers to the _____ (optimal use, non-use) of a natural resource.

Section 2: Market Failures

1. _____ occur when all the costs or benefits of an activity are not borne by parties directly involved in the activity.

2. _____ occur when social costs and benefits are not equal.

3. When social costs are higher than private costs, the market will produce _____ (too much, not enough) of the product.

4. Public goods are goods or services to which the principle of _____ does not apply.

5. You and your neighbors have decided to hire a private guard to patrol your neighborhood after dark to scare away burglars. Use your knowledge from this chapter to explain why your private guard is a public good, why problems with free riding are likely to appear, and why police services are usually provided by governments rather than private groups.

   _____

   _____

   _____

   _____

Section 3: Policies

1. The optimal level of pollution is reached when the marginal _____ from a cleaner environment equal the marginal _____ of cleaning up the environment.

2. Give the name of the environmental policy that matches each description.

   a. Pollution permits are issued and a market in permits develops. _____

   b. A maximum allowable level of pollution from a specific source is set. _____

   c. A firm can trade off one emission for another as long as the total remains below some standard.

   _____

3. Let's make you the director of the Environmental Protection Agency. You have to decide how much pollution a particular water treatment plant should be allowed to produce. Right now, the plant produces 4 tons of pollutants per day; the plant is owned by the federal government, so any cleanup costs must be paid for through taxes. The costs and benefits of reducing pollution are shown below. Find the amount of pollution that gives consumers the most net gain (total gains from pollution reduction minus total costs of pollution reduction).

Tons per Day	Marginal Benefits	Marginal Costs
3	$10 million	$ 1 million
2	5 million	4 million
1	2 million	16 million
0	1 million	100 million

Tons per day with highest net value _____

As director of the EPA, how do you explain to hostile environmentalists why you didn't require the plant to clean up all its pollution?

_____

_____

_____

_____

THINKING ABOUT AND APPLYING THE ENVIRONMENT

I. Oil Wells and Interest Rates

Let's suppose you own a small oil well that produces one barrel of oil per day if you run the pump. If you don't run the pump, the oil stays in the ground and you can produce it later. Running the pump costs you $1 for every barrel you pump; you don't have any other costs to consider.

1. Your oil today sells for $21 per barrel. If the interest rate is 10 percent per year and you expect oil to sell for $24 per barrel next year, are you better off to pump and sell a barrel of oil today, or leave it in the ground for next year? Explain why.

_____

_____

_____

_____

2. If the interest rate is 10 percent, what is the minimum price next year that will convince you to wait until next year to sell your oil? _____

3. If the interest rate is 5 percent, what is the minimum price next year that will convince you to wait until next year to sell your oil? _____

II. Hamburger Packaging and Pollution Policies

The "Economically Speaking" section of this chapter looks at the costs of trash, including fast-food packaging. The graph below shows the demand and marginal costs of producing hamburgers *(MC)*, not including the cost of disposing of the packaging, and the full cost of producing hamburgers *(MSC)*, which includes the costs of disposal.

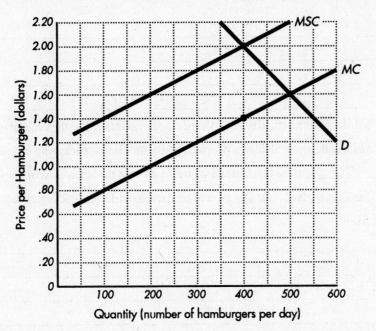

1. In a perfectly competitive market, how many hamburgers will be sold every day at what price?

   Number sold _____ Price _____

2. What is the optimal number of hamburgers and price, taking into account the cost of disposing of the packaging?

   Number sold _____ Price _____

3. What is the marginal social cost of disposing of the hamburger packaging? _____

4. Suppose the government wants to limit the amount of trash from hamburger packaging. If it sets an "emission standard" limiting the number of packages the hamburger stand can throw away, what would be an economically efficient emission standard? _____ Would setting this standard provide any incentives for the hamburger stand to develop different packaging techniques that reduced trash? Explain.

    _____

    _____

    _____

    _____

5. Suppose instead that the government sets an "effluent charge" to internalize the costs of disposing of the packaging. How much is the optimal charge per package for the current packaging technique? _____ If the effluent charge were based on the actual cost of disposing of the packaging, would the hamburger stand have any incentive to develop different packaging techniques that reduce trash? Explain.

    _____

    _____

    _____

    _____

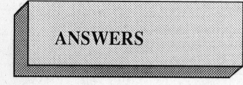

ANSWERS

Quick Check Quiz

Section 1: Natural Resources

1. d; 2. b; 3. b; 4. b; 5. c

If you missed any of these questions, you should go back and review pages 532–538 in Chapter 20 (pages 904–910 in *Economics*, Chapter 34).

Section 2: Market Failures

1. b; 2. d; 3. e; 4. d

If you missed any of these questions, you should go back and review pages 538–544 in Chapter 20 (pages 910–916 in *Economics*, Chapter 34).

Section 3: Policies

1. a; 2. a; 3. b; 4. d; 5. e

If you missed any of these questions, you should go back and review pages 544–555 in Chapter 20 (pages 916–927 in *Economics*, Chapter 34).

Practice Questions and Problems

Section 1: Natural Resources

1. exhaustible; cannot
2. nonexhaustible; can
3. rate of interest
4. faster
5. optimal use

Section 2: Market Failures

1. Externalities
2. Market failures
3. too much
4. mutual exclusivity
5. The guard is a public good because scaring away burglars benefits everyone in the neighborhood. If only some of your neighbors are willing to pay for the guard, everyone in the neighborhood will gain. Since people benefit even if they don't pay, free riding will be a problem. By levying taxes on everyone, governments get around free-rider problems, since you don't have a choice about paying taxes.

Section 3: Policies

1. benefits; costs
2. a. emissions offset
   b. emission standard
   c. bubble
3. 2 tons per day

   Removing the first ton of pollution (going from 4 tons to 3 tons) gives $10 million in benefits at a cost of only $1 million, for a net gain of $9 million. Removing the second ton of pollution (going from 3 tons to 2 tons) gives $5 million in benefits at a cost of $4 million, for a net gain of $1 million. Removing the third ton of pollution (going from 2 tons to 1 ton) gives only $2 million in benefits at a cost of $16 million, for a net loss of $14 million.

   Getting rid of the third ton of pollution isn't worth it, since the marginal benefits are less than the marginal cost. People value other things more highly than they value that additional pollution reduction.

Thinking About and Applying the Environment

I. Oil Wells and Interest Rates

1. You should leave it for next year. If you produce the oil now, you gain $20 now—the $21 price minus your $1 cost for pumping. If you save the $20 until next year at 10 percent interest, next year you will have $22 ($20 + $2 interest). If you wait till next year to produce the oil, you will have $23 next year ($24 price − $1 costs). $23 is better than $22.
2. $23. After you subtract your $1 cost, you would get $22 next year, the same as you would get by producing this year and saving the money for a year.

3. $22. If the interest rate is 5 percent, producing your oil now and saving the money gives you $21 next year—the $20 now plus only $1 interest. To make it worth waiting until next year, you will have to get at least $22 next year.

II. Hamburger Packaging and Pollution Policies

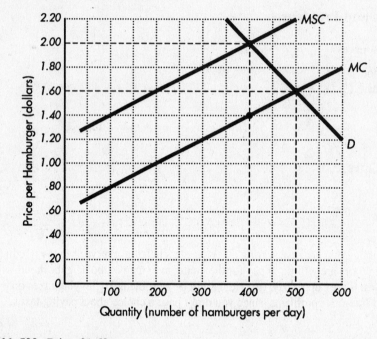

1. Number sold: 500 Price: $1.60
   In a perfectly competitive market, the equilibrium price and quantity are where the demand curve crosses the *MC* curve.
2. Number sold: 400 Price: $2.00
   The optimal number of hamburgers is where the demand curve and the *MSC* curve cross.
3. $.60 per hamburger—the difference between the *MSC* and *MC* curves at each quantity.
4. 400 packages per day—with this standard, the optimal number of hamburgers will be produced.
   No. Since the hamburger stand is limited to 400 packages per day and doesn't have to pay for the costs of disposing of the packaging, it has no incentive to find packaging materials that reduce disposal costs.
5. $.60—the cost of disposing of the packaging
   If the "effluent charge" is based on the actual cost of disposing of the packaging, the hamburger stand can save itself money by finding different techniques that reduce packaging costs. In general, using effluent charges provides more incentives for reducing pollution than does setting emission standards.

CHAPTER 21*
The Government and Public Choice

FUNDAMENTAL
QUESTIONS

1. Why is the government so heavily involved in our lives?

There's no doubt that government is heavily involved in our lives; its spending and rule making affect all of us. Economists give three general reasons for the growth of government. The **public interest theory of government** says that the government exists to serve the public interest. The **capture theory of government** says that the government exists to serve special-interest groups. The **public choice theory of government** combines elements of both viewpoints with basic economic concepts to analyze government.

2. What is the public choice theory of government?

Public choice theory takes the basic economic ideas of individual self-interest and maximizing behavior and uses them to examine government decision making. The fundamental assumption of public choice theory is that the objective of politicians and government workers is the maximization of their own self-interest or utility. For politicians, this implies doing the things that are most likely to get them re-elected.

3. How is the political market different from other markets?

In public choice theory, politicians sell government goods and services for votes; votes to politicians are like dollars to sellers in other markets. There are two main differences between political markets and other markets, however. As a consumer, you can buy individual goods and services from a variety of sellers. As a voter, you do not have that much choice: you have to choose among a few politicians, each one offering a **full-line supply** of positions on issues.

   The second difference comes from majority voting. Businesses try to maximize profits, whereas politicians do not have to maximize the number of votes they get; they only have to attract a majority of voters. The **median voter theorem** implies that politicians will choose positions that satisfy the average (or median) voter.

4. What role does rent seeking play in the economy?

Rent-seeking activities are directed toward gaining economic rents. They typically consume resources but do not increase output. Much special-interest legislation is based on rent seeking. For example, sugar beet growers in the United States hire lobbyists and make donations to political campaign funds in order to have import restrictions placed on sugar from other countries. The import restrictions generate economic rents for the sugar beet growers, but they do not increase output. Lobbying for import restrictions does use resources.

*Economics Chapter 35.

KEY TERMS

public interest theory of government
capture theory of government
public choice theory of government
full-line supply
median voter theorem

logrolling
excise tax
rents
rent seeking

QUICK CHECK QUIZ

Section 1: Justifications and Explanations of Government Activities

1. According to the public interest theory of government, government actions are taken in the interests of
   a. government policymakers.
   b. the median voter.
   c. special-interest groups.
   d. the public.
   e. those government employees who deal directly with the public.

2. According to the capture theory of government, government actions are taken in the interests of
   a. government policymakers.
   b. the median voter.
   c. special-interest groups.
   d. the public.
   e. those government employees who deal directly with the public.

3. According to the public choice theory of government, government actions are taken in the interests of
   a. government policymakers.
   b. the median voter.
   c. special-interest groups.
   d. the public.
   e. those government employees who deal directly with the public.

4. In public choice theory, politicians act
   a. in their own self-interest.
   b. in the best interests of the nation.
   c. in the best interests of their political party.
   d. to help special-interest groups in the economy.
   e. in the best interests of the neediest members of society.

Section 2: Public Choice and the Political Market

1. The median voter theorem says that
   a. politicians try to fool all of the people all of the time.
   b. on issues about which there is a continuum of views, politicians choose a position where half the voters want more and half want less.
   c. politicians try to provide the same average benefits to all voters.
   d. politicians decide how to vote by looking at the way other politicians vote.
   e. issues are decided on the basis of the average of what both sides want.

2. When economists talk about politicians' "full-line supply," they are referring to
   a. politicians who have speeches prepared on all possible subjects.
   b. the bundle of policies offered by a candidate.
   c. special-interest groups that try to buy politicians' votes regardless of their other positions.
   d. trading votes among politicians.
   e. the need of political parties to satisfy a wide range of viewpoints.

3. An excise tax is a tax on
   a. the sale of all commodities.
   b. the sale of all services.
   c. incomes above the poverty line.
   d. incomes below the poverty line.
   e. the sale of a particular commodity.

4. To politicians, logrolling refers to
   a. using log cabins as political props.
   b. trading votes or support in return for votes or support on other issues.
   c. bombarding voters with large amounts of printed materials.
   d. wealth provided to special-interest groups in return for political support.
   e. accepting contributions from special-interest groups on both sides of an issue.

Section 3: Rent Seeking

1. Rent-seeking activities are activities that produce
   a. zero output while consuming resources in an attempt to obtain economic rents.
   b. votes in exchange for votes on other issues.
   c. improvements in the well-being of the general public.
   d. increases in the price of land.
   e. increased occupancy of apartments.

2. Which of the following would NOT be classified as rent seeking?
   a. Barbers lobby a state legislature for restrictions on the number of barbers in the state.
   b. Wheat farmers lobby for government price supports.
   c. Small meat packers lobby for restrictions on the actions of larger, more efficient packers.
   d. Pacifists lobby for reductions in defense spending.
   e. All of the above are examples of rent-seeking behavior.

PRACTICE QUESTIONS AND PROBLEMS

Section 1: Justifications and Explanations of Government Activities

1. List the theory of government that matches the definition.

   a. _____ theory: Government actions benefit special-interest groups.

   b. _____ theory: Government actions promote the self-interest of politicians and
   government workers.

   c. _____ theory: Government actions improve the well-being of the general
   public.

2. In public choice theory, politicians act in ways that maximize their _____ .

Section 2: Public Choice and the Political Market

1. In public choice theory, what are the specific goals of each group listed below?

    a. political candidates: _____

    b. bureaucrats: _____

    c. voters and special-interest groups: _____

2. The _____ explains why political parties frequently take very similar positions.

3. _____ explains why a politician from New York may be willing to vote for a government project that only benefits people in Nevada.

Section 3: Rent Seeking

1. Wealth provided to special-interest groups in return for political support is called

    _____ .

2. Rent-seeking activities produce _____ output while consuming

    _____ in an attempt to obtain _____ .

3. Competition among rent seekers tends to _____ rents and may help force rent

    seekers to be more _____ .

THINKING ABOUT AND APPLYING THE GOVERNMENT AND PUBLIC CHOICE

I. Spending and Taxes

Use what you have learned in this chapter to explain why it is much easier for elected governments to raise spending than to raise taxes.

_____

_____

_____

_____

II. Pigging Out at the Public Trough

The "Economically Speaking" section for this chapter looks at a book listing federal government assistance programs and the costs and benefits to people in Congress of sponsoring legislation. Suppose that each piece of legislation that spent money had to contain a tax high enough to cover the money spent. Describe how this would affect the costs and benefits of special-interest legislation.

_____

_____

_____

_____

ANSWERS

Quick Check Quiz

Section 1: Justifications and Explanations of Government Activities

1. d; 2. c; 3. a; 4. a
   If you missed any of these questions, you should go back and review pages 562–567 in Chapter 21 (pages 934–939 in *Economics*, Chapter 35).

Section 2: Public Choice and the Political Market

1. b; 2. b; 3. e; 4. b
   If you missed any of these questions, you should go back and review pages 567–575 in Chapter 21 (pages 939–947 in *Economics*, Chapter 35).

Section 3: Rent Seeking

1. a; 2. d
   If you missed any of these questions, you should go back and review pages 575–579 in Chapter 21 (pages 947–951 in *Economics*, Chapter 35).

Practice Questions and Problems

Section 1: Justifications and Explanations of Government Activities

1. a. capture
    b. public choice
    c. public interest
2. utility (or self-interest)

Section 2: Public Choice and the Political Market

1. a. get elected
   b. acquire income, power, and prestige
   c. obtain wealth and privileges
2. median voter model
3. Logrolling

Section 3: Rent Seeking

1. rents
2. zero; resources; economic rents
3. dissipate; efficient

Thinking About and Applying the Government and Public Choice

I. Spending and Taxes

Spending creates benefits for at least some people within society, and these benefits are likely to translate into votes for the politicians supplying the spending. Taxes, on the other hand, are never popular with the people paying them, and they are likely to result in votes against politicians who raise taxes.

II. Pigging Out at the Public Trough

With current procedures, the costs to politicians of sponsoring legislation are the time and effort spent on logrolling. Tying a tax to each spending proposal would add voter dissatisfaction to the costs to politicians of sponsoring legislation. The equilibrium amount of legislation would be lower than under the current system.

CHAPTER 22*
World Trade Equilibrium

1. What are the prevailing patterns of trade between countries? What goods are traded?

   Trade occurs because specialization in production, based on **comparative advantage,** leads to increased output. Countries specialize in those products for which their opportunity costs are lower than costs in other nations; countries then trade what they produce beyond their own consumption and receive other countries' products in return.

   The bulk of world trade occurs within the industrialized group of countries; trade between the industrialized countries and developing countries accounts for most of the rest. Canada is the largest buyer of U.S. exports, and Japan is the largest source of U.S. imports. Oil, automobiles, and machinery are the goods that have the largest trading volume, although world trade occurs across a great variety of products.

2. What determines the goods a nation will export?

   A nation exports those goods for which it has a comparative advantage over other nations—that is, those goods for which its opportunity costs are lower than the opportunity costs of other nations. The **terms of trade**—how much of an exported good must be given up to obtain one unit of an imported good—are limited by the domestic opportunity costs of the trading countries.

3. How are the equilibrium price and the quantity of goods traded determined?

   As with most other markets, demand and supply determine the equilibrium price and quantity. For internationally traded goods, the **export supply curve** shows how much countries will be willing to export at different world prices. The **import demand curve** shows how much countries are willing to import at different world prices. Where the import demand curve and the export supply curve intersect is the international equilibrium price and quantity traded.

4. What are the sources of comparative advantage?

   There are two major sources of comparative advantage: productivity differences and factor abundance. Productivity differences come from differences in labor productivity and human capital, and from differences in technology. Factor abundance affects comparative advantage because countries have different resource endowments. The United States, with a large amount of high-quality farmland, has a comparative advantage in agriculture.

   Productivity differences and factor abundance explain most, but not all, trade patterns. Other sources of comparative advantage are human skills differences, product life cycles, and consumer preferences. Consumer preferences explain **intraindustry trade,** in which countries are both exporters and importers of a product. Some consumers prefer brands made in their own country; other consumers prefer foreign brands.

*Economics Chapter 36.

KEY TERMS

absolute advantage

comparative advantage

terms of trade

export supply curve

import demand curve

intraindustry trade

QUICK CHECK QUIZ

Section 1: An Overview of World Trade

1. The bulk of world trade occurs
   a. in the Eastern trading area.
   b. among the developing countries.
   c. among the industrial countries.
   d. between the developing and industrial countries.
   e. between the industrial countries and the Eastern trading area.

2. The United States imports the most from
   a. Canada.
   b. Germany.
   c. Japan.
   d. Mexico.
   e. the USSR.

3. The United States exports the most to
   a. Canada.
   b. Germany.
   c. Japan.
   d. Mexico.
   e. the USSR.

4. The most heavily traded good in the world is
   a. crude petroleum.
   b. airplanes.
   c. automobiles.
   d. televisions.
   e. wheat.

Section 2: An Example of International Trade Equilibrium

1. A nation has an absolute advantage in producing a good when
   a. it can produce a good for a lower input cost than can other nations.
   b. the opportunity cost of producing a good, in terms of the forgone output of other goods, is lower than that of other nations.
   c. it can produce a good for a higher input cost than can other nations.
   d. the opportunity cost of producing a good, in terms of the forgone output of other goods, is higher than that of other nations.
   e. the nation's export supply curve is below its import demand curve.

2. A nation has a comparative advantage in producing a good when
   a. it can produce a good for a lower input cost than can other nations.
   b. the opportunity cost of producing a good, in terms of the forgone output of other goods, is lower than that of other nations.
   c. it can produce a good for a higher input cost than can other nations.
   d. the opportunity cost of producing a good, in terms of the forgone output of other goods, is higher than that of other nations.
   e. the nation's export supply curve is below its import demand curve.

3. The terms of trade are the
   a. price of your country's currency in terms of another country's currency.
   b. price of another country's currency in terms of your country's currency.
   c. amount of an export good that must be given up to obtain one unit of an import good.
   d. amount of an import good that must be given up to obtain one unit of an export good.
   e. amount of imports divided by the amount of exports.

4. The limits on the terms of trade are determined by the
   a. difference between the domestic and world price.
   b. domestic opportunity costs of production within one country.
   c. domestic opportunity costs of production within each country.
   d. ratio of the domestic price to the world price.
   e. ratio of the world price to the domestic price.

5. The export supply and import demand curves for a country measure the
   a. international surplus and shortage, respectively, at different world prices.
   b. international shortage and surplus, respectively, at different world prices.
   c. domestic surplus and shortage, respectively, at different world prices.
   d. domestic shortage and surplus, respectively, at different world prices.
   e. domestic surplus and shortage, respectively, at different exchange rates.

Section 3: Sources of Comparative Advantage

1. The productivity-differences explanation of comparative advantage stresses
   a. differences in labor productivity among countries.
   b. the advantage that comes to a country that is the first to develop and produce a product.
   c. the relative amounts of skilled and unskilled labor in a country.
   d. differences in the amounts of resources countries have.
   e. differences in tastes within a country.

2. The factor-abundance explanation of comparative advantage stresses
   a. differences in labor productivity among countries.
   b. the advantage that comes to a country that is the first to develop and produce a product.
   c. the relative amounts of skilled and unskilled labor in a country.
   d. differences in the amounts of resources countries have.
   e. differences in tastes within a country.

322 / Chapter 22

3. The human-skills explanation of comparative advantage stresses
   a. differences in labor productivity among countries.
   b. the advantage that comes to a country that is the first to develop and produce a product.
   c. the relative amounts of skilled and unskilled labor in a country.
   d. differences in the amounts of resources countries have.
   e. differences in tastes within a country.

4. The product-life-cycle explanation of comparative advantage stresses
   a. differences in labor productivity among countries.
   b. the advantage that comes to a country that is the first to develop and produce a product.
   c. the relative amounts of skilled and unskilled labor in a country.
   d. differences in the amounts of resources countries have.
   e. differences in tastes within a country.

5. The consumer-preferences explanation of comparative advantage stresses
   a. differences in labor productivity among countries.
   b. the advantage that comes to a country that is the first to develop and produce a product.
   c. the relative amounts of skilled and unskilled labor in a country.
   d. differences in the amounts of resources countries have.
   e. differences in tastes within a country.

PRACTICE QUESTIONS AND PROBLEMS

Section 1: An Overview of World Trade

1. The country that imports the most from the United States is _____; the country that exports the most to the United States is _____.

2. World trade is _____ (distributed across many products, dominated by only a few products).

3. The product that accounts for the most world trade is _____.

4. Use Table 1 in the text to answer these questions.

   a. Trade within industrial countries accounts for what percentage of world trade?
      _____

   b. Trade within and between industrial and developing countries accounts for what percentage of world trade? _____

Section 2: An Example of International Trade Equilibrium

1. _____ (Comparative, Absolute) advantage is based on the relative opportunity costs of producing goods in different countries.

2. _____ (Comparative, Absolute) advantage occurs when a country can produce a good for a lower input cost than can other nations.

© 1991 Houghton Mifflin Company. All rights reserved.

3. The _____ are the amount of an export good that must be given up to obtain one unit of an import good.

4. The _____ (export supply, import demand) curve is derived from the domestic surplus at different world prices.

5. The _____ (export supply, import demand) curve is derived from the domestic shortage at different world prices.

6. The table below shows the number of hours of labor needed to produce a ton of mangos and a ton of papayas in Samoa and in Fiji.

	Samoa	Fiji
Mangos	2	6
Papayas	1	2

   a. Which country has an absolute advantage in producing mangos? _____

   b. Which country has an absolute advantage in producing papayas? _____

   c. What is the opportunity cost of 1 ton of papayas in Samoa? _____

   d. What is the opportunity cost of 1 ton of papayas in Fiji? _____

   e. Which country has a comparative advantage in papayas? _____

   f. What is the opportunity cost of 1 ton of mangos in Samoa? _____

   g. What is the opportunity cost of 1 ton of mangos in Fiji? _____

   h. Which country has a comparative advantage in mangos? _____

   i. The limits on the terms of trade are 1 ton of mangos for between _____ and _____ tons of papayas.

7. The graphs below show the soybean markets in the United States and in France (assuming that no other country in the world is involved in trade in soybeans).

   a. Before doing any analysis, let's look at the soybean markets in the United States and France. The price in the United States without trade is _____ per bushel; in France it is _____ per bushel. Since market prices reflect opportunity costs, which country has a comparative advantage in soybean production, and should export soybeans?

   _____

   b. On the "World" graph below, draw in the import demand and export supply curves for the United States and France; then find the equilibrium world price and quantity traded, and the amounts produced and consumed in the United States and France.

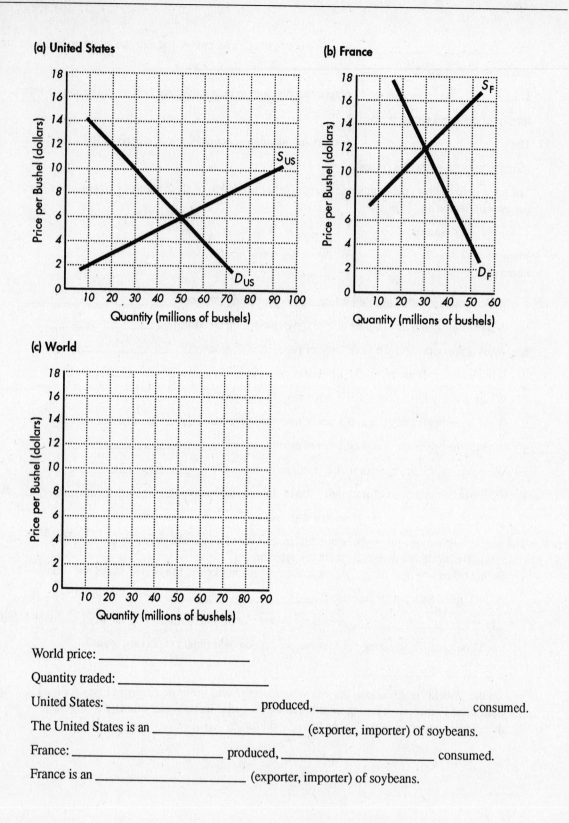

(a) United States

(b) France

(c) World

World price: _____

Quantity traded: _____

United States: _____ produced, _____ consumed.

The United States is an _____ (exporter, importer) of soybeans.

France: _____ produced, _____ consumed.

France is an _____ (exporter, importer) of soybeans.

c. In the problem above, what was the effect of trade on the price of soybeans in the United States and in France?

United States: _____

France: _____

Section 3: Sources of Comparative Advantage

1. Name the comparative-advantage theory that matches each explanation of comparative advantage listed below.

   a. _____ : differences in labor productivity among countries

   b. _____ : the advantage that comes to a country that is the first to develop and produce a product

   c. _____ : the relative amounts of skilled and unskilled labor in a country

   d. _____ : differences in the amounts of resources countries have

   e. _____ : differences in tastes within a country

2. The productivity-differences theory of comparative advantage is known as the _____ model.

3. The factor-abundance theory of comparative advantage is known as the _____ model.

4. Differences in consumer tastes within a country explain _____ , in which a country is both an exporter and importer of a differentiated product.

THINKING ABOUT AND APPLYING WORLD TRADE EQUILIBRIUM

I. World Trade Equilibrium

The graphs on the following page show the domestic markets for wheat in the United States, Canada, Argentina, and the USSR. Draw the import demand and export supply curves for the four countries, sum the import demand and export supply curves for the four countries to draw the world import demand and export supply curves on the world graph, find the equilibrium world price and quantity traded, and find the amounts produced and consumed in the four countries.

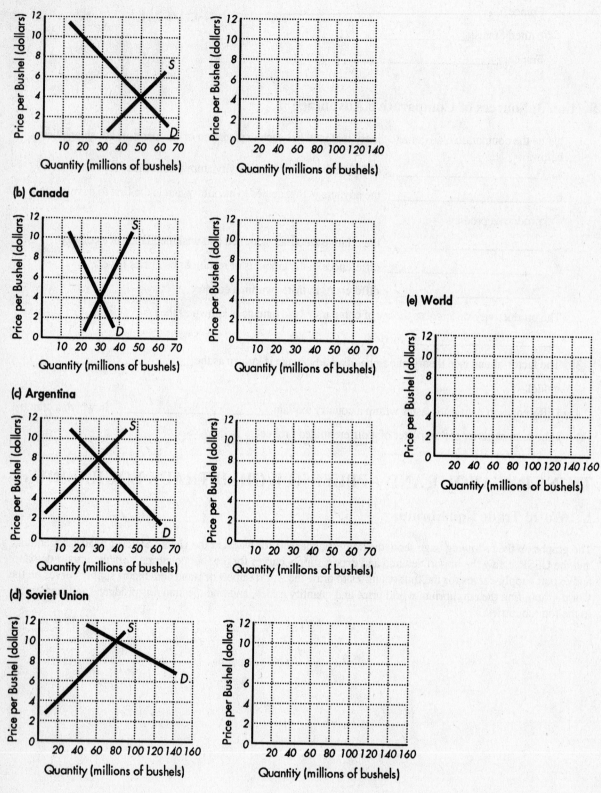

(a) United States

(b) Canada

(c) Argentina

(d) Soviet Union

(e) World

World price: _____

Quantity traded: _____

United States: _____ produced, _____ consumed.

The United States is a(n) _____ (exporter, importer, nontrader) of wheat.

Canada: _____ produced, _____ consumed.

Canada is a(n) _____ (exporter, importer, nontrader) of wheat.

Argentina: _____ produced, _____ consumed.

Argentina is a(n) _____ (exporter, importer, nontrader) of wheat.

USSR: _____ produced, _____ consumed.

The USSR is a(n) _____ (exporter, importer, nontrader) of wheat.

II. Triangular Trade

The "Economically Speaking" section for this chapter discusses the trade imbalance between the United States and Japan and the idea that trade between any two countries need not balance as long as each country's trade with all countries taken together is roughly balanced. Let's look a little further at this idea.

The graphs on the following page show the domestic markets for oranges, bananas, and sugar in Guatemala, Honduras, and Costa Rica. Draw the import demand and export supply curves for the three countries for each product, sum the import demand and export supply curves for each product to draw the world import demand and export supply curves on the world graphs, find the equilibrium world price and quantity traded for each product, the amounts produced and consumed of each product in each country, and the status of each country as an importer, exporter, or nontrader. Sketch the pattern of trade flows among the three countries. (Hint: Look at the picture in the "Economically Speaking" section.)

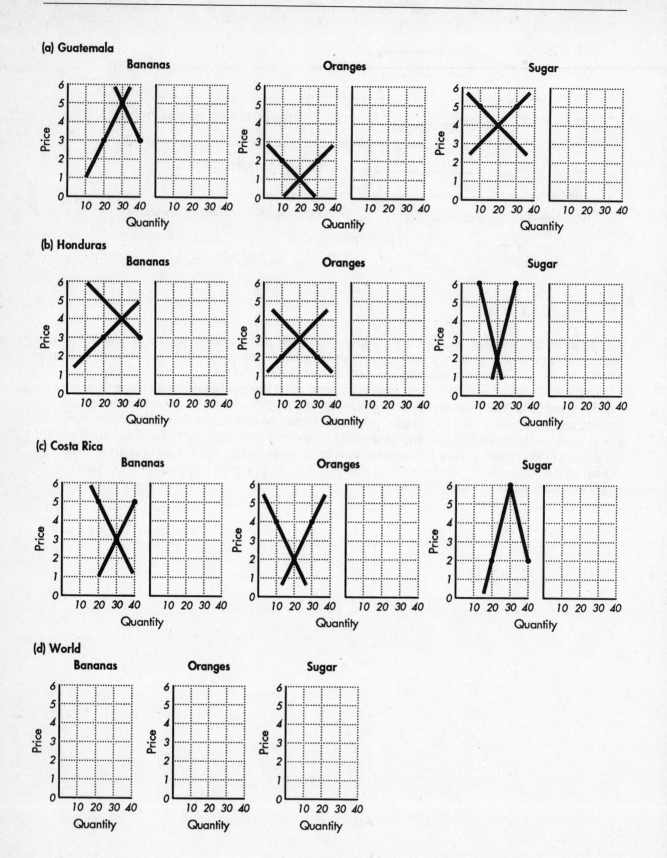

(a) Guatemala

Bananas   Oranges   Sugar

(b) Honduras

Bananas   Oranges   Sugar

(c) Costa Rica

Bananas   Oranges   Sugar

(d) World

Bananas   Oranges   Sugar

	World Price	Quantity Traded
Oranges	$_____	_____
Bananas	_____	_____
Sugar	_____	_____

	Amount Produced	Amount Consumed	Status
Guatemala			
Oranges	_____	_____	_____
Bananas	_____	_____	_____
Sugar	_____	_____	_____
Honduras			
Oranges	_____	_____	_____
Bananas	_____	_____	_____
Sugar	_____	_____	_____
Costa Rica			
Oranges	_____	_____	_____
Bananas	_____	_____	_____
Sugar	_____	_____	_____

Pattern of trade flows:

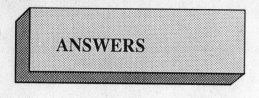

Quick Check Quiz

Section 1: An Overview of World Trade

1. c; 2. c; 3. a; 4. a

   If you missed any of these questions, you should go back and review pages 588–591 in Chapter 22 (pages 960–963 in *Economics*, Chapter 36).

Section 2: An Example of International Trade Equilibrium

1. a; 2. b; 3. c; 4. c; 5. c

   If you missed any of these questions, you should go back and review pages 591–599 in Chapter 22 (pages 963–971 in *Economics*, Chapter 36).

Section 3: Sources of Comparative Advantage

1. a; 2. d; 3. c; 4. b; 5. e

   If you missed any of these questions, you should go back and review pages 599–603 in Chapter 22 (pages 971–975 in *Economics*, Chapter 36).

Practice Questions and Problems

Section 1: An Overview of World Trade

1. Canada; Japan
2. distributed across many products
3. crude oil
4. a. 54.8 percent
   b. 85.5 percent

Section 2: An Example of International Trade Equilibrium

1. Comparative
2. Absolute
3. terms of trade
4. export supply
5. import demand
6. a. Samoa
      Mangos cost only 2 hours of labor in Samoa; they cost 6 hours of labor in Fiji.
   b. Samoa
      Papayas cost only 1 hour of labor in Samoa; they cost 2 hours of labor in Fiji.
   c. 1/2 ton of mangos
      Mangos take twice as much labor time as papayas in Samoa, so you can produce half as many mangos in the same amount of time.
   d. 1/3 ton of mangos
      Mangos take three times as much labor time as papayas in Fiji, so you can produce one third as many mangos in the same amount of time.

e. Fiji
Fiji has the lower opportunity cost: it has to give up only 1/3 ton of mangos to get a ton of papayas, whereas Samoa has to give up 1/2 ton.

f. 2 tons of papayas
Papayas take half as much labor time as mangos in Samoa, so you can produce twice as many papayas in the same amount of time.

g. 3 tons of papayas
Papayas take one-third as much labor time as mangos in Fiji, so you can produce three times as many papayas in the same amount of time.

h. Samoa
Samoa has the lower opportunity cost: it has to give up only 2 tons of papayas to get a ton of mangos, whereas Fiji has to give up 3 tons.

i. 2; 3

7. a. $6; $12; United States

b.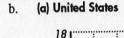

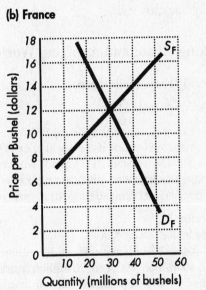

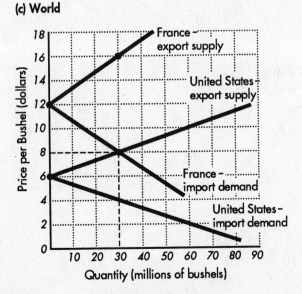

World price: $8
Quantity traded: 30 million
United States: 70 million produced, 40 million consumed; exporter
France: 10 million produced, 40 million consumed; importer

c. United States: price up from $6 to $8
    France: price down from $12 to $8

Section 3: Sources of Comparative Advantage

1. a. productivity differences
    b. product life cycle
    c. human skills
    d. factor abundance
    e. consumer preferences
2. Ricardian
3. Heckscher-Ohlin
4. intraindustry trade

Thinking About and Applying World Trade Equilibrium

I. World Trade Equilibrium

See solution on page 333.

The domestic prices before trade vary between $4 (United States and Canada) and $10 (USSR). The USSR will begin demanding imports if the world price is below $10; if the price goes below $8, Argentina will also demand imports. The United States and Canada will begin supplying exports if the world price goes above $4; if the price goes above $8, Argentina will also supply exports. The "World" graph shows the amounts these countries will supply (export) and demand (import) at various prices.

World price: $8
Quantity traded: 60 million
United States: 70 million produced, 30 million consumed; exporter
Canada: 40 million produced, 20 million consumed; exporter
Argentina: 30 million produced and consumed; nontrader
USSR: 60 million produced, 120 million consumed; importer

II. Triangular Trade

See solution on page 334.

	World Price	Quantity Traded
Oranges	$2	20
Bananas	4	20
Sugar	4	10

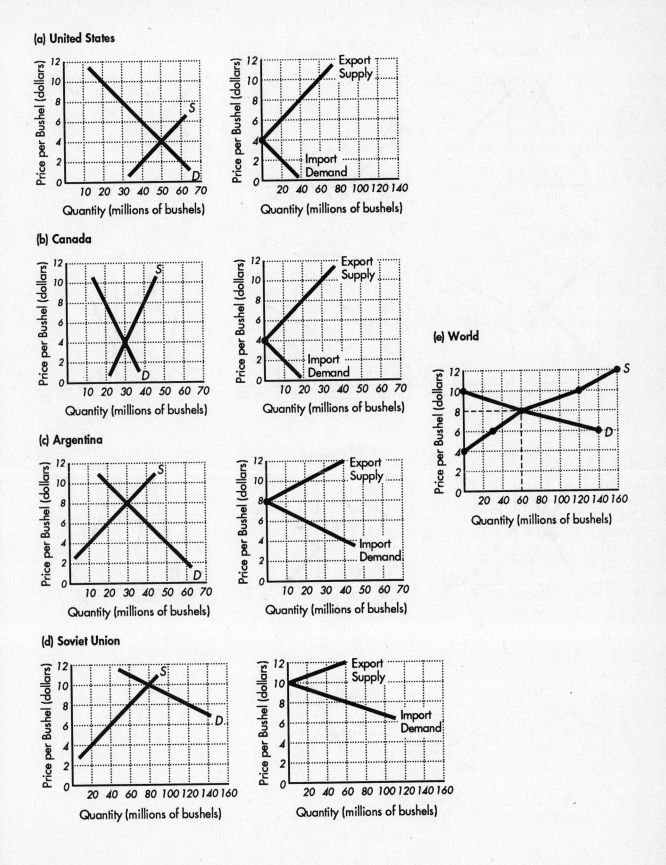

(a) United States

(b) Canada

(c) Argentina

(d) Soviet Union

(e) World

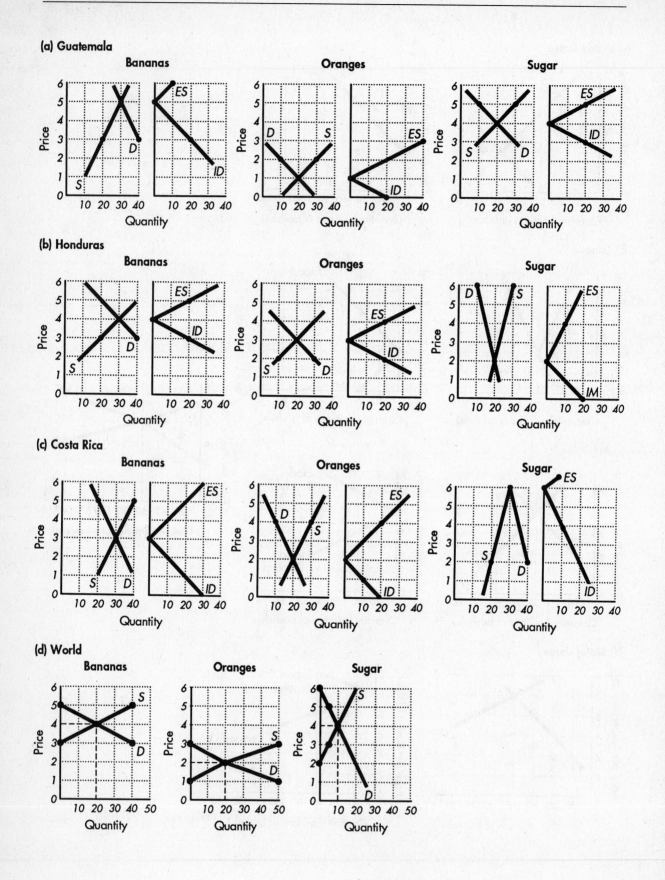

	Amount Produced	Amount Consumed	Status
Guatemala			
Oranges	30	10	Exporter
Bananas	25	35	Importer
Sugar	20	20	Nontrader
Honduras			
Oranges	10	30	Importer
Bananas	30	30	Nontrader
Sugar	25	15	Exporter
Costa Rica			
Oranges	20	20	Nontrader
Bananas	35	25	Exporter
Sugar	25	35	Importer

Pattern of trade flows:

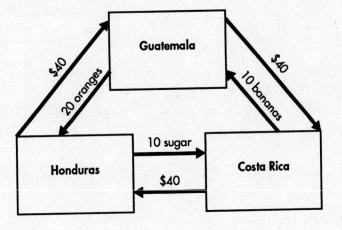

CHAPTER 23*
Commercial Policy

1. Why do countries restrict international trade?

    Most countries follow some sort of **commercial policy** to influence the direction and volume of international trade. Despite the costs to domestic consumers, countries frequently try to protect domestic producers by restricting international trade. Lobbying for trade restrictions is an example of the rent-seeking activities discussed in the chapter on government and public choice.

    To help hide the special-interest nature of most trade restrictions, several arguments are commonly used. These include saving domestic jobs, creating fairer trade, raising revenue through tariffs, protecting key defense industries, allowing new industries to become competitive, and giving **decreasing-cost industries** an advantage over foreign competitors. Although a few of these arguments have some validity, most have little or no merit.

2. How do countries restrict the entry of foreign goods and promote the export of domestic goods?

    Several tactics are frequently used for these purposes. **Tariffs,** or taxes on products imported into the United States, protect domestic industries by raising the price of foreign goods. Quotas restrict the amount or value of a foreign product that may be imported; **quantity quotas** limit the amount of a good that may be imported, and **value quotas** limit the monetary value of a good that may be imported. **Subsidies,** payments made by government to domestic firms, both encourage exports and make domestic products cheaper to foreign buyers. In addition, a wide variety of other tactics, such as health and safety standards, are used to restrict imports.

3. What sorts of agreements do countries enter into to reduce trade barriers to international trade?

    Groups of countries can establish **free trade areas,** where member countries have no trade barriers among themselves, or **customs unions,** where member countries not only abolish trade restrictions among themselves but also set common trade barriers on nonmembers. The United States and Canada established a free trade area in 1987. The best-known customs union is the European Economic Community (EEC), composed of most of the countries in Western Europe. Because they do not include all countries, free trade areas can result in both **trade diversion,** which reduces efficiency, and **trade creation,** which allows a country to obtain goods at lower cost.

Economics Chapter 37.

KEY TERMS

commercial policy
decreasing-cost industry
tariffs
quantity quota

value quota
subsidies
free trade area

customs union
trade diversion
trade creation

QUICK CHECK QUIZ

Section 1: Arguments for Protection

1. The basic objective of commercial policy is to
   a. promote free and unrestricted international trade.
   b. protect domestic consumers from dangerous, low-quality imports.
   c. protect domestic producers from foreign competition.
   d. protect foreign producers from domestic consumers.
   e. promote the efficient use of scarce resources.

2. Using trade restrictions to save domestic jobs
   a. usually costs consumers much more than the job saved is worth.
   b. usually just redistributes jobs from other industries to the protected industry.
   c. may provoke other countries to restrict U.S. exports.
   d. does all of the above.
   e. does only b and c above.

3. Some arguments for trade restrictions have some economic validity. Which of the following arguments has NO economic validity?
   a. the infant industry argument
   b. the national defense argument
   c. the government revenue creation from tariffs argument
   d. the creation of domestic jobs argument
   e. All of the above have some economic validity.

4. The objective of strategic trade policy is to
   a. protect those industries needed for national defense.
   b. provide domestic decreasing-cost industries an advantage over foreign competitors.
   c. develop economic alliances with other countries.
   d. carefully develop free trade areas to counteract customs unions.
   e. increase government revenues through tariffs.

Section 2: Tools of Policy

1. A tariff is a
   a. tax on imports or exports.
   b. government-imposed limit on the amount of a good that may be imported.
   c. government-imposed limit on the value of a good that may be imported.
   d. payment by government to domestic producers.
   e. payment by government to foreign producers.

2. A subsidy is a
   a. tax on imports or exports.
   b. government-imposed limit on the amount of a good that may be imported.
   c. government-imposed limit on the value of a good that may be imported.
   d. payment by government to domestic producers.
   e. payment by government to foreign producers.

3. A quantity quota is a
   a. tax on imports or exports.
   b. government-imposed limit on the amount of a good that may be imported.
   c. government-imposed limit on the value of a good that may be imported.
   d. payment by government to domestic producers.
   e. payment by government to foreign producers.

4. A value quota is a
   a. tax on imports or exports.
   b. government-imposed limit on the amount of a good that may be imported.
   c. government-imposed limit on the value of a good that may be imported.
   d. payment by government to domestic producers.
   e. payment by government to foreign producers.

5. Which of the following are NOT used to restrict trade?
   a. health and safety standards
   b. government procurement regulations requiring domestic purchasing
   c. subsidies
   d. cultural and institutional practices
   e. All of the above are used to restrict trade.

Section 3: Preferential Trade Agreements

1. An organization of nations whose members have no trade barriers among themselves but are free to fashion their own trade policies toward nonmembers is a
   a. customs union.
   b. trade group.
   c. international cartel.
   d. free trade area.
   e. internation economic alliance.

2. An organization of nations whose members have no trade barriers among themselves but impose common trade barriers on nonmembers is a
   a. customs union.
   b. trade group.
   c. international cartel.
   d. free trade area.
   e. internation economic alliance.

3. Trade diversion occurs when a preferential trade agreement
   a. allows a country to buy imports from a nonmember country at a lower price than that charged by member countries.
   b. reduces economic efficiency by shifting production to a higher-cost producer.
   c. allows a country to obtain goods at a lower cost than is available at home.
   d. reduces trade flows between nonmember countries.
   e. increases economic efficiency by shifting production to a higher-cost producer.

4. Trade creation occurs when a preferential trade agreement
   a. allows a country to buy imports from a nonmember country at a lower price than that charged by member countries.
   b. reduces economic efficiency by shifting production to a higher-cost producer.
   c. allows a country to obtain goods at a lower cost than is available at home.
   d. reduces trade flows between nonmember countries.
   e. increases economic efficiency by shifting production to a higher-cost producer.

PRACTICE QUESTIONS AND PROBLEMS

Section 1: Arguments for Protection

1. The main reason governments restrict foreign trade is to protect _____ producers from _____ competition.

2. Governments can generate revenues by restricting trade through _____; this is a common tactic in _____ (industrial, developing) countries.

3. The argument that new industries should receive temporary protection is known as the _____ argument.

4. Strategic trade policy aims at identifying industries with _____ and giving them an advantage over their foreign competitors.

5. Using trade restrictions to protect domestic jobs usually costs consumers _____ (more, less) money than the jobs are worth to the workers holding them.

6. Trade restrictions usually
   a. create more domestic jobs.
   b. just redistribute jobs within the economy.

Section 2: Tools of Policy

1. Tariffs are _____ on imports or exports. In the United States, tariffs on _____ (imports, exports) are illegal under the Constitution.

2. Quotas can be used to set limits on the _____ or _____ of a good allowed to be imported into a country.

3. When an exporting country agrees to limit its exports of a product to another country, the agreement is known as a _____ .

4. List three barriers to trade besides tariffs and quotas.

_____

_____

_____

5. The graph below shows the U.S. market for tangerines. The world price for tangerines is $10 per bushel. On the graph below, mark the quantity demanded and quantity supplied by U.S. sellers when the price is $10.

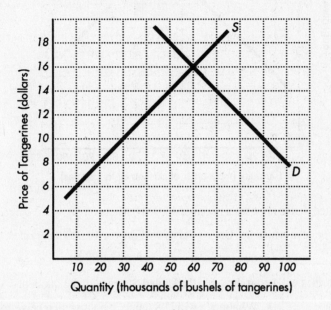

a. If the United States does not restrict imports of tangerines, it will import _____ tangerines at the price of _____.

b. Suppose the United States imposes a $4 per bushel tariff on imported tangerines. On the graph above, mark the quantity demanded and quantity supplied by U.S. sellers when the price is $14. The United States will then import _____ tangerines at a price of

_____.

c. With the $4 tariff, _____ tangerines will be produced in the United States, and U.S. growers will receive _____ per bushel.

6. The graph below shows the U.S. market for tangerines again. The world price for tangerines is again $10 per bushel.

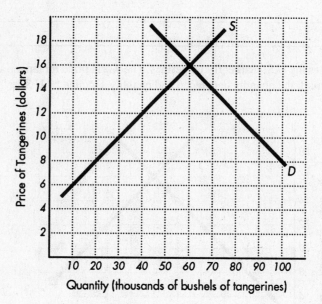

Quantity (thousands of bushels of tangerines)

a. Suppose the United States imposes a quota of 40,000 bushels on imported tangerines. On the graph above, mark the price at which the United States will import 40,000 tangerines. The price is

_____.

b. How many tangerines will be produced in the United States with the quota of 40,000?
_____ What price will U.S. tangerine growers receive for each bushel sold?

_____

Section 3: Preferential Trade Agreements

1. A _____ is a group of nations whose members have no trade barriers among themselves but impose common trade barriers on nonmembers.

2. A _____ is a group of nations whose members have no trade barriers among themselves but have their own trade policies toward nonmembers.

3. The European Economic Community is a _____ . List the six original member countries and the six that joined later.

Original Members	Later Members
_____	_____
_____	_____
_____	_____
_____	_____
_____	_____
_____	_____

THINKING ABOUT AND APPLYING COMMERCIAL POLICY

I.   Rent Seeking in the Textile and Auto Industries

Table 1 in the text shows the costs to consumers and the gains to producers from trade restrictions on various imports into the United States. The "Economically Speaking" section in the text looks at one of those industries—textiles—in detail. Let's explore some of these issues.

1. Look through Table 1. Can you find any industry for which the benefits of trade restrictions (producer

    gains) are larger than the costs (total consumer losses)? _____

2. Let's take a look at some of the reasons why trade restrictions cause net losses to the United States. Flip

    back to problem 6 in Section 2: the problem with an import quota on tangerines. Before the quota, how

    much did foreign tangerine growers receive for the tangerines they sold in the United States?

    _____ After the quota, how much did foreign tangerine growers receive for the

    tangerines they sold in the United States? _____ Do you think U.S. producers got

    to keep all the extra money U.S. consumers spent for tangerines after the quota was imposed? Explain.

    _____

    _____

    _____

    _____

3. Look back to Table 1 in your text again, and find the consumer losses and producer gains from trade restraints on automobiles.

    Consumer losses: _____

    Producer gains: _____

    In a good year, auto sales in the United States are around 10 million. How much extra per car are U.S. consumers paying, and how much extra per car are U.S. automakers receiving as a result of trade restraints?

    Consumer losses per car: _____

    Producer gains per car: _____

344 / Chapter 23

4. The most significant restriction on auto imports into the United States has been the voluntary export restraint agreement between the United States and Japan, whereby the Japanese agreed to set a quota on exports of automobiles to the United States and each Japanese automaker was given a specific number of cars that could be exported. Explain why the export quotas help prevent competition among Japanese automakers.

_____

_____

_____

_____

5. Use the ideas you learned in the chapter on government and public choice theory to explain why the U.S. government would encourage restrictions on importing Japanese autos, even though the restrictions cost U.S. car buyers large amounts of money. (Hint: Look at the title of this problem.)

_____

_____

_____

_____

ANSWERS

Quick Check Quiz

Section 1: Arguments for Protection

1. c; 2. d; 3. d; 4. b
   If you missed any of these questions, you should go back and review pages 610–616 in Chapter 23 (pages 982–988 in *Economics*, Chapter 37).

Section 2: Tools of Policy

1. a; 2. d; 3. b; 4. c; 5. e
   If you missed any of these questions, you should go back and review pages 616–622 in Chapter 23 (pages 988–994 in *Economics*, Chapter 37).

Section 3: Preferential Trade Agreements

1. d; 2. a; 3. b; 4. c
   If you missed any of these questions, you should go back and review pages 622–625 in Chapter 23 (pages 994–997 in *Economics*, Chapter 37).

Practice Questions and Problems

Section 1: Arguments for Protection

1. domestic; foreign
2. tariffs; developing
3. infant industry
4. decreasing costs
5. more
6. b

Section 2: Tools of Policy

1. taxes; exports
2. quantity; value
3. voluntary export restraint
4. subsidies
   government procurement
   health and safety standards
5.

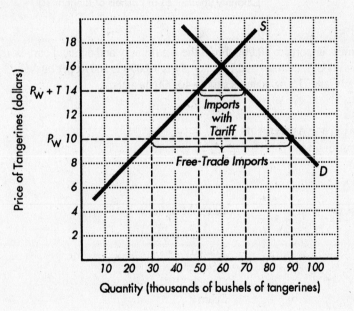

a. 60,000; $10
   At the world price of $10, the United States will demand 90,000 bushels but will produce only 30,000 bushels. The difference (90,000 – 30,000) is how much the United States will import.
b. 20,000; $14
   The tariff raises the price of tangerines in the United States to $14 (the $10 world price + the $4 tariff). At this price, U.S. consumers demand 70,000 tangerines, and U.S. producers supply 50,000, leaving 20,000 to be imported.
c. 50,000; $14

6.

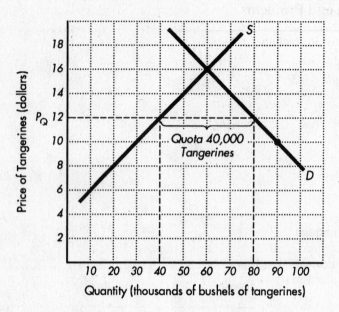

a. $12

The quota limits imports to 40,000. From the U.S. supply and demand curves, the price where the difference between U.S. demand and U.S. supply is 40,000 is at $12 per bushel: U. S. consumers buy 80,000 bushels, and U.S. producers supply 40,000 bushels.

b. 40,000; $12

Section 3: Preferential Trade Agreements

1. customs union
2. free trade area
3. customs union

Original Members	Later Members
France	United Kingdom
West Germany	Ireland
Italy	Denmark
Belgium	Greece
Netherlands	Spain
Luxembourg	Portugal

Thinking About and Applying Commercial Policy

I. Rent Seeking in the Textile and Auto Industries

1. no (Except for peanuts, where the gains are estimated to equal the losses, the losses to consumers are larger than the gains to producers.)
2. $10; $12

No; some of the extra money U.S. consumers paid went to foreign sellers of tangerines, who received a higher price.

3. Consumer losses: $5,800,000,000
    Producer gains: $2,600,000,000
    Consumer losses per car: $580
    Producer gains per car: $260
4. Cartels try to raise prices by cutting back output. From the point of view of an individual firm in a cartel, cutting price to expand sales is usually profitable; such cheating contributes to the eventual collapse of most cartels. By using the Japanese government to enforce limits on output, Japanese car makers were able to raise prices without worrying about any cheating their competitors might do.
5. Trade restraints are an example of rent-seeking behavior. Import quotas on automobiles transfer wealth from consumers (a relatively small amount from many car buyers) to automakers and auto workers (a relatively large amount to each one). The cost to car buyers is hidden in the price of the automobile and so does not provoke consumer resentment against politicians who vote for restraints. The automakers and auto workers, of course, know who is responsible for their added wealth and reward cooperative politicians with campaign contributions and votes.

CHAPTER 24*
Exchange-Rate Systems and Practices

1. How does a commodity standard fix exchange rates between countries?

   A commodity standard exists when exchange rates are based on the values of different currencies in terms of some commodity. The **gold standard,** in general use between 1880 and 1914, fixed the value of countries' currencies in terms of how much currency was needed to buy an ounce of gold. Fixing the value of currencies in terms of gold also fixes the relative value of all currencies to each other. For example, if the value of an ounce of gold is 20 U.S. dollars and its value is also 200 Mexican pesos, then a U.S. dollar has the same value as 10 Mexican pesos. As long as countries fix the value of their currencies in terms of some commodity, the relative values of those currencies also stay the same.

2. What kinds of exchange-rate arrangements exist today?

   The gold standard ended with World War I; since then many exchange-rate systems have been tried. At the present time, nations use a variety of exchange-rate arrangements, including fixed exchange rates, freely floating exchange rates, and **managed floating exchange rates.**

3. How is equilibrium determined in the foreign-exchange market?

   Equilibrium is determined in foreign-exchange markets the same way it's determined in other markets: by the intersection of supply and demand curves. The demand for a currency, such as the U.S. dollar, comes from the desire of people in other countries to buy things in the United States; the supply of U.S. currency to the foreign-exchange market comes from U.S. residents' desire to buy things from foreign countries.

4. How do fixed and floating exchange rates differ in their adjustment to shifts in supply and demand for currencies?

   With floating exchange rates, the foreign-exchange market adjusts automatically to shifts in supply and demand, the same way perfectly competitive markets for products adjust. With fixed exchange rates, a government can try to maintain the fixed rate through intervention in the foreign-exchange market, although this is unlikely to work unless the shifts in supply and demand are temporary. A **fundamental disequilibrium** usually requires a currency devaluation.

5. What are the advantages and disadvantages of fixed and floating exchange rates?

   Fixed exchange rates require that a nation match its macroeconomic policies to those of the country or countries to which its currency is pegged; this limits a country's ability to set its own policies. Floating exchange rates allow countries to follow their own macroeconomic policies.

*Economics Chapter 38.

6. What determines the kind of exchange-rate system a country adopts?

Countries can in general choose what kind of exchange-rate system they want to use. The choice seems to depend on four characteristics: how large the country is (in terms of economic output), how **open** the country's **economy** is (how large a fraction of GNP is devoted to international trade), the country's experience with inflation, and how diversified the country's international trade is.

KEY TERMS

gold standard
gold exchange standard
reserve currency
International Monetary Fund
   (IMF)
World Bank
foreign-exchange market
   intervention

equilibrium exchange rates
devaluation
managed floating exchange
   rates
special drawing right
European Monetary System
   (EMS)

appreciate
depreciate
fundamental disequilibrium
speculators
open economy
multiple exchange rates

QUICK CHECK QUIZ

Section 1: Past and Current Exchange-Rate Arrangements

1. Which of the following describes a gold standard?
   a. a currency that is used to settle international debts and that is held by governments to use in foreign-exchange market interventions
   b. an exchange-rate system in which each nation fixes the value of its currency in terms of gold but buys and sells the U.S. dollar rather than gold to maintain fixed exchange rates
   c. the buying or selling of currencies by a government or central bank to achieve a specified exchange rate
   d. the exchange rates that are established in the absence of government foreign-exchange market intervention
   e. a system whereby national currencies are fixed in terms of their value in gold, thus creating fixed exchange rates between currencies

2. Which of the following describes a gold exchange standard?
   a. a currency that is used to settle international debts and that is held by governments to use in foreign-exchange market interventions
   b. an exchange-rate system in which each nation fixes the value of its currency in terms of gold but buys and sells the U.S. dollar rather than gold to maintain fixed exchange rates
   c. the buying or selling of currencies by a government or central bank to achieve a specified exchange rate
   d. the exchange rates that are established in the absence of government foreign-exchange market intervention
   e. a system whereby national currencies are fixed in terms of their value in gold, thus creating fixed exchange rates between currencies

3. Which of the following describes a reserve currency?
   a. a currency that is used to settle international debts and that is held by governments to use in foreign-exchange market interventions
   b. an exchange-rate system in which each nation fixes the value of its currency in terms of gold but buys and sells the U.S. dollar rather than gold to maintain fixed exchange rates
   c. the buying or selling of currencies by a government or central bank to achieve a specified exchange rate
   d. the exchange rates that are established in the absence of government foreign-exchange market intervention
   e. a system whereby national currencies are fixed in terms of their value in gold, thus creating fixed exchange rates between currencies

4. Which of the following describes foreign-exchange market intervention?
   a. a currency that is used to settle international debts and that is held by governments to use in foreign-exchange market interventions
   b. an exchange-rate system in which each nation fixes the value of its currency in terms of gold but buys and sells the U.S. dollar rather than gold to maintain fixed exchange rates
   c. the buying or selling of currencies by a government or central bank to achieve a specified exchange rate
   d. the exchange rates that are established in the absence of government foreign-exchange market intervention
   e. a system whereby national currencies are fixed in terms of their value in gold, thus creating fixed exchange rates between currencies

5. Which of the following describes equilibrium exchange rates?
   a. a currency that is used to settle international debts and that is held by governments to use in foreign-exchange market interventions
   b. an exchange-rate system in which each nation fixes the value of its currency in terms of gold but buys and sells the U.S. dollar rather than gold to maintain fixed exchange rates
   c. the buying or selling of currencies by a government or central bank to achieve a specified exchange rate
   d. the exchange rates that are established in the absence of government foreign-exchange market intervention
   e. a system whereby national currencies are fixed in terms of their value in gold, thus creating fixed exchange rates between currencies

6. The Bretton Woods system
   a. created the International Monetary Fund and the World Bank.
   b. was a gold exchange standard.
   c. used the U.S. dollar as a reserve currency.
   d. tried to maintain exchange rates through foreign-exchange market intervention.
   e. was and did all of the above.

Section 2: Fixed or Floating Exchange Rates

1. Currency appreciation is
   a. a decrease in the value of a currency under floating exchange rates.
   b. an increase in the value of a currency under floating exchange rates.
   c. a decrease in the value of a currency under fixed exchange rates.
   d. an increase in the value of a currency under fixed exchange rates.
   e. resetting the pegged value of a currency.

2. Currency depreciation is
   a. a decrease in the value of a currency under floating exchange rates.
   b. an increase in the value of a currency under floating exchange rates.
   c. a decrease in the value of a currency under fixed exchange rates.
   d. an increase in the value of a currency under fixed exchange rates.
   e. resetting the pegged value of a currency.

3. Which of the following statements about fixed and floating exchange rates is false?
   a. Fixed exchange rates put pressure on a nation to manage its macroeconomic policy in concert with other nations.
   b. Floating exchange rates put pressure on a nation to manage its macroeconomic policy in concert with other nations.
   c. Speculators are more likely to be a problem under fixed exchange rates than under floating exchange rates.
   d. Fixed exchange rates can force a devaluation in the event of fundamental disequilibrium.
   e. Floating exchange rates adjust automatically to changes in demand and supply.

Section 3: The Choice of an Exchange-Rate System

1. Economically, an open economy is one in which
   a. no trade with other countries takes place.
   b. there are no trade restraints.
   c. a large fraction of the country's GNP is devoted to internationally traded goods.
   d. exchange rates are freely floating, with no government intervention in foreign-exchange markets.
   e. other nations may freely invest.

2. Which of the following circumstances would make it likely that a country would choose a fixed exchange rate?
   a. The country is large, in terms of GNP.
   b. The country has an open economy.
   c. The country's inflation experience has diverged from its trading partner's.
   d. The country has a very diversified trading pattern.
   e. Both a and d above would make it unlikely that a country would choose floating exchange rates.

3. Multiple exchange rates
   a. are impossible.
   b. eventually lead to fixed exchange rates.
   c. eventually lead to a gold standard.
   d. have the same effects as taxes and subsidies.
   e. are easier to administer than a single exchange rate.

PRACTICE QUESTIONS AND PROBLEMS

Section 1: Past and Current Exchange-Rate Arrangements

1. From about 1880 to 1914, most currencies were fixed in value in terms of _____ .

2. The Bretton Woods agreement of 1944 set up two international financial institutions that are still active today. Name the two institutions that match the descriptions below.

   a. _____ : supervises exchange-rate arrangements and lends money to member countries experiencing problems meeting their external financial obligations

   b. _____ : makes loans and provides technical expertise to developing countries

3. A _____ is a deliberate decrease in the official value of a currency.

4. Today, the major industrial countries determine the value of their currencies through

   _____

5. The _____ is an artificial unit of account averaging the values of the U.S. dollar, German mark, Japanese yen, French franc, and British pound.

6. The European monetary system maintains _____ (fixed, floating) exchange rates among its member nations and maintains _____ (fixed, floating) exchange rates with the rest of the world.

7. Under a gold standard, if gold is worth $35 per ounce in the United States and 175 francs per ounce in France, how many francs will exchange for $1? _____

8. Under a gold standard, if gold is worth $20 per ounce in the United States and 10 marks per ounce in Germany, how many marks will exchange for $1? _____

Section 2: Fixed or Floating Exchange Rates

1. The U.S. demand for German marks comes from the desire of _____ (U.S., German) citizens for _____ (U.S., German) goods.

2. The U.S. supply of German marks comes from the desire of _____ (U.S., German) citizens for _____ (U.S., German) goods.

3. If U.S. citizens decide that they want to buy more Mercedes automobiles from Germany, the U.S. _____ (demand for, supply of) marks will _____ (increase, decrease).

4. If German citizens decide they want to buy fewer IBM computers from the United States, the U.S. _____ (demand for, supply of) marks will _____ (increase, decrease).

5. The two graphs below show the current U.S. demand for and supply of German marks. The exchange rate between marks and dollars is freely floating.

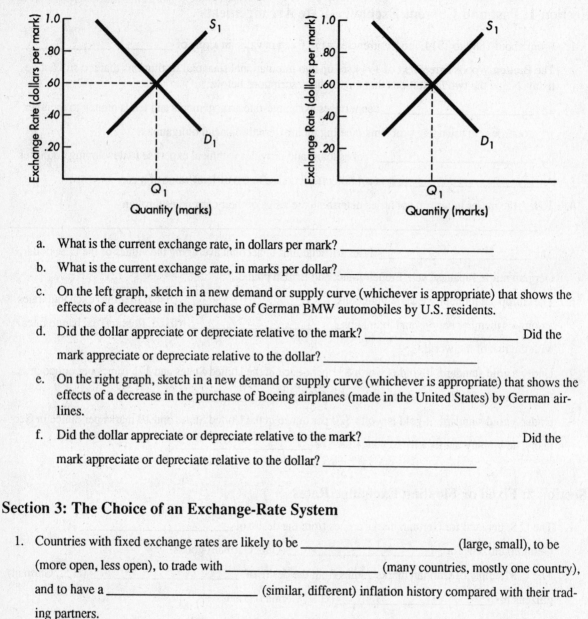

a. What is the current exchange rate, in dollars per mark? _____

b. What is the current exchange rate, in marks per dollar? _____

c. On the left graph, sketch in a new demand or supply curve (whichever is appropriate) that shows the effects of a decrease in the purchase of German BMW automobiles by U.S. residents.

d. Did the dollar appreciate or depreciate relative to the mark? _____ Did the mark appreciate or depreciate relative to the dollar? _____

e. On the right graph, sketch in a new demand or supply curve (whichever is appropriate) that shows the effects of a decrease in the purchase of Boeing airplanes (made in the United States) by German airlines.

f. Did the dollar appreciate or depreciate relative to the mark? _____ Did the mark appreciate or depreciate relative to the dollar? _____

Section 3: The Choice of an Exchange-Rate System

1. Countries with fixed exchange rates are likely to be _____ (large, small), to be _____ (more open, less open), to trade with _____ (many countries, mostly one country), and to have a _____ (similar, different) inflation history compared with their trading partners.

2. Some countries use _____ exchange rates to effectively provide subsidies for favored activities and taxes for activities that are discouraged.

3. Section 3.b in the text, on multiple exchange rates, cites Venezuela as a country that was using multiple exchange rates in 1985. Use the exchange rates listed there to find the costs in Venezuelan bolivars (Bs) of the transactions below.

   a. _____: $10,000 interest payment on debt owed by a Venezuelan company to Citibank in New York

   b. _____: $10,000 purchase of drilling supplies by the Venezuelan national oil company

   c. _____: $10,000 purchase of personal computers by the Venezuelan education agency

   d. _____: $10,000 purchase of a Chevrolet by a Venezuelan citizen

THINKING ABOUT AND APPLYING EXCHANGE-RATE SYSTEMS AND PRACTICES

I. Stable Exchange Rates and Foreign-Exchange Risk

When we compared fixed and floating exchange rates, one of the important differences was that fixed exchange rates forced countries to adapt their macroeconomic policies and inflation rates to match those of their trading partners. Why would any country want to give up the flexibility of setting its own policies? The "Economically Speaking" section for this chapter gives part of the answer: businesses prefer stable exchange rates because they minimize foreign-exchange risk.

The next chapter discusses foreign-exchange risk in detail, but we don't need much detail yet. Read through the "Preview" section of the next chapter (the one on foreign-exchange risk), review the "Economically Speaking" section of this chapter, and summarize the arguments for and against a system of fixed exchange rates.

_____

_____

_____

_____

_____

_____

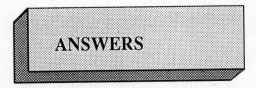

ANSWERS

Quick Check Quiz

Section 1: Past and Current Exchange-Rate Arrangements

1. e; 2. b; 3. a; 4. c; 5. d; 6. e
   If you missed any of these questions, you should go back and review pages 632–638 in Chapter 24 (pages 1004–1010 in *Economics*, Chapter 38).

Section 2: Fixed or Floating Exchange Rates

1. b; 2. a; 3. a

If you missed any of these questions, you should go back and review pages 638–644 in Chapter 24 (pages 1010–1016 in *Economics*, Chapter 38).

Section 3: The Choice of an Exchange-Rate System

1. c; 2. b; 3. d

If you missed any of these questions, you should go back and review pages 644–648 in Chapter 24 (pages 1016–1020 in *Economics*, Chapter 38).

Practice Questions and Problems

Section 1: Past and Current Exchange-Rate Arrangements

1. gold
2. a. International Monetary Fund (IMF)
   b. World Bank
3. devaluation
4. managed floating exchange rates
5. special drawing right (SDR)
6. fixed; floating
7. 5 francs

   It takes 5 times as many francs as dollars to buy an ounce of gold (175 francs per ounce/$35 per ounce), so one dollar would be equivalent to five times as many francs.
8. .5 mark

   It takes .5 times as many marks as dollars to buy an ounce of gold (10 marks per ounce/$20 per ounce), so one dollar would be equivalent to half as many marks.

Section 2: Fixed or Floating Exchange Rates

1. U.S.; German
2. German; U.S.
3. demand for; increase

   The Mercedes factory in Germany wants to be paid in its own currency (marks). U.S. buyers of German products have to buy marks with dollars. Since we want to buy more marks than before, the demand for marks will increase.
4. supply of; decrease

   IBM in the United States wants to be paid in its own currency (dollars). German buyers of U.S. products have to sell marks to get dollars. Since they want to sell fewer marks than before, the supply of marks will decrease.

5.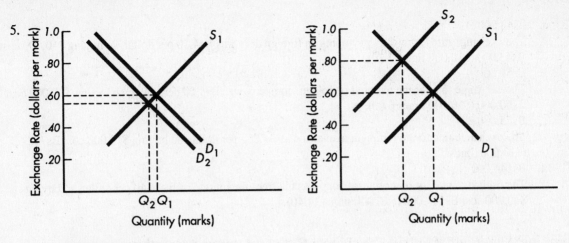

a. .60 dollar per mark
   It takes $.60 to buy 1 mark, in dollars per mark. You can read this value from the intersection of demand and supply on the graph.
b. 1.67 marks per dollar
   The exchange rate in marks per dollar is the inverse of the exchange rate in dollars per mark: $1/.60 = 1.67$. Exchange rates can be expressed either way around.
c. U.S. buyers of German products are the demanders of marks (they need to buy marks to pay Germans), so the demand curve will shift. If we buy fewer BMWs, the demand for marks will decrease, as shown on the graph above. The size of the shift on the graph does not matter.
d. appreciate; depreciate
   It takes fewer dollars now to buy a mark than it did before (.55 dollar per mark instead of .60), so the dollar is more valuable relative to the mark.
   It now takes 1.82 marks to buy a dollar (1/.55). It takes more marks now to buy a dollar than before, so the mark is less valuable relative to the dollar.
e. German buyers of U.S. products are the sellers of marks (they need to sell marks to get dollars to pay Americans), so the supply curve will shift. If they buy fewer Boeing airliners, the supply of marks will decrease, as shown on the graph above. The size of the shift on the graph does not matter.
f. depreciate; appreciate
   It takes more dollars now to buy a mark than it did before (.80 dollar per mark instead of .60), so the dollar is less valuable relative to the mark.
   It now takes only 1.25 marks to buy a dollar (1/.80). It takes fewer marks now to buy a dollar than before, so the mark is more valuable relative to the dollar.

Section 3: The Choice of an Exchange-Rate System

1. small; more open; mostly one country; similar
2. multiple

3. a. Bs43,000

    The exchange rate for interest payments on foreign debt was Bs4.30 per dollar, so buying $10,000 cost Bs43,000 ($10,000 times 4.30).

    b. Bs60,000

    The exchange rate for the national petroleum company was Bs6.00 per dollar, so buying $10,000 cost Bs60,000 ($10,000 times 6.00).

    c. Bs75,000

    The exchange rate for government agencies was Bs7.50 per dollar, so buying $10,000 cost Bs75,000 ($10,000 times 7.50).

    d. Bs144,000

    The exchange rate for other transactions was the free-market rate of Bs14.40 per dollar, so buying $10,000 cost Bs144,000 ($10,000 times 14.40).

Thinking About and Applying Exchange-Rate Systems and Practices

I. Stable Exchange Rates and Foreign-Exchange Risk

Arguments for fixed exchange rates:
1. They reduce foreign-exchange risk, improving the accuracy and efficiency of business decisions.
2. They force discipline in macroeconomic policy making.

Arguments against fixed exchange rates:
1. They reduce macroeconomic policy flexibility.
2. They create difficulties in reacting to shifts in demand and supply.

CHAPTER 25*
Foreign-Exchange Risk and International Lending

1. What is foreign-exchange risk, and how does it affect international traders?

    In the last chapter, we looked at how foreign-exchange rates are determined and how they can change when the international demand or supply of a country's goods changes. For firms importing or exporting products, there is usually some time lag between the date a contract in international trade is signed and the date payment will be made. If exchange rates change during that time, the value of the payment will change.

    For example, let's say that you want to buy a Mercedes-Benz automobile direct from the factory and pick up the car in three months during your vacation in Germany. You will have to pay 150,000 marks when you pick up the car. Today, the **spot exchange rate** is 1.5 marks per dollar: your Mercedes would cost you $100,000 if you paid for it today. But you won't pay for it until three months from now. If the value of the mark depreciates to 2 marks per dollar in three months, you will get a bargain: your Mercedes will only cost you $75,000. But what if the value of the mark appreciates to 1 mark per dollar: now your Mercedes will cost you $150,000. It's hard to make good decisions when you don't know what the price will be.

2. How do the forward, futures, and options markets in foreign exchange allow a firm to eliminate foreign-exchange risk?

    The forward, futures, and options markets in foreign exchange allow a firm expecting to receive or make payments in a foreign currency in the future to change an **open position,** whereby the firm is exposed to foreign-exchange risk, to a **covered position,** whereby the firm knows today what the domestic value of its foreign payment will be in the future.

    Although all three types of markets allow a firm to reduce or eliminate foreign-exchange risk, they work in somewhat different ways. The foreign-exchange forward market is a global market in which any amount of foreign currency is bought and sold for delivery at a future date. The foreign-exchange futures market is an organized market in which standardized contracts for future delivery of some currencies are bought and sold. Foreign-currency options give the purchaser the right to buy or sell a specified amount of currency at a set price on or before a particular date.

3. What caused the international debt crisis?

    Buying and selling products are not the only international economic transactions; international lending and borrowing are also an important source of financing, particularly for developing countries. In the 1970s, many developing countries borrowed large amounts from commercial banks in the industrial countries. In the early 1980s, a global recession led to high interest rates, at the same time reducing the demand for the exports of developing countries. With less earnings from exports and higher loan payments due to high interest rates, many developing countries in Latin America were not able to keep up payments on their loans.

*Economics Chapter 39.

4. What solutions have been proposed for the debt crisis?

A variety of solutions have been proposed. Initially, **debt rescheduling** was used to stretch out payments, with new loans given to help pay the interest on older loans. When financial conditions in the debtor countries did not improve, other possible solutions were considered. Debt buy-backs, debt-for-equity swaps, and debt-for-bonds swaps have all been used in limited cases. The Baker Plan, by which countries would implement free-market reforms in exchange for expanded loans, has not been implemented.

KEY TERMS

spot exchange rate	forward exchange rate	striking price
foreign-exchange risk	call	LIBOR
open position	put	debt rescheduling
covered position		

QUICK CHECK QUIZ

Section 1: Foreign-Exchange Transactions

1. The spot exchange rate is the foreign-exchange rate established today for delivery of a foreign currency
   a. at a specified location.
   b. immediately.
   c. at a specified time in the future.
   d. at some unspecified time in the future.
   e. at some specified time and location in the future.

2. The forward exchange rate is the foreign-exchange rate established today for delivery of a foreign currency
   a. at a specified location.
   b. immediately.
   c. at a specified time in the future.
   d. at some unspecified time in the future.
   e. at some specified time and location in the future.

3. Which of the following describes the forward exchange market?
   a. a market where you can buy the right to buy or sell a specified amount of currency at a set price on or before a particular date
   b. a market where you can buy $1 million or more in foreign currency to be delivered at a specific date in the future
   c. a market where you can buy or sell foreign currency for delivery immediately
   d. a market where you can buy a standardized contract for immediate delivery of some foreign currencies
   e. a market where you can buy a standardized contract for future delivery of some foreign currencies

4. Which of the following describes the spot foreign-exchange market?
   a. a market where you can buy the right to buy or sell a specified amount of currency at a set price on or before a particular date
   b. a market where you can buy $1 million or more in foreign currency to be delivered at a specific date in the future
   c. a market where you can buy or sell foreign currency for delivery immediately
   d. a market where you can buy a standardized contract for immediate delivery of some foreign currencies
   e. a market where you can buy a standardized contract for future delivery of some foreign currencies

5. Which of the following describes the foreign-exchange futures market?
   a. a market where you can buy the right to buy or sell a specified amount of currency at a set price on or before a particular date
   b. a market where you can buy $1 million or more in foreign currency to be delivered at a specific date in the future
   c. a market where you can buy or sell foreign currency for delivery immediately
   d. a market where you can buy a standardized contract for immediate delivery of some foreign currencies
   e. a market where you can buy a standardized contract for future delivery of some foreign currencies

6. Which of the following describes the foreign-currency options market?
   a. a market where you can buy the right to buy or sell a specified amount of currency at a set price on or before a particular date
   b. a market where you can buy $1 million or more in foreign currency to be delivered at a specific date in the future
   c. a market where you can buy or sell foreign currency for delivery immediately
   d. a market where you can buy a standardized contract for immediate delivery of some foreign currencies
   e. a market where you can buy a standardized contract for future delivery of some foreign currencies

7. A call option
   a. gives you the right to sell currency at a certain price.
   b. gives you the right to buy currency at a certain price.
   c. is a contract requiring you to buy a specified amount of currency at the future spot price.
   d. is a contract requiring you to sell a specified amount of currency at the future spot price.
   e. gives you the choice of either buying or selling currency at a specific time in the future.

8. A put option
   a. gives you the right to sell currency at a certain price.
   b. gives you the right to buy currency at a certain price.
   c. is a contract requiring you to buy a specified amount of currency at the future spot price.
   d. is a contract requiring you to sell a specified amount of currency at the future spot price.
   e. gives you the choice of either buying or selling currency at a specific time in the future.

Section 2: The International Debt Problem

1. Which of the following is NOT among the causes of the international debt problem?
   a. increases in LIBOR
   b. decreased demand for exports because of global recession in the early 1980s
   c. loans with variable interest rates
   d. careless lending to countries that were involved in regional wars
   e. increases in the U.S. prime rate

2. Which of the following is NOT true of the Baker Plan for dealing with developing countries' debt problems?
   a. It is named after James Baker, who was the U.S. Treasury Secretary.
   b. Government intervention in the economies of developing countries would be expanded.
   c. Countries would continue to receive new loans.
   d. Developing countries would emphasize free markets.
   e. Economic changes in the developing countries were expected to lead to improved growth and eventual repayment of all loans.

3. Which of the following has NOT been one of the ways proposed or used to reduce developing countries' debt?
   a. debt buy-backs
   b. debt-for-equity swaps
   c. the Baker Plan
   d. debt-for-bonds swaps
   e. complete debt forgiveness

PRACTICE QUESTIONS AND PROBLEMS

Section 1: Foreign-Exchange Transactions

1. When you are waiting to buy foreign currency in the future in the spot market, you have a(n) _____ (open, covered) position and _____ (are, are not) exposed to foreign-exchange risk.

2. You can eliminate foreign-exchange risk by using the _____, _____, or _____ markets in foreign exchange. When you use these markets, you can convert an open position into a _____ position.

3. In the foreign-currency options market, a call option gives you the right to _____ (buy, sell) currency at a certain price, and a put option gives you the right to _____ (buy, sell) currency at a certain price. The price at which currency can be bought or sold in this market is called the _____.

4. Match the following descriptions with the three types of foreign-exchange markets.
   a. The _____ market trades the rights to buy and sell foreign currency in the future.
   b. The _____ market trades standardized contracts to buy or sell foreign currency for delivery in the future.
   c. The _____ market is for large-scale buying and selling of foreign currency for future delivery at a price set today.

5. In late February 1990, the Red Cedar Shingle Company ordered 2,000,000 cedar shingles from a Canadian lumber company; the shingles cost 1 Canadian dollar (C$) each. The shingles were scheduled for delivery and payment in September 1990.

a. What was the cost of the shingles in U.S. dollars when the order was placed? (Figure 1 in the text has the exchange rate you need; use the Wednesday rate.) _____

b. If the exchange rate changes so that a Canadian dollar is worth .87 U.S. dollar when the order is delivered, what will be the cost of the shingles in U.S. dollars then? _____

c. To avoid foreign-exchange risk, the Red Cedar Shingle Company plans to use the forward exchange market. Assuming there were no service charges, what was the cost of C$2,000,000 on Wednesday, February 21, 1990, for delivery 180 days later? (Figure 1 in the text has the information you need; use the Wednesday rate.) _____

d. If Red Cedar uses the foreign-exchange futures market, how many Canadian-dollar contracts will it need to buy? _____ Ignoring the commissions charged in the futures market, what was the cost in U.S. dollars of using September futures contracts to buy C$2,000,000? (Figure 2 in the text has the information you need; use the settle price.) _____

6. In late February 1990, the Yellow Cedar Shingle Company ordered 500,000 cedar shingles from a Canadian lumber company; the shingles cost 1 Canadian dollar (C$) each. The shingles were scheduled for delivery and payment in March 1990.

a. What was the cost of the shingles in U.S. dollars when the order was placed? (Figure 1 in the text has the exchange rate you need; use the Wednesday rate.) _____

b. If the exchange rate changes so that a Canadian dollar is worth .80 U.S. dollar when the order is delivered, what will be the cost of the shingles in U.S. dollars then? _____

c. Why can't the Yellow Cedar Shingle Company use the forward market to avoid foreign-exchange risk?

_____

d. If Yellow Cedar uses the foreign-exchange futures market, how many Canadian-dollar contracts will it need to buy? _____ Ignoring the commissions charged in the futures market, what was the cost in U.S. dollars of using March futures contracts to buy C$500,000? (Figure 2 in the text has the information you need; use the settle price.) _____

e. If Yellow Cedar uses the foreign-exchange options market, how many Canadian-dollar contracts will it need to buy? _____ Will it buy put or call options? _____ If Yellow Cedar would be satisfied with an exchange rate of US$.83 = C$1.00, how much would an option ensuring it would pay no more than $.83 cost? (Figure 3 in the text has the information you need.) _____

f. If Yellow Cedar would be satisfied with an exchange rate of US$.835 = C$1.00, how much would an option ensuring it would pay no more than $.835 cost? (Figure 3 in the text has the information you need.) _____

364 / Chapter 25

Section 2: The International Debt Problem

1. The developing-country debt crisis began when Mexico was unable to _____.

2. The main cause of the debt crisis was a combination of rising _____ ____ and worldwide _____.

3. During the 1982–1985 period, the initial response to debt-repayment problems was _____, which extended payments and offered new loans.

4. Variable-interest-rate loans to developing countries based interest rates on the U.S. _____ or on _____, the rate charged for loans between major banks in London.

5. In a _____, the lender agrees to eliminate the debt in exchange for immediate payment of less than the face value of the debt.

6. In a _____ swap, a private firm buys a country's debt for less than face value and sells the debt back to the developing country in exchange for an ownership position in a firm in the developing country.

7. In a _____ swap, new debtor-country bonds are exchanged for existing commercial-bank debt.

THINKING ABOUT AND APPLYING FOREIGN-EXCHANGE RISK AND INTERNATIONAL LENDING

I. Debt-Reduction Strategies: Debt Buy-Backs

Section 2.b.2 in the text and the "Economic Insight" section entitled "Buying Back Bolivian Government Debt" look at one way that developing countries have reduced their debt. Bolivia, for example, offered to buy back some of its debt to commercial banks at a price of 11 cents for each dollar of debt.

1. How much debt did banks buy back from Bolivia, and how many dollars did Bolivia pay?

   _____

   _____

2. What did the banks gain from selling Bolivian debt for a small fraction of the amount Bolivia owed?

   _____

   _____

   _____

   _____

© 1991 Houghton Mifflin Company. All rights reserved.

3. Bolivia had made no payments on its debt for the four years before the buy-back offer. Why did Bolivia use some of its foreign aid to buy back its debt, instead of just keeping on paying nothing? (Hint: Look at the "Economic Insight" article entitled "Country Risk.")

_____

_____

_____

_____

II. Debt-Reduction Strategies: Debt-for-Equity Swaps

Section 2.b.3 in the text discusses debt-for-equity swaps, including a 1986 swap involving Mexico, Nissan Motors, and U.S. commercial banks.

1. What did Nissan gain from the swap?

_____

_____

_____

_____

2. What did Mexico gain from the swap?

_____

_____

_____

_____

3. What did U.S. banks gain from the swap?

_____

_____

_____

_____

III. Debt-Reduction Strategies: Debt-for-Bonds Swaps

Section 2.b.4 examines another method of reducing developing country debt, swapping commercial bank debt for government bonds. The text section analyzes a 1987 Mexican debt-for-bonds swap. Let's apply that analysis to a hypothetical debt-for-bonds swap.

1. Suppose that Brazil offers to swap $5 billion of its commercial bank debt for Brazilian bonds, using U.S. Treasury bonds as collateral; Brazil has made no payments on its debt for several years. If Brazil offers to swap the debt for bonds at a rate of 70 cents per dollar, the commercial banks will get bonds worth how much? _____

2. Why would the banks be willing to make the swap?

_____

_____

_____

_____

3. How does the swap help Brazil?

_____

_____

_____

_____

IV. Clipping the Wings of "Flight Capital"

This chapter's "Economically Speaking" section examines the phenomenon of "capital flight" from Latin American countries, of wealthy investors in these countries sending their money to places like the United States or Switzerland for investing rather than investing the money in their own countries. One key to a permanent solution to the international debt problem is to encourage people in developing countries to invest their money "at home" rather than in other countries. Read over the "Economically Speaking" section, list the factors mentioned there that motivate capital flight, and explain what parts of the Baker Plan would be helpful in discouraging capital flight.

_____

_____

_____

_____

_____

_____

ANSWERS

Quick Check Quiz

Section 1: Foreign-Exchange Transactions

1. b; 2. c; 3. b; 4. c; 5. e; 6. a; 7. b; 8. a

If you missed any of these questions, you should go back and review pages 654–662 in Chapter 25 (pages 1026–1034 in *Economics*, Chapter 39).

Section 2: The International Debt Problem

1. d; 2. b; 3. e

If you missed any of these questions, you should go back and review pages 662–670 in Chapter 25 (pages 1034–1042 in *Economics*, Chapter 39).

Practice Questions and Problems

Section 1: Foreign-Exchange Transactions

1. open; are
2. forward; futures; options; covered
3. buy; sell; striking price
4. a. options
   b. futures
   c. forward
5. a. $1,668,400

   The Wednesday spot exchange rate from Figure 1 was .8342 U.S. dollar for 1 Canadian dollar. Red Cedar was buying 2 million shingles at C$1 each, or C$2 million of shingles. To find the value in U.S. dollars, multiply the C$2 million times .8342 US$ per C$.

   b. $1,740,000

   Multiply C$2 million times .87 US$ per C$. This increase shows the effects of foreign-exchange risk.

   c. $1,634,800

   The 180-day forward exchange rate was .8174 US$ per C$, so the cost to Red Cedar was C$2 million times .8174.

   d. 20 contracts; $1,631,000

   The Canadian-dollar futures contracts in Figure 2 are for C$100,000, as listed in the figure on the Canadian Dollar line. To cover the C$2 million purchase, Red Cedar needs to buy 20 contracts (C$2 million/C$100,000 per contract).

   The settle rate in the futures market was .8155 for September contracts. This is the cost in US$ per C$ bought, so the cost of futures contracts for C$2 million is C$2 million times .8155 US$ per C$ (not including commissions).

6. a. $417,100

   The Wednesday spot exchange rate from Figure 1 was .8342 U.S. dollars for 1 Canadian dollar. Yellow Cedar was buying 500,000 shingles at C$1 each, or C$500,000 of shingles. To find the value in U.S. dollars, multiply the C$500,000 times .8342 US$ per C$.

   b. $400,000

   Multiply C$500,000 times .80 US$ per C$. Foreign-exchange risk can work to a buyer's benefit if the exchange rate falls. Converting an open exchange position to a covered exchange position avoids foreign-exchange risk but also prevents any gains from changes in exchange rates.

   c. The forward market deals only in transactions of $1 million or more.

   d. 5 contracts; $415,700

   The Canadian-dollar futures contracts in Figure 2 are for C$100,000, as listed in the figure on the Canadian Dollar line. To cover the C$500,000 purchase, Yellow Cedar needs to buy 5 contracts (C$500,000/C$100,000 per contract).

   The settle rate in the futures market was .8314 for September contracts. This is the cost in US$ per C$ bought, so the cost of futures contracts for C$500,000 is C$500,000 times .8314 US$ per C$ (not including commissions).

   e. 10 contracts; call options; $2,350

   The Canadian-dollar options contracts in Figure 3 are for C$50,000, as listed in the figure on the Canadian Dollar line. To cover the C$500,000 purchase, Yellow Cedar needs to buy 10 contracts (C$500,000/C$50,000 per contract).

Call options give you the right to buy foreign currency: you can "call" the money and it comes to you. Put options give you the right to sell foreign currency: you can "put" the money into the market.

To avoid paying more than US$.83 for C$1, Yellow Cedar should buy call options with a strike price of .83. The cost of the March call option with a strike price of .83 is listed as .47 cent per C$, or US$.0047 per C$. To cover C$500,000 would cost $2,350 (C$500,000 times .0047).

f. $1,250

To avoid paying more than US$.835 for C$1, Yellow Cedar should buy call options with a strike price of .83 1/2. The cost of the March call option with a strike price of .83 1/2 is listed as .25 cent per C$, or US$.0025 per C$. To cover C$500,000 would cost $1,250 (C$500,000 times .0025).

Section 2: The International Debt Problem

1. make its debt payments on schedule
2. interest rates; recession
3. debt rescheduling
4. prime rate; LIBOR
5. debt buy-back
6. debt-for-equity
7. debt-for-bonds

Thinking About and Applying Foreign-Exchange Risk and International Lending

I. Debt-Reduction Strategies: Debt Buy-Backs

1. The article says that the banks sold back $270 million of debt. If they received 11 cents per dollar, they received $29.7 million ($270 million times .11).
2. Bolivia had not been making payments on the debt and might never pay back any of the debt. Through the buy-back, the banks received some money back and removed the uncertainty about the value of the debt.
3. By reducing the amount of its debt and demonstrating its willingness to make at least partial payment, Bolivia probably increased its credit worthiness and its ability to borrow in the future. Also, with the amount of debt reduced, Bolivia has a better chance of being able to pay off its other creditors.

II. Debt-Reduction Strategies: Debt-for-Equity Swaps

1. Nissan received $54 million in pesos to pay for expanding its factories in Mexico at a cost of only $40 million, so Nissan got a $54-million factory for $40 million, saving $14 million.
2. Mexico paid off $60 million of debt at a cost of $54 million, using its own currency instead of some of its limited supply of U.S. dollars. Also, Mexico has an expanded Nissan factory that generates more jobs in Mexico; without the swap, Nissan might have decided to build the factory in another country.
3. As with debt buy-backs, banks receive at least some payment on their loans. Getting $40 million back on $60 million in loans is better than getting nothing back.

III. Debt-Reduction Strategies: Debt-for-Bonds Swaps

1. $3.5 billion ($5 billion times .70)
2. Once again, a bird in the hand is worth two in the bush. Being sure you receive at least partial payment (guaranteed by the U.S. Treasury bonds in this case) is better than receiving no payment at all.
3. By reducing the amount of its debt, Brazil can improve its credit worthiness and increase its chances of paying off other creditors.

IV. Clipping the Wings of "Flight Capital"

Factors that motivate capital flight:
  avoidance of high inflation rates
  high taxes
  economic mismanagement and political instability
  higher interest rates abroad
  possible expropriation
  overvalued exchange rates

Elements of the Baker Plan:
  stimulate economic growth through continued lending
  restructure economies to emphasize free markets
  de-emphasize government intervention in markets
  de-emphasize government subsidies
  de-emphasize government enterprises

 The objective of the Baker Plan was to create local economies that have a foundation of economic efficiency and that will provide long-term growth. The Baker Plan would, if successful, not only enable the debtors to eventually repay their debts, but also create local economic conditions that would encourage local investment, removing many of the incentives for capital flight. A stable, growing local economy should create lower inflation and competitive interest rates and exchange rates. De-emphasizing the role of government in markets should reduce taxes and economic mismanagement, as well as the fear of expropriation.